In this book Charles Ziegler develops the concept of learning in foreign policy by exploring the link between Mikhail Gorbachev's domestic reforms and the radical transformation of Soviet relations with Northeast Asia in the 1980s. He argues that, although international factors may have played a role, it was pressures for domestic change, and economic reform in particular, which had the greatest impact on new Soviet thinking. The history of Soviet relations with Northeast Asia is briefly traced, highlighting the extent to which ideology impeded foreign policy learning under Stalin, Khrushchev, and Brezhnev. The author then turns to Gorbachev's determined efforts to reverse thirty years of Sino-Soviet hostility, his mixed record on Soviet–Japanese relations, and the abrupt turnaround in Soviet policy toward South Korea. Finally Soviet national security interests in the Far East and Western Pacific are explored in the context of US–Soviet military competition and changing Soviet conceptions of the utility of military force in international relations.

Foreign policy and East Asia will be of interest to students of Soviet, post-Soviet and Asian politics, international relations and foreign policy, and to all those concerned with the sources of change during the Gorbachev era.

T0381870

Foreign policy and East Asia

Cambridge Soviet Paperbacks: 10

Editorial Board

Mary McAuley (General editor)   Timothy Colton
Karen Dawisha   David Dyker   Diane Koenker
Gail Lapidus   Robert Legvold   Alex Pravda
Gertrude Schroeder

Cambridge Soviet Paperbacks is a completely new initiative in publishing on the Soviet Union. The series will focus on the economics, international relations, politics, sociology and history of the Soviet and Revolutionary periods.

The idea behind the series is the identification of gaps for upper-level surveys or studies falling between the traditional university press monograph and most student textbooks. The main readership will be students and specialists, but some 'overview' studies in the series will have broader appeal.

Publication will in every case be simultaneously in hardcover and paperback.

Cambridge Soviet Paperbacks

1 NICOLA MILLER
   Soviet relations with Latin America
   0 521 35193 6 (hardback) / 0 521 35979 1 (paperback)

2 GALIA GOLAN
   Soviet policies in the Middle East
   From World War II to Gorbachev
   0 521 35332 7 (hardback) / 0 521 35859 0 (paperback)

3 STEPHEN WHITE
   Gorbachev and after
   0 521 43374 6 (hardback) / 0 521 43984 1 (paperback)

4 PHILIP R. PRYDE
   Environmental management in the Soviet Union
   0 521 36079 X (hardback) / 0 521 40905 5 (paperback)

5 PEKKA SUTELA
   Economic thought and economic reform in the Soviet Union
   0 521 38020 0 (hardback) / 0 521 38902 X (paperback)

6 GAIL LAPIDUS and VICTOR ZASLAVSKY with
   PHILIP GOLDMAN (eds.)
   From Union to Commonwealth
   Nationalism and separatism in the Soviet Republics
   0 521 41706 6 (hardback) / 0 521 42716 9 (paperback)

7 RICHARD STITES
   Russian popular culture
   Entertainment and society since 1900
   0 521 36214 8 (hardback) / 0 521 36986 X (paperback)

8 LEWIS H. SIEGELBAUM
   The Soviet state and society between revolutions, 1918–1929
   0 521 36215 6 (hardback) / 0 521 36987 8 (paperback)

9 ANNA LAWTON
   Kinoglasnost: Soviet cinema in our time
   0 521 38117 7 (hardback) / 0 521 38814 7 (paperback)

10 CHARLES E. ZIEGLER
    Foreign policy and East Asia
    Learning and adaptation in the Gorbachev era
    0 521 41547 0 (hardback) / 0 521 42564 6 (paperback)

Foreign policy and East Asia

Learning and adaption in the Gorbachev era

CHARLES E. ZIEGLER

Associate Professor of Political Science,
University of Louisville, Kentucky

CAMBRIDGE
UNIVERSITY PRESS

CAMBRIDGE UNIVERSITY PRESS
Cambridge, New York, Melbourne, Madrid, Cape Town, Singapore,
São Paulo, Delhi, Dubai, Tokyo

Cambridge University Press
The Edinburgh Building, Cambridge CB2 8RU, UK

Published in the United States of America by Cambridge University Press, New York

www.cambridge.org
Information on this title: www.cambridge.org/9780521425643

© Cambridge University Press 1993

First published 1993
Re-issued in this digitally printed version 2010

A catalogue record for this publication is available from the British Library

Library of Congress Cataloguing in Publication data

Ziegler, Charles E.
Foreign policy in East Asia: learning and adaptation in the
Gorbachev era / Charles E. Ziegler.
    p.   cm. – (Cambridge Soviet paperbacks: 10)
ISBN 0 521 41547 0 (hardback) – ISBN 0 521 42564 6 (pbk.)
1. East Asia – Foreign relations – Soviet Union. 2. Soviet Union
– Foreign relations – East Asia. 3. Soviet Union – National security.
4. Soviet Union – Foreign relations – 1985–1991.   I. Title.   II. Series.
DS517.7.Z53 1993
327.4705 – dc20   92–36268 CIP

ISBN 978-0-521-41547-7 Hardback
ISBN 978-0-521-42564-3 Paperback

Contents

Preface

The conceptual underpinnings of this study date from 1985 to 1986, when the author was in residence at the Hoover Institution as a National Fellow. It was then that I began searching for a framework that would make some analytical sense of the link between domestic politics and foreign policy in the Soviet Union. The task was more daunting than it appeared at first glance, and I benefited greatly from conversations with Thomas Rochon, Condoleeza Rice, Richard Staar, Brian Latell, David Granick, and Sidney Hook. The support of Hoover's National Fellow program, under the able direction of Thomas Henriksen, is gratefully acknowledged.

An initial draft of the manuscript was written during 1989, while the author was an International Affairs Fellow of the Council on Foreign Relations. Much of the research for the manuscript was carried out at the International Institute for Strategic Studies in London, where the Director François Heisbourg, the staff, and fellow researchers all made my stay extraordinarily pleasant and productive. The Council on Foreign Relations and IISS also generously provided travel funds for the fellowship year. As Director of the IAF program, Tony Dunn was a welcome source of encouragement and support.

At the University of Louisville, the College of Arts and Sciences, the Provost's Office, and the Office of Graduate Programs and Research all provided generous support for travel to the Soviet Union in 1989 and 1991. Additional support was provided through grants from the Southern Regional Education Board.

Dr. Mikhail Titarenko, Director of the Institute of Far Eastern Studies kindly arranged an invitation for a research trip in 1989, and scholars from his Institute, the Institute of the USA and Canada, and the Institute of Oriental Studies answered all my questions in the true spirit of glasnost.

I am deeply indebted to many individuals for their insightful comments on various parts of the manuscript – Gerald Segal, Rodger

Payne, Andy Butfoy, John Chipman, Renee DeNevers, James McCoy, David Bradford, James O'Sullivan, Roger E. Kanet, Steven Blank, and David Morrison. I am grateful to Louie Greenwell, who designed the maps for chapters 4, 5, and 7, and Dianne O'Regan, who compiled the index. I profited immeasurably from many hours of conversation with Rajan Menon, and from his extensive comments on the manuscript. Of course, even with all this help mistakes can be made, and the author is willing to take credit for whatever errors remain.

I have followed the Library of Congress system for transliteration of the Russian, with occasional modification of names of persons or places where convention dictates. Chinese, Japanese and Korean names appear as cited most commonly in the English-language press. Sources in the end notes are cited in full where they first occur in each chapter, and thereafter appear in abbreviated form.

1   Introduction

> We do not claim to be able to teach others. Having heard endless
> instructions from others, we have come to the conclusion that this is a
> useless pastime. Primarily, life itself teaches people to think in a new
> way. We ourselves have come gradually to it, mastering it stage by
> stage ...
>
> Mikhail Gorbachev, *Perestroika: New Thinking for Our Country and
> the World* (New York: Harper and Row, 1987), p. 144.

Readers fatigued by the profusion of studies on Soviet politics may
question the need for a book that analyzes the foreign policy of a state
which no longer exists. There are several reasons why a study of this
sort is justifiable. First, and easiest for the author to rationalize to
himself, is the countless hours of research and writing that went into
the manuscript prior to the dissolution of the USSR in December 1991.
Few specialists have suffered the indignity of having so many of their
basic assumptions called into question, not to mention seeing their
main object of study simply disappear. It is a humbling experience, but
then humility is a key element of learning, as I shall argue in the
following chapter.

A second, less flippant reason for this book lies in attempting an
explanation of the pressures that contributed to what is undoubtedly
the most remarkable transformation of a major political-economic
system in the twentieth century. Soviet learning *vis-à-vis* relations with
Northeast Asia is one small, relatively manageable component of the
broader process of learning that occurred in both domestic politics and
foreign policy. Ideally, it should aid historians of Soviet affairs,
students of political change, and policy-makers interested in understanding the democratization process and the emergence of Soviet
new thinking.

Third, this study seeks to build on the various theories of learning as one of the most promising conceptual tools for understanding foreign policy change. I suggest that the underlying premises of American foreign policy, based on the realist school of international relations, hindered timely recognition of the revolutionary changes that were taking place in both Soviet foreign and domestic policies. A learning perspective would have attributed far more significance to domestic influences on Soviet foreign policy and, as suggested in this study, would have reinforced the contention that new thinking was "genuine" early in the Gorbachev era.[1]

Finally, this book seeks to make a contribution to the substantive literature on Soviet relations with the countries of Northeast Asia – China, Japan, North and South Korea – together with US–Soviet security interactions in the Western Pacific. Gorbachev's efforts realized several major accomplishments in foreign policy toward this region, but these developments tended to be overshadowed by the revolutionary transformations taking place in Europe. One objective of this study is to provide a succinct overview of the evolution of Soviet policy toward Northeast Asia, on the assumption that a regional approach better incorporates the linkages among issues in that region of the world.

In Chinese Taoist philosophy, the path, or "way," to learning is distinguished by openness, non-resistance, and humility. Soviet communism had through most of its history exhibited the opposite characteristics – it was a closed, repressive political system, outwardly confrontational and ideologically arrogant. Gorbachev may never have considered his reform program to be Taoist, but the intended effect was to introduce a much-needed balance into his country's internal politics and foreign policies. Glasnost opened the country to new information and ideas. The "silk" of economic cooperation supplanted the "iron" of military force, and a new readiness to learn from other countries and philosophies replaced Marxist–Leninist utopian dogma. In one decade, the intellectual and political elite progressed from relative complacency, to the realization that Soviet-style communism was seriously flawed, to the complete rejection of communism and the search for a better path toward the twenty-first century.

A decisive decade

As the 1980s drew to a close, the collapse of communist regimes in Eastern Europe forced analysts to revise their theories of Soviet foreign policy. Basic assumptions about the motivations and parameters of

Soviet decision-making changed almost overnight. However, a close look at events in East Asia, where evolutionary processes have produced far less drama than in Europe, illustrates the protracted and complex developments that have led to fundamental changes in Soviet foreign policy. This book traces the evolution of new thinking throughout the 1980s, focusing on Soviet relations with Northeast Asia, and US–Soviet security interactions in the West Pacific.

The Soviet Union, as former Foreign Minister Eduard Shevardnadze was fond of saying, aspired to be both a European and an Asian power. Although approximately three-fourths of the Soviet population was concentrated west of the Urals mountains, some two-thirds of Soviet territory and the bulk of its natural wealth lay in the Asian part of the Soviet Union. Soviet leaders from Lenin onward claimed an Asian role for the USSR, either as a model of socialism or as the inherent right of a great power. In the early Brezhnev years, the Soviet Union sought to establish a dominant position in the Far East through expansion of military power. Yet Soviet influence in the region never matched its military presence. Lacking political or economic clout, the USSR found its influence in one of the world's most dynamic economic regions severely circumscribed at the start of the 1980s.

Mikhail Gorbachev's major speeches in Vladivostok (July 1986) and Krasnoiarsk (September 1988) received a great deal of attention in Asia and the West as indications of new Soviet interest in improving relations with the countries of Asia and the Pacific. However, Gorbachev's initiatives, which rejected policies proven to be ineffective and attempted to formulate more balanced and flexible approaches to a rapidly changing environment, were actually one stage in a learning process that had begun in the waning years of the Brezhnev era. Gorbachev deserves much of the credit for his boldness as leader, but as this study suggests, Soviet foreign policy was undergoing a fundamental systemic transformation throughout the decade of the 1980s. In both domestic politics and external relations, the extraordinary pressures for change faced by the Soviet Union initiated a process of political learning that continued into the 1990s.

Developments in Soviet Northeast Asian policy are closely linked to the domestic economic and political reforms initiated in the mid-1980s. Marxist–Leninist ideological motivations were superseded by pragmatic considerations in foreign policy, conditioned if not dictated by the exigencies of internal reform. This study conceptualizes the basic shifts in policy evident through the 1980s in Soviet relations with the People's Republic of China, Japan, and both North and South Korea as part of a larger process of foreign policy learning that completely revolutionized the Soviet position in the world.

Soviet "new thinking" (*novoe myshlenie*) was applied to Northeast Asia and the Pacific region as well as to the United States and Europe. A demonstrably new approach became evident under Gorbachev – less overtly aggressive, more sophisticated diplomatically, more conciliatory, ready to establish good relations with all countries in the region. Soviet reformers abandoned an ideologically based, conflict-oriented, isolationist policy in favor of a pragmatic policy based on universal human values, interested in commerce and stability, and eschewing revolutionary violence in favor of peaceful reform. In place of economic autarky, the Soviet Union expressed its intention to become a responsible participant in Asian-Pacific economic and political organizations.

This reorientation of Soviet policy toward the region was linked to domestic reform efforts in the USSR; more specifically, to the restructuring – perestroika – of the Soviet economy. Improved relations with the Asia-Pacific states were expected to permit some economizing militarily, provided that perceived threats to Soviet security from China and the US in the Far East could be contained or reduced.

Optimistic reformers expected that Asian investment and economic cooperation would help create in the Soviet Far East a diversified export structure capable of earning significant hard currency to replace the heavy reliance on raw materials and fuel exports. A high-technology export economy focused around value-added products, science, tourism, and services was to link the country's economy into the Asian miracle. For these goals to be achieved, the USSR would need to establish better political relations with individual countries in the region, with economic organizations, and with the United States, than existed in the post-war era.

Soviet economic reforms did make possible new types of economic cooperation – joint ventures and special economic zones, for example – designed to attract Asian technology, investment, management skills, and work habits. These policies reflected the adaptation of Soviet views to current economic realities, based on the poor performance record of the Soviet and other socialist planned economies in contrast to more open, market-oriented exporting countries. However, the unwillingness or inability of Soviet leaders to adopt the necessary economic and legal mechanisms for a true market economy frustrated significant integration into the Asian-Pacific economic system.

Changing approaches to national security interests in the Asian-

Pacific region reflected an increasingly comprehensive and subtle Soviet perspective on the limited utility of military force in international relations. Over time, the leadership came to realize that Soviet military expansion under Brezhnev had not enhanced Soviet security, but rather threatened the security of other countries and exacerbated tensions in the region. Alarmed by the Soviet military build-up in the 1960s and 1970s, the United States and its allies responded by modernizing and expanding their armed forces, and shifting to a more aggressive naval doctrine to counter the perceived threat from the USSR.

Prior to new thinking, ideological constraints made it impossible to acknowledge Soviet behavior as a factor contributing to international tensions. Under Gorbachev, this dogma was replaced by a more honest, critical evaluation of Soviet policies. Moreover, the fixation on military power as the sole guarantor of Soviet security was replaced by a more balanced and comprehensive view of security encompassing military, economic, and political components. In concrete terms, this new policy translated into developing the economic infrastructure of the USSR through fundamental reform; presenting a more benign, accommodative political stance diplomatically through new thinking; and reconstituting Soviet military forces to eliminate their threatening force posture.

Soviet relations with Northeast Asia must be viewed in the context of post-war Soviet goals, developments in the regional political and economic situation, and the American presence in the region. The approach used in this study conceptualizes the USSR as a system that responded both to internal demands, and to pressures and constraints in the international environment. By the late 1970s strains had accumulated to the point where a fundamental reassessment of foreign policy methods, goals, and priorities was clearly needed. Soviet political learning occurred in both foreign and domestic policies during the 1980s and, as is often the case with learning, proved to be a painful and difficult experience. While this process did not start precisely in 1980, nor was it completed by 1990, this study suggests that the decade of the 1980s was pivotal and deserves close scrutiny.

The purpose of this book is to explicate the linkages between domestic changes and constraints in the USSR, and Soviet policies toward the Asia-Pacific. Complex ties among various countries in East Asia make it difficult to justify arbitrarily restricting the analysis to one country or a narrow geographic zone. However, a discussion of Soviet policy toward the entire East Asia and Pacific region would be either unmanageable or superficial. This study will concentrate on Soviet relations with the major countries of Northeast Asia – the People's Republic of China, Japan, and the two Koreas. Soviet policies in the Gorbachev period attached the highest priority to improving political and economic relations with these nations, while reducing perceived military challenges from China, and from the United States in collaboration with its Japanese and South Korean allies. Any discussion of Soviet policy toward this region must therefore include an examination of Soviet security interests and American presence in the West Pacific.

The remaining East Asian and Pacific states became more important to Soviet policy in the Gorbachev era, but remained distinctly secondary in Soviet calculations. Relations with the remaining newly industrializing states (Hong Kong, Taiwan and Singapore), the Association of Southeast Asian Nations member-nations (Indonesia, Philippines, Thailand, Malaysia, Singapore and Brunei), Australia, New Zealand, and the Pacific island states were predicated on supporting the central goals of reducing tensions in the region, creating pressures for the elimination of US bases and withdrawal of American forces, and facilitating Soviet economic development. Discussion of these states will be included only insofar as they factor into US–Soviet security interactions.

Plan of the book

In the following chapter, the concept of learning in foreign policy is developed. Learning, which involves significant changes in belief systems, and the more efficient alignment of means to ends in foreign policy, is analytically distinct from adaptation. Adaptation, or what is at times referred to as "simple" learning, consists of a shift in behavior prompted by failure, in which neither basic goals nor values are subject to reassessment. Shifts in Soviet ideas and behavior on foreign policy, as reflected in new thinking, evolved exponentially, culminating in a major break point in the late 1980s. Evidence for individual learning in foreign policy can be discerned from the middle of the Khrushchev period, but the rigid ideological structure of Marxism–Leninism frustrated the dissemination of innovative ideas to the organizational and governmental levels. In the 1980s a generational change in the leadership, the presence of a General Secretary committed to rational decision-making, and a series of foreign and domestic policy failures combined to create an ideal learning environment.

Chapter 3 sets out the historical context of Soviet relations with Northeast Asia, starting with the immediate post-war period and continuing into the late Brezhnev era. Strikingly, the basic parameters of relations established under Stalin were maintained essentially intact until Gorbachev. There are clearly instances of adaptive behavior during this period, especially in Sino-Soviet relations, but Soviet policy toward the region is characterized more by continuity than by change. Ideological rigidity and the closed nature of Soviet decision-making appear to account for the absence of genuine learning.

Chapter 4 analyzes the major developments in relations between the Soviet Union and the People's Republic of China during the Gorbachev era. China was the key element in Soviet policy toward the region. The Sino-Soviet rift constituted the single greatest setback for Soviet foreign policy in the post-war period. In addition, China was one of the two most serious military threats in the region. China and the Soviet Union shared common, albeit not identical interests in economic reform during the 1980s, and sizeable trade between the two countries developed late in the decade.

Learning in Soviet–Japanese relations is the subject of chapter 5. Japan occupied a position of importance for Soviet decision-making in Northeast Asia subordinate only to China. As the world's second most powerful economy, and a growing military power in its own right, Japan commanded Soviet attention. Post-war animosity between the two countries was reinforced by Japan's formal defense alliance with the United States, and by the intractable Northern Territories issue. However, the failure to settle longstanding differences and a policy of Soviet intimidation had proved increasingly counterproductive in the reform era. Although prospects for extensive economic cooperation between the USSR and Japan were problematic barring successful resolution of the islands issue, many Soviet reformers viewed Japanese technology and investment as instrumental in modernizing the Soviet Far East, and urged a breakthrough in relations. Finally, trade disputes with the United States, resurgent Japanese nationalism, and the search for a redefinition of Japan's role in the world presented new opportunities and risks for Soviet policy-makers.

Soviet policy toward North and South Korea is a useful case study of learning in foreign policy. Although Korea was a lower priority than China or Japan, Soviet support for a volatile and unpredictable North Korea, whose leader demanded non-recognition of the economic powerhouse to the south, made little sense to Soviet reformers. Under new thinking, Soviet leaders faced the difficult task of trying to normalize relations with South Korea, and thereby reap the potential benefits of economic cooperation, while attempting not to alienate Kim Il-sung. Chapter 6 analyzes the dynamics of Soviet policy toward both Koreas in the 1980s.

Chapter 7 analyzes Soviet military developments in the Asian-Pacific region, outlining changes in security positions and force deployments after Gorbachev came to power. Learning is evident in security policies regarding the use of force, the concept of sufficiency in defense, and in a retreat from attempts at power projection in the Pacific. The Brezhnev leadership refused to acknowledge that Soviet military expansion threatened other states in the region. By contrast, the Gorbachev leadership accepted some responsibility for fueling the military build-up in the region. Moreover, Soviet strategy attempted to reverse developments of the 1970s and early 1980s by initiating a reciprocal build-down of forces in the Far East. These initiatives were highly successful in Sino-Soviet relations, although the Chinese deserve some credit for having started the process through unilateral military reductions. Responses from the United States and Japan were much more cautious, and were only beginning to be enacted in the final year or so of Gorbachev's tenure.

One significant question to be addressed involves the much slower pace and narrower scope of force reductions in the Soviet Far East and Western Pacific compared with the revolutionary build-down in Europe. Although Soviet ground forces and the Pacific fleet experienced significant quantitative cutbacks, the modernization of Soviet forces in the region continued until the August 1991 coup. As indicated in chapter 7, this anomaly in Northeast Asian security was most likely the result of political or contextual factors, rather than a specific inability to learn.

Chapter 8 concludes by evaluating the utility of a learning process model for understanding Soviet relations with Northeast Asia. Although this study applied the learning concept to one area (divided into four case studies), the same approach could also provide broader insights into the revolutionary changes that transformed Soviet politics in the 1980s. Other scholars have applied the concept of learning to such areas of Soviet foreign policy as relations with Eastern Europe, the United States, Western Europe, and the Third World. This approach would appear to have considerable value for conceptualizing change in both foreign and domestic politics, and deserves further elaboration.

Finally, a learning perspective on Soviet politics may have avoided the rather myopic approach to international affairs that governed Washington's policies toward the USSR. The neo-conservative view of Soviet international behavior, which dominated American foreign policy throughout the 1980s, conceptualized the Soviet political system as fundamentally illegitimate, yet so repressive as to be virtually impervious to domestic pressures for change, at least over the short term.

An American foreign policy based on a reassertion of US military strength, I suggest, does not deserve much of the credit for transforming the Soviet system. Internal factors were far more important. Moreover, a preoccupation with the military aspects of Soviet power, and with Soviet external behavior, made it very difficult for Washington's analysts to accept the evidence that real change was taking place in Soviet politics. A learning approach would not have predicted the massive, rapid changes which resulted in the dissolution of the Soviet external and internal empires. And yet it might have alerted us much earlier to the subtle indicators that portended major change in the socialist world.

2 Learning, adaptation, and foreign policy change

> We have thoroughly studied the lessons of the past and present realities and taken account of the ideas and initiatives of others, including, of course, socialist countries in Asia.
>
> Mikhail Gorbachev, Krasnoiarsk speech (TASS, 19 September 1988).

Investigating the factors causing or contributing to the fundamental changes in Soviet foreign policy that have taken place under Gorbachev is an extraordinarily complex task. Ideally, a conceptual framework should accommodate both international environmental factors, and the domestic determinants of foreign policy. The approach should be able to consider varying levels of input into decision-making – at the individual, the institutional, and the systemic level. Finally, the framework must be dynamic, able to account for change, or stasis, over time in foreign policy.

The concept of learning appears to be an especially useful intellectual tool for making sense out of a complicated and chaotic transition period. First, foreign policy learning in a system may be stimulated by the actions of other relevant states, or through the assessment of foreign policy successes or failures of the state in question. Second, learning can be depicted as taking place at distinct levels – by the individual, within various foreign policy and academic organizations, and by government as a whole. Learning is an interactive process in which new ideas generated at one level may prompt a reevaluation of longstanding positions held at another level. The resultant changes may then stimulate a spiral of learning among the various levels.

Finally, learning is a process that occurs over an extended period of time. It is dynamic, but not linear, and may even be regressive. That is, one should not simplistically assume that progress toward the researcher's subjective concept of "rationality" is necessarily learning. Learning takes place as the subject reassesses the appropriateness of earlier beliefs or behavior, and consequently adjusts toward a (subjectively defined) better fit of means and ends. Likewise, it should be recognized that regression, or "unlearning," may take place. Individuals can easily forget lessons learned, and the problem becomes more acute as one moves to the institutional and systemic levels.

There are additional limitations in using a model of learning to illuminate foreign policy behavior. Robert Legvold has argued that learning is an evaluative standard useful in assessing changes in decision-makers' belief systems. It may be possible to develop an objective definition of learning in foreign policy as moving toward a more efficient alignment of ends and means, but this does not explain why leaders change their minds or why they adopt new foreign policies. Learning cannot provide us with a causal theory of change.[1]

I would caution against trying to impose excessive structure when conceptualizing foreign policy change as a learning process. The notion of learning as utilized in this study cannot easily be developed into an elegantly systematic, rigorous explanatory framework, because learning is itself a disjointed, largely trial-and-error process. Certainly change in the period and place under review – the Soviet Union in the 1980s – unfolded as a chaotic and unplanned sequence of events culminating in fundamental transformations. For our purposes, a flexible framework is more appropriate.

A learning approach to comparative foreign policy

Although far from perfect, a learning approach toward studying Soviet relations with Northeast Asia can make a significant contribution to our understanding of change in foreign policy more generally. The approach utilized in this book develops four case studies illustrating the pressures contributing to a rethinking of foreign policy fundamentals in one country. James Rosenau has suggested that a single country theory of foreign policy can contribute to our theoretical understanding of foreign policy decision-making. The single country method maintains the rigor of comparative foreign policy studies by using across-time comparison. This approach preserves the in-depth knowledge of the area specialist, who has an appreciation of the unique characteristics of the Soviet system, while combining this specific knowledge with the theory-building capabilities of the comparativist. As Rosenau explains,

The investigator compares the patterns in different units as they might vary and/or break in response to specified stimuli or the emergence of different conditions. What renders these conditions scientific is not the nature of the units, but the availability of enough data points to form patterns and enough evidence of stimuli and/or conditions that are sufficiently different to justify before-and-after comparisons. If the data are sufficient and the breakpoints separating the before-and-after patterns clear-cut, therefore, it does not matter whether the comparisons are made across several units or within one. The latter offers a laboratory for scientific inquiry in the sense that its structures, processes and policy outcomes at different moments in time constitute different system states and outcomes – and thus different data points – that can be analyzed for patterns and fitted (or not) to theory. If the unit is the Soviet Union, the patterns are those of a single country and an explanation of them can thus be viewed as a single-country theory.[2]

One focus for the single-country theory, Rosenau suggested, is "that realm of politics wherein domestic and foreign dynamics converge." A growing world interdependence forces states to adapt to rapid changes: "increasingly they will have to devote resources and energy to balancing the complex internal and external demands to which growing interdependence have given rise."[3] Domestic political, economic, and social pressures, in conjunction with a transformed international environment, generated new demands on the Soviet system in the later years of the Brezhnev regime. Although the aging generation of conservative Soviet rulers resisted acknowledging the serious problems confronting the USSR, they could not ignore reality indefinitely. Gradually, the need for fundamental change came to be accepted by key elements of the Soviet leadership.

This new attitude emerged from an extended learning process affecting primarily the younger generation of Soviet leaders who, influenced by a freer exchange of ideas under glasnost, came to recognize and admit past mistakes and, in the Soviet lexicon, "draw the necessary conclusions." This learning process is central to adapting the Stalinist system designed for the 1930s to the radically changed international environment of the late twentieth century. To better understand the dynamics affecting Soviet foreign policy decision-making in the 1980s, a clearer definition of the terms "learning" and "adaptation" is necessary.

Learning and adaptation

There is a good deal of disagreement among scholars over the precise meaning of learning. For the purposes of our analysis, it is useful to start by distinguishing between learning and adaptation. Adaptation may be defined as a process of utilizing new knowledge for adjustments within existing structures, to achieve a closer approximation to regime goals. Adaptation does not challenge the dominant motivating ideology, basic system values, decision-making structures, or central goals of an organization. Adaptive behavior seeks to preserve the existing order. The status quo may not be tolerable to elites, since problems are perceived as serious enough to warrant a change from "business as usual." However, fundamental changes in the ideology, governing structures, or basic goals – changes that would indicate genuine learning – may not be acceptable unless conditions have reached a crisis stage.

Learning is dependent on quantitatively and qualitatively higher levels of new knowledge. Learning in institutions involves a process of building consensus, through new knowledge, on the seriousness of existing problems, on the inadequacy of current problem-solving strategies, and on the need for fundamental changes to realign methods with goals. Basic goals may be called into question. According to this definition, there need not be a solid consensus on the form changes should take. There is agreement, however, among a significant number of elites that fundamental change is warranted.

Learning occurs at varying rates, depending on organizational structure and ideological flexibility. In general, obstacles to learning are greater in closed systems than in open systems. In closed systems central decision-makers are relatively isolated from lower level foreign policy organizations, and from factors in the domestic environment that might constrain their behavior. Closed systems also tend to buffer their populations from influences in the international environment which might introduce ideas challenging the structural basis of the system. The outside world is perceived as highly threatening. Information is obtained indirectly, through authorities, rather than directly from the competing systems. Finally, closed systems embody a narrow perspective preoccupied with the remote future. Since it is impossible to refute assertions connected with the future, virtually any inconsistencies in the present may be explained away.[4]

Open systems, by contrast, are highly penetrated internally and internationally. Since they are more dependent on the external environment, there is relatively less suspicion of foreign cultural influences. Open systems, being less threatened from outside, are more receptive to new ideas. Foreign policy decision-makers in open systems are subject to a higher degree of influence by governmental and non-governmental organizations, by public opinion, and by other domestic factors. In contrast to closed systems, open systems

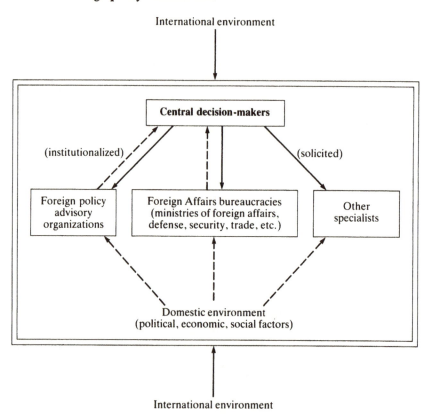

Figure 2.1   Learning process in closed systems

have a more balanced conception of how past, present, and immediate future relate to each other. They are less concerned with a utopian distant future than are closed systems. The differences between these two ideal types are illustrated in Figure 2.1 and Figure 2.2.

Of course, no system is either perfectly open or perfectly closed. In the latter half of the twentieth century few political systems have been able to maintain a hermetically sealed domestic environment. The communist states were the most successful, but even they were fighting a losing battle against the pervasiveness of the electronic media, the spread of information technology, and the growing mobility of the global village. Internally, success in educational development created the foundation for an incipient civil society, notwithstanding the regime's efforts to stifle creative thought. In other words, these systems were at best *imperfectly* closed, unable to seal off completely

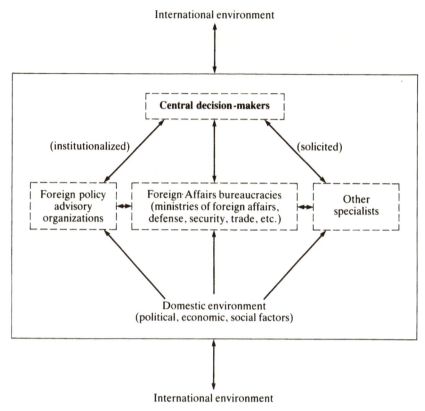

Figure 2.2   Learning process in open systems

the pressures for change (read learning) originating from within and outside their boundaries.

Political learning and adaptation in the Soviet context must be understood in relation to the Marxist–Leninist ideology that has conditioned and colored all policies, both foreign and domestic, since 1917. Many Western analysts have minimized the role of ideology in Soviet foreign policy decision-making. Although Marxism–Leninism was never used as an inflexible and ready-made prescription for certain courses of action in either routine or crisis situations, general beliefs about historical development, political motivations, and desirable goals and the means for attaining these goals were rooted in Marxist–Leninist theory. Throughout Soviet history ideology performed a critical function as an "operational code," a framework that conditioned decisions and imposed limits on decision-makers' rationality.[5]

Fundamental reform in the Gorbachev period, I argue, was the direct albeit not inevitable consequence of the inability of the Brezhnev regime to adapt to rapidly accumulating domestic and international pressures. Rosenau has defined adaptation as a process of coping with or stimulating changes that contribute to keeping the essential structures of a system within acceptable limits.[6] In the Brezhnevite USSR, the "acceptable limits" of adaptive change were very narrowly defined. Adaptation could only take place within highly confined parameters bounded by Soviet leaders' unimaginative interpretations of Soviet ideology. Ideological rigidity was reinforced by other factors – negative attitudes toward change among the leadership, highly centralized and highly formalized decision-making organs, and the closed nature of the system – which further inhibited policy innovations.[7]

The marginal changes in foreign and domestic politics and economics acceptable to the Brezhnev leadership and enacted into policy were not really adaptive; that is, they did not successfully contribute to system preservation. Instead, minor formalistic modifications to the status quo guaranteed that pressures would continue to accumulate, to the point where the official ideology and basic assumptions were brought into question. Foreign policy specialists in Soviet research institutes and think tanks were the earliest individuals to question the wisdom and effectiveness of certain policies and programs. These scholars, as innovators, were the first to examine critically the means, and ultimately many of the ends, of Soviet foreign policy. Individual learning, through a long, complex and conflict-ridden process, eventually translated into systemic learning – the decision to implement new thinking in Soviet foreign policy.

The process of individual foreign policy learning among scholars in the research institutes and universities, in the form of rather esoteric debates, has received considerable attention from Western Sovietologists. Organizational and systemic learning, however, is much more difficult to analyze. The structure of virtually all organizations in the Soviet Union was designed to frustrate innovation – that is, the consideration and adoption of new ideas. Just as innovation in Soviet industry was discouraged by a system that rewarded only maintenance of the status quo (fulfilling the plan), so too the propagation and adoption of new ideas in social, economic, and political organizations was not rewarded. The authoritarian milieu in the USSR frustrated organizational learning, which then lowered the potential for systemic learning. Open systems, by contrast, maintain a continuous exchange with their environment that improves the potential for social innovation.[8]

In the Soviet authoritarian system, the capacity for systemic learning was highest during periods of leadership succession.[9] Historically, major policy changes have occurred in the years immediately following the death or retirement of a General Secretary. In the post-Stalin and post-Brezhnev succession periods, elderly and inflexible executives were replaced by leaders who recognized the need for significant changes. In the case of Khrushchev, who was summarily ejected from the Kremlin in October 1964, his questionable experiments ("harebrained schemes" as they were derogatorily referred to by his successors) were reversed in favor of greater conservativism. However, William Zimmerman's classic study of Soviet foreign policy discerned a process of individual learning continuing, as reflected in the greater attention devoted to methodology and theory in international relations studies, for several years into the Brezhnev period.[10] Unfortunately, conditions were not favorable to organizational or systemic learning, particularly after the Prague Spring experience soured the conservative Brezhnev politburo on economic and political experimentation.[11]

Periods of leadership transition, before a single figure has consolidated control and advanced an agenda, have provided windows of opportunity for innovators to persuade leaders to experiment with new approaches in foreign and domestic policy. The highly restrictive nature of decision-making in foreign affairs inhibited development of a large pool of talented foreign policy personnel inside the Soviet government. Newly promoted officials who lacked experience and confidence with foreign policy would be more likely than their predecessors to turn to specialists for advice. In addition, officials not definitively linked to past policies would be more amenable to exploring creative new solutions.

Although succession periods provide unique opportunities for innovative ideas to be considered, this does not mean that the potential for learning did not exist at other times. Clearly, individual learning continued through the Brezhnev era; quite possibly, some organizational learning was also occurring among foreign policy institutes. However, the Soviet system during the entire post-Stalin period was highly resistant to innovation. This was partly attributable to the closed, authoritarian nature of the Soviet polity. In addition, the stranglehold of a single political generation recruited and promoted through the ranks during the Stalinist purges, that had dominated

Soviet affairs for nearly fifty years, frustrated consideration of new ideas.[12]

The generation of leaders that moved rapidly into the upper echelons of Soviet officialdom during the 1930s was not amenable either philosophically (in beliefs and values), or experientially (in political socialization experiences, and their basic isolation from problems of the modern USSR) to ideas that would significantly alter the status quo – what is now called "old thinking." The Gorbachev generation, by contrast, could be distinguished from the Brezhnev/Gromyko generation both philosophically and experientially. Members of this younger generation tended to be more educated, more capable of critical thinking, and therefore more receptive to learning.

For the reformers of this generation, perestroika was initially viewed as a form of adaptation that would enable the Soviet Union to meet the demands of the late twentieth century without radically reforming the party-state system. Glasnost and democratization were supposed to complement perestroika by further undermining systemic constraints on adaptation. Glasnost would introduce a competition of ideas to stimulate new solutions to economic and social problems. Democratization would reestablish contact between Soviet leaders and the public lost during the Stalinist era of repression, enabling the Party and government to better ascertain and meet the genuine needs of the population. Finally, new thinking was expected to harmonize Soviet foreign policy with this more realistic approach to domestic issues.

This study suggests that the Gorbachev leadership pursued an adaptive strategy during the period 1985–87. By 1987–88, however, the contradictions of piecemeal reform had become increasingly apparent. Soviet leaders were confronted with the choice of trying to preserve the essential elements of a system that had proved unworkable, or abandoning many of the defining principles of Soviet communism. The period from 1987 to 1989, then, was the decisive phase, with genuine learning evident in Soviet foreign and domestic policy.

The international environment and Soviet learning

Soviet policy toward Northeast Asia in the Brezhnev era had centered on the issue of national security, dominated primarily by a perceived military threat from China and the United States. Economic and political relations were generally subordinated to security considerations. Conditions facing the Soviet Union in the region in the 1980s were considerably different from those present in the 1960s or 1970s. China's economic reform program and its moderation in foreign policy, the broadening of the Asian economic miracle to the Newly Industrialized Countries (NICs) and more recently the member-nations of the Association of Southeast-Asian Nations (ASEAN), and the expansion of US military power under the Reagan administration are only several of the more conspicuous developments of the past decade. In contrast to a relatively successful European policy, Soviet actions in the Asian-Pacific region were acknowledged by Soviet analysts to have been clumsy and often counterproductive to pro-fessed Soviet goals. This legacy of failure stimulated a profound rethinking of Soviet Asian policies.

Second, Soviet policies in the 1960s and 1970s had not proved effective at enhancing Soviet security in East Asia, nor did they augment Soviet influence. The extraordinary expansion of naval, land, and air forces throughout the 1970s gave the Soviet Union a for-midable military presence in the Far East. Military power, however, was the sole asset available to the USSR in that region. Economically, politically, technologically, and culturally, the Soviet Union had little to offer the Asian-Pacific nations. Moreover, Soviet military inter-vention in Afghanistan, its material support for an aggressive Vietnam,· and intimidation through troop and naval deployments reinforced anti-Soviet attitudes in the region. In sum, exclusive reliance on the military component of policy was counterproductive, and limited the range of Soviet options.

Third, the international environment in the Asian-Pacific region changed dramatically in the decade of the 1980s, promising an increas-ing role for the region in world politics over the ensuing decades. The emergence of a pragmatic China largely preoccupied with internal reforms and good relations abroad, the dynamic economic perform-ance of Japan and the NICs and consequent tensions with the United States over trade issues, growing anti-nuclear sentiment combined with nationalist resentment of US presence and influence in the region in some countries, and the potential for instability in several key states presented the Soviet Union with fresh challenges and opportunities early in the Gorbachev era. The Eurocentric approach of the Brezhnev regime was ill-equipped to appreciate and cope with these develop-ments. Soviet new thinking, premised on a more realistic appraisal of the weaknesses and limitations on Soviet influence in international affairs, adjusted Soviet Asian policy to accommodate to new circum-stances.

Internal factors and Soviet learning

Several internal factors contributed to the reevaluation of basic foreign policies during the Brezhnev regime. First, the accumulation of domestic problems throughout the Soviet Union in the 1970s and 1980s (declining growth rates, low productivity, food shortages, the potential for rising ethnic discontent, alcohol and drug abuse) demanded attention at the highest levels, and indirectly led to a reexamination of expensive foreign policy commitments. Domestic issues supplanted foreign policy concerns as economic restructuring and modernization moved to the forefront of the Kremlin's policy agenda.

In the Brezhnev period, natural resources located in the European USSR became increasingly depleted, and fossil fuels came to provide the bulk of Soviet hard-currency earnings. Given these factors, resource-rich Siberia and the Far East should have received a growing share of Soviet capital investment. Yet the high costs of extraction, the extraordinarily harsh living conditions of the Far East, and aggressive Soviet foreign policies combined with the inefficiencies of central planning to frustrate regional development goals.

Perestroika's emphasis on economic development renewed interest in exploiting the massive natural resource base of the Soviet Far East. Soviet economists were encouraged to assess the potential for applying Asia's highly successful export-oriented growth model to the backward Soviet Far Eastern region. In addition, economic co-operation with the Asian-Pacific countries was to be pursued in an effort to obtain the capital investment, technology, and management skills necessary to develop Siberia and the Soviet Far East.

Another significant domestic factor influencing Soviet foreign relations was the restructuring of the foreign policy establishment. These reforms came in several stages. The first stage, within a year of Gorbachev's appointment as General Secretary, involved a number of personnel changes. Eduard Shevardnadze succeeded the venerable Andrei Gromyko as Minister of Foreign Affairs in July 1985. Gromyko's chief Asia advisors, Leonid Il'ychev and Mikhail Kapitsa, were moved out of the foreign ministry and Igor Rogachev, a pragmatic China expert, was appointed Deputy Minister of Foreign Affairs for Asia. Evgenii Primakov, Middle East expert and former Director of the Institute of Oriental Studies who would serve as a close foreign policy advisor to Gorbachev, was appointed Director of the Institute of World Economy and International Relations (IMEMO). At about the same time, Mikhail Titarenko replaced M.I. Sladkovskii as Director of the Academy of Sciences' Institute of Far East Affairs.

The system of departments within the Ministry of Foreign Affairs was reorganized during 1985–86. A new Pacific Ocean Department was formed to handle relations with Japan, Australia, New Zealand, and Papua New Guinea. The Japan "Section" was upgraded to a "Division," and a new Southeast Asian Department was formed. The Foreign Ministry also established a special bureau for relations with Asian socialist countries.[13]

A second wave of foreign policy restructuring took place in 1988, coincident with the acceleration of domestic political reform. At the 19th Party Conference in June, the entire Soviet political system, including the foreign policy establishment, was subjected to a withering examination. Following the conference, Foreign Minister Shevardnadze delivered a major critique of Soviet foreign policy to his staff, where he rejected the class approach to foreign affairs in favor of universal human values, and praised recent moves to abolish much of the secrecy that had characterized foreign policy decision-making. Ministry personnel had been polled to determine their attitudes, and were urged to submit proposals to revamp foreign policy in advance of the conference. Shevardnadze noted that new ideas had been solicited from ministry personnel during and after the April 1985 Central Committee plenum, but the results had not been very productive.[14]

The third major stage in foreign policy restructuring occurred in 1991, as the centralized Soviet political system collapsed. The year began with Boris Pankin replacing Shevardnadze, who warned the nation of an impending coup by hardliners opposed to new thinking's accomplishments, as Foreign Minister. Republic-level foreign affairs ministries became more active in diplomacy and external trade relations. Following the August coup, each Soviet republic asserted its sovereignty in foreign relations, the Baltic states achieved independence, and a struggle over former Soviet military resources began.[15]

This last phase of "restructuring" has radically changed foreign policy in what was the Union of Soviet Socialist Republics. With the formal dissolution of the USSR at the close of 1991, it was no longer possible to speak of a "Soviet foreign policy." For this reason, an assessment of this most recent learning process on foreign policy will be reserved for subsequent study. The present volume is concerned with those factors leading to the rejection of longstanding Soviet foreign policy axioms, and the adoption of a fundamentally new course in foreign relations during the Gorbachev period, rather than with foreign policy learning in the post-Soviet era.

Old and new thinking in Soviet foreign policy

The process of discarding "old thinking" and adopting "new thinking" in foreign policy was, like any learning process, gradual and evolutionary, marked by frequent setbacks and contradictions. Learning is not necessarily a linear process leading toward a more rational alignment of means and ends. As with biological evolution, some new elements may prove successful in helping the organism cope with a changed environment, and are retained. Others may initially look promising, but later prove unsuccessful and must ultimately be discarded.

Consider the following examples of how old thinking hindered adaptation in Soviet foreign policy. First, a dichotomized perspective emphasizing conflict between socialist and capitalist nations, later referred to as the "image of the enemy," needlessly aggravated tensions with the non-socialist world. Adherence to an ideology premised on irreconcilable hostility was recognized to be increasingly outmoded and dangerous given the presence of nuclear weapons. In addition, belligerent attitudes between the superpowers made it difficult to achieve mutually advantageous cooperation in economic development, trade, scientific research, and in finding peaceful solutions to regional conflicts. Gorbachev's December 1988 speech to the United Nations explicitly rejected this conflictual perspective by "de-ideologizing" Soviet foreign policy. The Leninist tenet of international class struggle was replaced by a pluralist concept accepting a global "balance of interests."[16]

Second, the one-sided pursuit of security through a massive Soviet arms build-up was acknowledged to be counterproductive, fueling the arms race and generating coalitions against the USSR. East Asia provided ample evidence of the futility of such a policy of intimidation. National security could be accomplished at lower cost by seeking mutual security, relying on a minimum of force to provide for an adequate defense, while making offensive operations unfeasible. A less heavily armed and hence less threatening Soviet Union was judged preferable in this period of severe economic stringency.

Third, a pattern of constant falsehoods and deception in Soviet foreign policy justifiably fueled the suspicions of other nations. Resistance to on-site verification in arms control negotiations and blatant distortions of history, for example, contributed to an atmosphere of mistrust in foreign relations. By abandoning patently absurd claims, revising the official historical record, and acknowledging some responsibility for international tensions, the Soviet Union earned itself a fair amount of goodwill and respect in the international community.

Fourth, the Brezhnev doctrine of limited sovereignty, as exercised in 1956, 1968, 1979, and 1981, was inherently threatening to putative allies, client states, and non-socialist neighboring states. Moreover, these actions did not enhance Soviet national security by "restoring or protecting socialism." Soviet reformers recognized that forcible interventions did not serve Soviet interests, and the events of 1989 in Eastern Europe confirmed the definitive rejection of the Brezhnev doctrine.[17]

Although most serious scholars would agree that Soviet foreign policy has been driven by more complex forces than a simple ideological plan to dominate the world militarily, many would also agree that past Soviet behavior did little to ameliorate international tensions. Soviet foreign policy supported revolutionary forces around the world, displayed a self-righteous conviction that the USSR was free from blame for international tensions, and exhibited deep-seated feelings of insecurity and fears of capitalist aggression. Soviet international behavior was characterized by obsessive secrecy, particularly in matters of national security and foreign policy, that led others to make worst-case assumptions about Soviet intentions and capabilities. Finally, Soviet leaders relied on the misguided belief that the international balance of power – the "correlation of forces" – was shifting inexorably in their favor.[18]

This linkage between domestic politics and foreign policy is crucial to understanding Soviet new thinking. From Gorbachev's perspective, restructuring could not be successful under conditions of international tension. A benign international environment was necessary for Soviet leaders to concentrate the bulk of their attention and scarce resources on modernizing the economy, improving the supply of food and other consumer products to the population, managing ethnic tensions, dealing with alcohol and drug addiction, and addressing the loss of direction that resulted from the Brezhnev years. As Party First Secretary from Stavropol province, and from 1978 to 1985 Central Committee Secretary for Agriculture, Gorbachev came to the general secretaryship with a greater sensitivity to economic and social problems than many of the Brezhnev generation. His top associates and closest advisors were frequently recruited from outside the insular Moscow establishment and in general shared Gorbachev's appreciation for the limitations on Soviet foreign policy.[19]

The conviction that the Soviet Union faced serious, even critical problems emerged toward the end of Brezhnev's tenure. Poland's near-revolutionary situation, together with serious deficiencies in the Soviet economy, science and technology, sparked animated discussion among social scientists, ideologists and officials over the state of social-ism.[20] The younger, more reform-minded members of the Politburo began searching for solutions to the country's massive internal prob-lems prior to Brezhnev's death. Gorbachev later told US Secretary of State George Shultz that he and Nikolai Ryzhkov held extensive discussions in 1982, and appointed hundreds of experts to make policy recommendations.[21]

In the wake of Brezhnev's death, the Communist Party leadership ordered a thorough evaluation of domestic and foreign policy prob-lems. At the June 1983 plenum of the Party Central Committee, General Secretary Iurii Andropov outlined as one of the Party's prin-ciple tasks stimulating new ideological and theoretical work in the social sciences, natural sciences, and economics. Domestic issues were to have top priority. Anticipating Gorbachev's retrenchment in foreign relations, Andropov warned the former colonial countries that although the USSR would provide political, military and economic support "to the extent of our possibilities," the principal responsibility for building socialism rested with the people and their leaders.[22]

Gorbachev was given a major role in following up on the mandate of this plenum. In December 1984 he delivered the keynote speech to an All-Union Scientific and Practical Conference, in which he criticized social scientists for their timid approach to solving key theoretical problems of Soviet development. Gorbachev stressed many of the themes that would become part of his perestroika program – less bureaucracy, more openness, revitalizing Marxism–Leninism, greater attention to the human factor in production, and recognizing the needs of diverse interests in Soviet society. Only by intensifying economic productivity, he maintained, could the Soviet Union guaran-tee itself a strengthened position in the international arena.[23]

The policy recommendations assembled after the June 1983 plenum comprised the preparatory work for the April 1985 plenum of the Party Central Committee, which set out the general outline of perestroika. Much later, Gorbachev noted that both he and Prime Minister Nikolai Ryzhkov had 110 documents on file dating to well before the April plenum. These documents, which formed the basis for perestroika, glasnost, and new thinking in foreign policy, contained the expert conclusions of academicians, writers, prominent specialists, and other public figures.[24]

The official contours of Soviet new thinking were elaborated in Gorbachev's book *Perestroika*, published in 1987. In it, Gorbachev rejected nuclear war as unwinnable and unthinkable, since war would mean mutual destruction of the superpowers and possibly extinction of the human species. National security was presented as dependent on mutual security; Soviet security, he argued, could not be assured as long as its excessive military might threatened other nations. Furthermore, the arms race was inherently destabilizing and could not be "won" by any **single** power. Mirror imaging by the superpowers stimulated a continual spiral that wasted huge amounts of money and talent on both sides. All states, no matter how small, should be guaranteed "freedom of choice" to determine their internal political, economic, and social arrangements without interference from the superpowers.

Finally, anticipating his United Nations address, Gorbachev rejected the validity of a zero-sum perspective on international relations. In place of a dichotomous world view, in which conflict was inevitably a consequence of the larger class struggle, Gorbachev stressed the functional interdependence of states. This organic relationship underscored the need for mutually advantageous cooperation in economic development, environmental protection, and scientific research, and in finding peaceful solutions to regional conflicts.[25]

A central aspect of the new thinking in Soviet foreign policy incorporated a revised view of the Soviet role in promoting and supporting national liberation movements. Although Soviet decision-makers followed a pragmatic foreign policy from the earliest years, avoiding direct conflicts with the United States or other Western powers, during the period from 1955 to 1982 Moscow supported diverse radical movements in Asia and Africa. Such support often took the form of stimulating violent uprisings in an attempt to deny influence to Soviet competitors. A profound reevaluation of Soviet Third World policy was taking place among Soviet scholars even before Brezhnev's death.[26] Gorbachev acted on many of their recommendations, shifting policy away from a preoccupation with class analysis and the concomitant promotion of instability in international affairs, in favor of a cooperative approach to regional conflicts.

Consensus on Soviet foreign policy goals and methods was far from automatic. Gorbachev's positive references to growing international interdependence and mutually beneficial cooperation contrasted sharply with the zero-sum perspective on international relations that continued to be voiced by some members of the Soviet elite. Politburo member Egor Ligachev staunchly defended the Stalinist perspective of the world as divided ideologically into two fundamentally irreconcilable camps, socialist and capitalist. International relations were governed by class contradictions and antagonisms. Ligachev warned against a policy based on common human values which might result in a reduced commitment to support for national liberation struggles.[27]

While defenders of this conservative outlook on foreign affairs remained evident in Soviet politics through the late 1980s, and even experienced a resurgence in late 1990 and early 1991, new thinking was highly popular among Moscow's foreign policy establishment. Even the August coup leaders, the most reactionary elements of the Kremlin hierarchy, were unwilling to revise Gorbachev's foreign policy line.

The broad consensus on new thinking is striking. Virtually all Soviet leaders realized they could no longer simply adapt to new challenges by replacing personnel or making minor adjustments in policies and structures, as in the past. Domestic issues necessitated key changes in foreign policy doctrine. Soviet reformers understood that internal problems, particularly the economy, had reached a critical point – a "break-point," to use Rosenau's terminology. As the momentum for change accelerated, it became increasingly apparent that real progress could not be achieved barring the fundamental restructuring of Soviet political life.

The implications of the domestic reform process for foreign policy meant it would not be feasible to restrict information on foreign affairs while relaxing control over information on domestic issues, although foreign policy was one of the later policy areas to be opened for discussion. Second, it would be problematic to hold officials accountable for domestic policy decisions and not for foreign policy decisions, especially when the latter involved the expenditure of scarce resources (military spending) or lives (as in Afghanistan). Third, it would be difficult for Soviet leaders to acknowledge major structural failures in the Soviet economic and political system, and then expect the East Europeans and other client states, whose systems demonstrated even more acutely the weaknesses of the Soviet model, not to reject Soviet tutelage. Finally, it would present a major dilemma to continue to posit a dichotomized world-view while seeking full participation in an increasingly interdependent world order, a move necessary to overcome the harmful autarkic practices of the past.

Without the pressure of public opinion, a free flow of information, or democratic mechanisms that would ensure that political leaders were responsible to the people, conditions for systemic learning had been largely dependent on succession periods, which were neither regular nor predictable. In any case, earlier succession periods did not coincide with generational changes, so pressures for change were offset by continuities in philosophy and experience.

History may show that we have erred in focusing on Gorbachev and present developments in the USSR as anomolous. The real anomaly, one might argue, is the unique combination of circumstances, particularly the fifty-year political monopoly of a single generation, that perpetuated essentially static conditions throughout the post-Stalin period. There is evidence that learning occurred throughout this period, but this learning was for the most part by isolated individuals. Systemic and institutional learning were frustrated by continued adherence to a relatively inflexible ideological framework, as an examination of Soviet relations with Northeast Asia indicates.

New thinking and Northeast Asia

The geographically defined approach utilized in this study has certain advantages in exploring the Soviet foreign learning process. Learning at the individual, institutional, and systemic level, at least effective learning, is influenced by diverse experiences and information. Regimes may have a tendency to compartmentalize learning (for example, the lessons learned in administering housing policy probably will not be adapted to security issues), but it is reasonable to assume some cross-fertilization takes place among elites and advisors in similar fields. Thus, insights derived from policy toward Latin America might have application to relations with Africa or other Third World nations.

A regional, geographic approach is broad enough to include a range of cases, yet narrow enough to keep the study manageable. Northeast Asia as defined here incorporates two actors of central importance to Soviet foreign policy – one communist and one capitalist – an economic powerhouse, and two smaller countries with radically divergent socio-economic systems. Occasional references to reform in Soviet–American relations, Soviet–East European relations, and domestic political and economic change illustrate the parallel nature of learning in these policy areas during the latter half of the 1980s.

Outlining the basic Soviet beliefs and values which motivated, conditioned, and constrained policy toward the region contributes toward our understanding of Soviet learning in relations with Northeast Asia. Beyond that, it is also important to determine Soviet goals in the region prior to new thinking, together with the methods employed by Soviet policy-makers to realize these goals.

The official basis for Soviet new thinking toward the Asian-Pacific region was elaborated in Gorbachev's major speeches at Vladivostok and Krasnoiarsk, in his interview with the Indonesian newspaper *Merdeka*, through official policy statements from the 27th Party Congress and the April 1986 "Asian Programme," and in remarks by leading scholars and officials. The central components were, first, the Asian-Pacific region was to be accorded greater attention in Soviet foreign policy, in keeping with its growing importance for world affairs. Second, the USSR would seek actively to reduce tensions in the region through political means, while maintaining good relations with all states. Third, the Soviet Union would attempt to halt the arms race, calling for limitations and reductions in both nuclear and conventional weapons in the Pacific. Specific elements included working out confidence building measures, guaranteeing the security of sea lanes of communication and free passage through international straits, promoting the concept of nuclear-free and peace zones, limiting the naval presence of both superpowers, and eliminating foreign military bases in the region.

A fourth component of Soviet policy involved the expansion of trade and other forms of economic cooperation with all states in the region. Economic ties were to become far more complex and organic than in the past; full integration into the dynamic Asian system was to be sought through participation in the Pacific Economic Cooperation Conference, the UN Economic and Social Commission for Asia and the Pacific, the Asian Development Bank, and other international forums. Fifth, the Soviet Union renewed its support for the Asian non-aligned movement. Finally, Soviet policy adopted a less confrontational approach to regional organizations – ASEAN, for example – and encouraged the evolution of multipolar political alignments in the area.

Soviet policies toward the Asian-Pacific region were acknowledged by reformers to have been counterproductive and frequently self-defeating. One group of specialists, reviewing progress made in the two years after Gorbachev's Vladivostok speech, decried the secondary position accorded the region by previous regimes, and linked weak Soviet influence there to exclusive reliance on military power.[28]

Moscow's traditional allies and client states in the region – Mongolia, North Korea, Vietnam, Laos, and Cambodia – had a history of being governed by the most repressive political systems, and proved to be the weakest economic performers. Two pivotal states, Japan and China, wielded considerably more influence in the Far East despite their military inferiority to the Soviet Union. By attempting to reduce their threatening military posture in the Far East, while appealing for good political and economic relations with all states, the Gorbachev leadership hoped to regain some of the ground lost under Brezhnev.

A concomitant element of Soviet new thinking viewed superpower status as heavily dependent on political, economic, and cultural factors. Military strength remained critical to superpower status, but military force alone had proved to be a rather ineffectual instrument of foreign policy. Soviet reformers recognized that the Soviet empire was seriously over-extended, with some retrenchment and considerable rebuilding needed to avoid permanent damage to the Soviet state. The Soviet Union fielded impressive military forces in Asia, but could not convert this presence into an effective instrument of statecraft.[29]

In the Asian-Pacific region, Japan's extensive presence provided convincing evidence that economic strength could be as effective a source of influence, if not more so, than purely military power.[30] South Korea's growing prominence in the region contrasted sharply with North Korea's increasing isolationism and poor economic perform-ance. China's market-oriented reforms had stimulated extraordinary growth rates and the rapid expansion of trade and international investment. Clearly, there were many potential lessons to be derived from the Asian experience.

Conclusion

The revolutionary events that took place in the Soviet Union can be seen in a new light if these changes are viewed as the end result of an extended learning process. The intellectual seeds were planted shortly after the 20th Party Congress in 1956, germinated during the thaw, but then went underground during the period of stagnation under Brezh-nev. Many of the ideas for reform, and an awareness of Soviet economic, social, political, and foreign policy problems emerged in the later years of Brezhnev regime, at least in embryonic form. An intel-lectual flowering took place during the transition phase, spurred on by directives from Andropov and Gorbachev, two leaders who were more rationalist than ideological in their approach. Chernenko's unimaginative tenure was brief enough to have little impact on the process – we have seen that expert recommendations were being gathered during this period, even if most specialists were still reluctant to risk recommending far-reaching changes.

When Gorbachev became General Secretary in March 1985, much of the preparatory work for perestroika and new thinking was already in place. Gorbachev did not have a clear plan for the specific shape reforms should take, but by this time he did have a good idea of what was wrong with the country. Over the next six years Gorbachev's and the reformers' thinking evolved, as they became aware of the contradictions between their ultimate goals and the inherently conservative, repressive nature of the system. Reforms that were originally envisioned as preserving the system while making it more humane, more democratic, and more efficient, eventually were forced to confront the reality that it was the essential structures of the system itself – the Communist Party's political monopoly, state bureaucratic control of the economy, and the pervasive influence of a quasi-religious ideology – that were responsible for the crisis of socialism.

3 Learning and adaptation in the historical context

there are still attempts to turn away from painful matters in our history. We cannot agree to this ... a truthful analysis must help us solve today's problems ...

Mikhail Gorbachev, speech on the seventieth anniversary of the October Revolution, 2 November 1987, in J.L. Black, ed., *USSR Documents 1987* (Gulf Breeze, Florida: Academic International Press, 1988), p. 95.

Soviet decision-makers, no less than their counterparts in the United States, have relied on past experience to guide the formulation of foreign and domestic policies. In any political system there is considerable variation in how effectively leaders perceive and utilize history to address contemporary problems. Much depends on the particular time frame in which leaders grew to political maturity, on their training and ideological perspective, and on the major events that conditioned their world view.[1]

For Khrushchev, Brezhnev, and the foreign policy executives and advisors of their generation, the years of terror and repression under Stalin, the trauma of the Second World War, and Cold War tensions were vitally important formative experiences. This history was viewed through the prism of Marxist–Leninist ideology, which obscured or distorted the lessons that might be drawn from experience, and was further influenced by the imperial chauvinism of Russian nationalism. Soviet communism had narrowly escaped annihilation during the war, and, from the Kremlin's perspective, continued to face an aggressively hostile capitalist world bent on its downfall. These threats, however, were balanced by the gratifying successes in replicating the Soviet model throughout Eastern Europe and Asia. Events had corroborated the historical determinist expectations of Marxism, and the bipolar Leninist view of world politics as class warfare writ large.

Shortly after Stalin's death, the leadership was confronted with stark evidence that refuted Soviet pretensions to universal hegemony among the infant socialist states, based on the ideological conviction that socio-economic affinities would supersede national distinctions. Confront-ation in Poland, revolution in Hungary, and above all the rupture with China, challenged regime dogma on Soviet foreign policy in a pro-foundly changed international system. Although Khrushchev indi-cated some capacity for learning how to deal with the challenges of this new order when he advanced the concept of "separate national paths to socialism," Soviet leaders were clearly not ready to tolerate much vari-ation in the socialist camp. His conservative successors were consider-ably more dogmatic, and less willing to question the fundamental premises of Soviet foreign policy – in a word, less open to learning.

Glasnost was an integral component of Mikhail Gorbachev's plan to restructure the Soviet Union, by opening for critical discussion topics that had previously been ignored or distorted. One of the goals of this campaign was the elimination of "blank spots" in Soviet history. His-torical revision was needed in order to transcend the stifling legacy of Stalinism. By reevaluating the past, candidly analyzing the failures and successes of Soviet foreign policy, reformers could more effectively align external goals with the system's internal capabilities and limi-tations.

This chapter reviews the historical record of Soviet relations with China, Japan, and North and South Korea in the period from 1945 through the Brezhnev period, with the aim of assessing how Soviet leaders perceived, evaluated, and reacted to relations with each country and to major events in the region. What assumptions governed Soviet policy under Stalin? Did significant changes occur in Soviet relations with Northeast Asia from the Stalin to the post-Stalin periods, or was Soviet policy characterized by continuity? Is there any evidence that a process of learning or adaptation was taking place during the Khrush-chev and Brezhnev periods, and what were the significant variables facilitating or hindering learning and adaptation? Exploring the Soviet post-war experience provides the context for understanding the devel-opment of new thinking toward Northeast Asia under Gorbachev.

The post-war setting

Northeast Asia in the years following World War Two presented Soviet leaders with a substantially different situation from that existing during the interwar period. The threat of an aggressive, militaristic

Japan had been eliminated. Rapid advances of Soviet troops in the Far East ensured control of Manchuria, together with the acquisition of south Sakhalin and the Kurile islands, territories surrendered to Japan during the late tsarist period. However, the dominant American presence in Japan and much of the Pacific region constrained further Soviet ambitions toward expansion and influence. Compared with Europe, Asia appeared to offer few opportunities, but it also posed no immediate dangers for the USSR.[2]

Stalin's approach to Northeast Asia was conditioned by the Manichaean ideological perspective of two irreconcilably hostile camps, enunciated by Andrei Zhdanov at the founding congress of the Cominform in 1947 and formally propounded at the 19th Congress of the Soviet Communist Party in 1952. According to this perspective, North Korea and (after 1949) China were loyal allies of socialism's leading representative. South Korea and Japan, by contrast, were regarded as mere vassals of the United States.

Khrushchev's pronouncements on peaceful coexistence notwithstanding, this ideological frame of reference was modified only slightly by Stalin's successors. Zero-sum thinking limited Soviet leaders to triangular diplomacy aimed at maintaining a balance of power in the region, to counter a perceived threat from the United States, China, or some combination of the two major powers, reinforced by South Korea and Japan. Relations with these countries fluctuated over time, but the underlying premises of Soviet policy toward the region persisted through the Brezhnev era.

Following Stalin's death in 1953, the Soviet leadership sought a quick resolution of some of the more acute trouble spots in East–West relations, most notably the Korean conflict, as part of an overall effort to reduce tensions. Relations were normalized with Japan in 1955–56, although the two countries were at that time unable to resolve the issue of the Kuriles and conclude a peace treaty.[3] Further moves toward a more accommodating stance with the West were evident in Khrushchev's speech to the 20th Party Congress, in 1956, where he abandoned the two-camps doctrine in favor of peaceful coexistence of states, rejected the feasibility of warfare in the nuclear era, and accepted the notion of separate national paths to socialism. Khrushchev also emphasized Soviet willingness to expand relations with the newly emerging Third World nations. The first Soviet visit to the Third World had been to Asia (India, Burma, and Afghanistan, in 1955), and Soviet leaders had voiced strong support for the Bandung founding conference of the non-aligned movement. Overtures were made to

India, Afghanistan, Burma, Indonesia, and other Asian countries that had been largely ignored under Stalin.

Despite this seemingly new attention to and respect for Asia, the single most disastrous foreign policy setback of the post-war period – the break with China – evolved during the Khrushchev period. The reasons for the deterioration in relations are many and complex, and have been extensively analyzed over the years.[4] More important for the purposes of this analysis is arriving at an understanding of the central themes in Soviet relations with the People's Republic of China, specifically from the Soviet perspective of learning and adapting from its interactions with China.

The growing US involvement in Vietnam in the 1950s and 1960s complicated Soviet relations with the PRC, but also offered new opportunities for the Soviet Union to demonstrate its commitment to the forces of national liberation in Asia. Soviet military assistance to North Vietnam, totalling more than $3 billion from 1965 to 1972, paid handsome dividends in the form of a humiliating American withdrawal and subsequent move toward isolationism. From the Soviet perspective, America's withdrawal from Vietnam signaled a new era in the Asian-Pacific region, and in the Third World more generally, as the "correlation of forces" shifted in favor of the USSR. But as American presence and influence in Asia waned, Chinese radicalism and chauvinism presented a new threat. The Ussuri river clash of 1969 heightened Soviet fears of Chinese aggression, while US–China *rapprochement* in the 1970s reinforced Soviet anxieties and accelerated the Soviet military build-up in the Far East.

Moscow's global activism in the 1970s was built almost entirely on expanding military power, and was facilitated by the American retreat from international commitments. The post-Vietnam reticence of America to get involved in distant conflicts made it easier for the Soviet Union to support radical movements worldwide, in the belief that such actions would not significantly affect East–West relations. Soviet power and influence appeared to be expanding in Asia during the latter part of the 1970s, as US influence declined. Vietnam and the USSR signed a Treaty of Friendship and Cooperation in 1978, and Soviet aid to Vietnam increased to approximately $2–3 billion annually. In exchange for this largesse, the Soviet Union acquired basing rights at Cam Ranh Bay and Danang, and Vietnam was brought into the Council for Mutual Economic Assistance. Soviet assistance to Afghanistan increased after the April 1978 revolution, culminating in the December 1979 invasion and a decade-long bloody commitment.

Finally, Soviet military forces in the Far East and the Pacific Ocean were enlarged and modernized during this period.

A more aggressive international posture and behavior had consequences that were not appreciated or acknowledged by the Brezhnev generation of Soviet leaders. The following can be attributed in whole or part to Soviet bellicose actions in the Asia-Pacific: the Sino-Japanese Friendship Treaty of 1978, with its much-publicized anti-hegemony clause; a resurgence of American military spending and the expansion of America's military presence, initiated in President Carter's last years but expanded dramatically under President Reagan; the modernization and expansion of Japanese and South Korean military forces; and the establishment of diplomatic relations between the US and PRC in 1979, followed by tentative steps toward military cooperation between the two countries in the 1980s. Moscow's foreign policy elite, however, refused to acknowledge Soviet responsibility for these developments.

There are some rather revealing parallels in Soviet foreign policies toward the Far East in the years following Stalin's death, and those pursued by the Soviet leadership following the death of Leonid Brezhnev, nearly thirty years later. In each case, a period of conservatism was followed by a period of reassessing policy, both domestic and foreign. As the new functionaries jockeyed for position, internal reforms generally took precedence. However, priorities and approaches in foreign policy were also subject to review. The emphasis was on attempting to preserve earlier gains, recognizing opportunities that had previously been overlooked, and correcting some of the more egregious blunders of the previous regime. Stalin's successors were faced with resolving the stalemated Korean conflict; Brezhnev's with the "bleeding wound" of Afghanistan, as Gorbachev so aptly put it.

Sino-Soviet relations furnish a useful illustration. After Stalin's death in 1953 the Chinese communists were treated less as vassals and more as equal partners in communism. Similarly, improved relations with the Chinese were actively sought following Brezhnev's death. Here it should be noted that several initiatives for improved Sino-Soviet relations were taken during Brezhnev's lifetime. Initial feelers were advanced in 1979, and continued even after the invasion of Afghanistan. Brezhnev's Tashkent speech of March 1982 overtly demonstrated Soviet interest in negotiations, and normalization talks began soon afterward. Moreover, China's internal reforms under Deng Xiaoping had clearly improved the political climate from the peak of hostilities during the Cultural Revolution.

But these surface similarities do not negate the fact that the post-Brezhnev transition marked a fundamental break with the Stalinist past in foreign policy. A confluence of domestic factors and foreign policy setbacks over time produced an awareness that Stalinist policies were ineffective or counterproductive in the late twentieth century, and that new approaches were needed. This recognition led to a basic reassessment of Soviet assumptions and methods in foreign policy.

There are, of course, significant differences between the end of the Stalin and Brezhnev periods. The comparison should not be exaggerated. In each case, however, we find a new set of leaders seeking enhanced external stability in order to deal first with an acute set of domestic problems. In both cases, one faction of the new leadership promoted a more innovative, or accommodative, foreign policy in an attempt to take advantage of changing external circumstances. And in both periods it is possible to discern a new appreciation of the limits on Soviet power, or at least an acknowledgment of the overextension of Soviet commitments in the region.

The purpose of the following sections is not to offer any new evidence of the causes of the Sino-Soviet split, or to shed new light on Soviet relations with Japan and Korea, but rather to suggest that Soviet policies toward the region under Khrushchev and Brezhnev were essentially a continuation of Stalinist policy. This is not to suggest that policies were inflexible – there is evidence of limited adaptation to take advantage of changing circumstances. However, genuine learning, as defined in Chapter 2, is noticeably absent in Soviet policy toward Northeast Asia prior to the Gorbachev period.

China

Chiang Kai-shek's apparently secure position and Stalin's satisfaction with a weak and divided China had convinced Stalin to pursue normal relations with the Quomindang in the first years after the war. A Treaty of Friendship and Alliance was concluded between the Nationalist government and the Soviet Union in August 1945. Defying the expectations of both the West and Moscow, Mao's communists quickly routed the Quomindang and established the People's Republic of China in October 1949. This victory gave an impressive boost to the world communist movement, encouraged the communist parties active in various Asian countries after the war, and reinforced the Western perception that an inexorable communist advance was taking place under Soviet tutelage.

There are three main elements in Sino-Soviet relations that remained essentially constant through the Stalin, Khrushchev, and Brezhnev periods. First, Soviet leaders were unwilling or unable to treat China as a fully co-equal power. China was perceived as an underdeveloped country lagging far behind the USSR economically, technologically, and politically. A second and related consideration was the Soviet claim to ideological primacy. As long as the Soviet Communist Party was held to be the leading and guiding force in world socialism, Chinese communism was relegated to either a subordinate or heretical position. Third, relations between the two powers evolved from ideological competition in the late Khrushchev period to military confrontation by the end of the 1960s. Although the Soviet military build-up generated a perception of superiority and confidence, especially after the USSR achieved nuclear parity with the United States in the late 1960s, it also encouraged new alignments of forces against a more aggressive Soviet force posture.

Sino-Soviet relations were marred by tensions and resentments from the beginning.[5] Stalin and the other Soviet leaders displayed a paternalistic attitude toward the new Communist state. They regarded China as a junior partner in world communism, albeit a far more important ally than any other socialist state. During Mao's initial visit to Moscow, from December 1949 to February 1950, the Chinese were praised as "little brothers" of the USSR. Stalin went out of his way to apologize for underestimating the CCP's potential in the immediate post-war period, and the Chinese delegation appeared to accept the Soviet Union's role as "elder brother" and teacher. A common Chinese slogan in the early 1950s even exhorted communists to "learn from the USSR."[6]

Stalin's condescending attitude rankled the Chinese, who were sensitive about maintaining the appearance of an egalitarian relationship. During Mao's 1950 visit the Chinese delegation was adamant in urging Stalin to attend an official reception held in the Metropol' hotel, rather than in the Kremlin, as a recognition of sovereign Chinese authority.[7] In his memoirs, Khrushchev asserts that Stalin's general attitude during Mao's visit was one of neglect and condescension. However, Khrushchev himself agreed with Stalin's view that Mao held a narrow peasant's position, ignored the urban working class, and had a poor understanding of Marxism.[8] While Khrushchev rejected Stalin's peculiar personality quirks in dealing with foreign communists as counterproductive, accepted the theoretical right of each socialist country to follow distinct national paths to socialism, and claimed to base relations between socialist systems on principles of genuine equality, the foundations of his China policy do not appear to have been substantively different from Stalin's.

Under Khrushchev, the Soviet Union began a policy of employing economic assistance to cement political ties with selected Third World nations, and to link the socialist world more closely through the Soviet-led Council for Mutual Economic Assistance. Stalin's plundering of the East European states was reversed, and a series of economic assistance projects was initiated with China in 1953. The payoffs for the USSR were the expected emulation of Soviet central planning, the implicit recognition of the USSR as an ideal developmental model, and additional benefits from gratitude for Soviet generosity. The Soviet Union's impressive growth rates and significant technological achievements in the 1950s were, from Khrushchev's perspective, clear evidence that the Soviet model was superior to any alternate form of development, either socialist or capitalist.

From early in the post-Stalin period, however, the Chinese emerged as potential competitors of, rather than collaborators with, the Soviet Union in the Third World. A standard Soviet history of the Brezhnev period notes indignantly that the Chinese tried to assert their leadership of Asian revolutionary movements as early as December 1949, by urging the Indian and Indonesian communists to emulate China's revolutionary experience.[9] China's effective support of North Korea, its participation in the 1954 Geneva accords, China's prominent role at the April 1955 Bandung Conference of Afro-Asian nations, and the formulation of the five principles of peaceful coexistence as the basis for Sino-Indian relations marked the beginnings of Beijing's independent foreign policy.

Since the genesis of the Soviet shift in Third World policy can be traced to Stalin's last year, it seems reasonable that Khrushchev's Asian opening of 1955–56 was primarily oriented toward competing with the West for influence. Competition with China, however, appears to have been a factor even at this early stage. China's natural affinity with the lesser developed countries and its growing independence in foreign policy may have encouraged Soviet leaders to adopt a more activist stance.

China's Hundred Flowers campaign of 1957 and the Great Leap Forward launched the following year created serious strains between Moscow and Beijing. From the Soviet perspective, these adventurist policies challenged the "proven" model of socialist development pioneered by the USSR. More importantly, this period of radical change was perceived by Moscow as a power struggle between two rival factions within the CCP. One, the Marxist-internationalist faction, accepted the Soviet developmental model and Khrushchev's foreign policy line. The petty-bourgeois Maoist faction, by contrast, favored nationalistic, anti-Soviet policies, rejecting the goals expressed at the 20th Party Congress. The Maoists sought to isolate the USSR from other socialist states, establish a bloc of national liberation movements hostile to the Soviet Union, undermine Soviet ideological authority, and sabotage peaceful coexistence.[10]

China's tumultuous experiments offended the Soviet leaders' obsession with political order, even during the more adventurist Khrushchev years. Of the Hundred Flowers notion of contending schools of thought, Khrushchev observed that "certain flowers ought to be cultivated but others should be cut down," and instructed Soviet newspapers and propagandists to avoid any discussion of the subject.[11] Despite the "thaw" in Soviet cultural life of the late 1950s, the idea of openly expressing a plurality of opinions was anathema to the Soviet leadership.

China's bid for economic self-sufficiency clearly annoyed the Soviets. At the 20th Party Congress, Khrushchev had praised China's gradual economic transformation, based on a Soviet-style five-year plan. Three years later, in the midst of the Great Leap Forward, the 21st Soviet Party Congress was convened to herald the achievements of the Soviet centrally planned system and announce a revised seven-year plan. According to the First Secretary's report, the USSR expected by 1970 to be the world's leader in total volume of production and per capita output. Khrushchev graciously commended China's ambitious goal of surpassing Britain's industrial output within a few years, but the message of the Congress was clear – the Soviet method of development was demonstrably superior to either capitalism or the Chinese model. All communist parties might have been theoretically equal, but none could match Soviet experience or achievements. By developing the Soviet Union into the most powerful socialist country and (very shortly) the world's most advanced nation, the CPSU had proved the efficacy of its methods.[12]

In any case, the Soviet leadership suspected Mao and the Chinese communists were not satisfied with an equal partnership in leading the international communist movement, but instead sought political and ideological hegemony. The Soviets also had second thoughts about contributing to China's military potential, especially given that country's bellicose statements about a socialist victory emerging from global nuclear war. Khrushchev's July 1958 visit to Beijing attempted to ensure joint control over China's nuclear research and military programs. When Soviet efforts failed, Khrushchev canceled an earlier offer to provide the PRC with a sample atomic weapon. In August 1960, piqued at Chinese "ingratitude" for Soviet assistance in industrial construction projects, he abruptly ordered some 1400 Soviet advisors to return home.[13]

Underlying Soviet relations with China, and for that matter the entire socialist community, was a fundamental contradiction which Soviet leaders consistently refused to recognize. Soviet claims to a dominant role in the world communist movement were predicated on the fiction of an objective, Marxist–Leninist position unencumbered by nationalistic interests. Of course, Khrushchev's revisions to Soviet ideology were in line with Soviet national interests, but he (and his successors) failed to realize that Chinese (or Yugoslav, or Albanian, or Hungarian) interests might not coincide perfectly with fluctuations in Soviet policy. It was illogical to base relations with other socialist countries on a malleable ideology without also accepting the premise of a plurality of interests, and this the Soviets were unwilling to do. Chinese nationalism, therefore, was simply equated with anti-Sovietism.

The Khrushchev and Brezhnev leaderships dealt with this conundrum through a strategy of denial. A facade of unity may have been less satisfactory than a genuine identity of views, but it was clearly preferable to open discord. At the fall 1960 Moscow conference of eighty-one communist parties, for example, the CPSU went to great lengths to preserve the impression of international unity, exerting pressure on the Chinese delegation to adhere to the Soviet line. During a July 1963 meeting of representatives of the Chinese and Soviet parties, headed by Deng Xiaoping and Mikhail Suslov, the Soviets again tried and failed to gain Chinese adherence to a general line of the international communist movement.[14]

Following Khrushchev's ouster, both sides explored the possibility of normalizing relations. The Chinese party leadership sent "warm congratulations" to General Secretary Leonid Brezhnev, Premier Alexei Kosygin and President Anastas Mikoian, expressing the hope that the fraternal friendship of the two peoples could develop without interruption.[15] The Chinese sent a delegation headed by Zhou Enlai to Moscow for the November 7th celebrations, and Premier Kosygin visited Beijing twice early in 1965. However, Soviet overtures seemed premised on the belief that Khrushchev's personal antagonism toward

Mao had been a significant factor in the split. It soon became apparent that the USSR was not about to concede its claim to ideological hegemony or to compromise on any of its basic positions. China's slide into the radicalism of the Cultural Revolution decisively ended Soviet hopes for reconciliation on their terms. Party relations between the CCP and CPSU were severed in March 1966, and diplomatic relations were suspended for three years beginning in 1967.

Paradoxically, the early years of the Sino-Soviet conflict supported the efforts of Soviet reformers who were determined to continue Khrushchev's destalinization program. These more progressive forces, in directing their criticisms toward Mao's cult of personality, were utilizing a potent weapon against those Stalinists opposed to the "liberal" themes of the 20th and 22nd Party congresses. The Chinese, by attacking the results of these congresses and openly promoting the cult of personality, further strengthened the cause of Soviet reformers.[16] However, a series of developments in 1967–69 shifted the conflict away from its ideological basis toward largely military considerations. These included the Cultural Revolution, Iurii Andropov's transfer in 1967 from the Central Committee Department for Liaison with the Socialist Countries to the KGB, the Czechoslovak Prague Spring and subsequent Warsaw Pact invasion, and the clashes between Soviet and Chinese forces along the Ussuri river border in 1969.

The Brezhnev leadership's increasing reliance on amassing military force as the primary instrument of Soviet statecraft coincided with a conservative turn in Soviet politics after the middle of the 1960s. As efforts to contain China politically became increasingly problematic, Moscow shifted toward a military strategy designed to contain a possible threat from the East. China had exploded its first atomic bomb just two days after Khrushchev was deposed. Additional tests were conducted in 1965 and 1966, and a thermonuclear device was tested in June 1967.[17] These alarming developments, coinciding with the vituperative Chinese attacks on Soviet "revisionism" during the Cultural Revolution, contributed to a build-up of Soviet military forces on the Sino-Soviet border. From approximately seventeen to twenty divisions deployed along the Sino-Soviet border and in the Soviet Far East in 1965, Soviet troop strength eventually peaked at some fifty-three to fifty-five divisions in the early 1980s, or approximately one-fourth of all ground forces.

By fall of 1968, following the Soviet invasion of Czechoslovakia and the enunciation of the Brezhnev doctrine of limited sovereignty, the USSR had evidently replaced the United States as China's premier enemy.[18] In late November the Chinese proposed to the outgoing Johnson administration (with Nixon's approval) resuming the meetings in Warsaw between the two nation's representatives.[19] Armed clashes between Soviet and Chinese forces over Damansky (Zhenbao) island on the Ussuri river in March 1969, and additional engagements from April to June, convinced the Brezhnev regime to accelerate the build-up of nuclear and conventional forces in the Far East. Given Beijing's earlier stated willingness to absorb a nuclear strike from the United States in order to precipitate socialism's ultimate victory, Soviet leaders were understandably apprehensive about their country's security. In Washington, a Soviet embassy official contacted the State Department to sound out America's response to a hypothetical Soviet strike against Chinese nuclear facilities.[20]

The Kremlin also supplemented military actions with a series of diplomatic initiatives. Premier Kosygin met Zhou at the airport in Beijing in September 1969, following a visit to Hanoi. In his speech to the 24th Party Congress, Brezhnev approvingly noted this meeting of the heads of government, which was followed by border talks in Beijing. There were signs of "a certain normalization" in state relations over the past eighteen months, he noted, although there had been no moves to restore party ties. Diplomatic relations were revived late in 1970, and several economic agreements were signed which marginally increased trade in the first half of the decade. However, Brezhnev took the opportunity to condemn Chinese leaders for advancing their own special ideological-political platform incompatible with Leninism, for disrupting the international communist movement, and for demanding the CPSU renounce its 20th Party Congress line and the Soviet Party Program.[21]

Within the international communist movement, the Kremlin sought to contain and isolate China. In his speech to the June 1969 Moscow conference of seventy-five communist parties (the Chinese, Japanese, and North Korean parties were not in attendance), Brezhnev devoted considerable space to criticizing the Chinese for fragmenting communist solidarity, exhibiting great-power aspirations through territorial claims on other countries, and displaying a cavalier approach to the possibility of armed conflict. In passing, Brezhnev suggested that the recent course of events mandated the creation of an Asian collective security system, a proposal, despite later Soviet claims to the contrary, clearly directed against the PRC.[22] This proposal, which would be resurrected later by Gorbachev, met with an overwhelmingly negative reaction among the Asian nations to which it was directed.[23]

Chinese-American *rapprochement*, inaugurated with Secretary of State William Roger's 1969 Canberra speech and publicly expressed in Henry Kissinger's July 1971 visit to Beijing, both surprised and angered Soviet leaders. The Shanghai Communiqué, signed following Richard Nixon's February 1972 visit, included a provision opposing any attempt to establish "hegemony" in the Asian-Pacific region, an unmistakeable reference to Soviet presence in the area. For the Kremlin, this developing relationship signaled more than merely an enhanced physical threat. America's China policy challenged Soviet aspirations to be recognized as one of the world's two superpowers, and the ascendant one at that. To the extent that the triangle was equilateral, the United States at least implicitly recognized China's claim to represent an alternative ideological-political world view separate from and in competition with Soviet-led socialism. As Nixon and Kissinger expected, Soviet concern over the developing Sino-American relationship prompted Moscow to respond more forthrightly to American initiatives.

The Sino-Soviet relationship in the 1960s and 1970s was further complicated by competition for influence in the Third World. The typical Soviet criticism of China charged Beijing with seeking to arouse mistrust and hostility toward the USSR among Third World nations, attempting to persuade these countries that the developmental experience of the Soviet Union was irrelevant to their situation, and in general fueling the fires of extremism in the developing world. Policies toward Asian and African developing nations sought to demonstrate the superiority of the Soviet model of political control and economic development over either the capitalist or Chinese models.

Soviet commentators were particularly incensed at the Chinese claim to a unique identity of interest with the Third World that neither the capitalist nor the Soviet-led socialist systems could match. Mao's division of the globe into three zones and his claim to leadership of the developing third group (comprised of Asian and African states) equated the USSR with the United States and the forces of imperialism. Considering China's lack of tangible resources to support its Third World policies, these political and ideological challenges posed a greater problem for Soviet leaders than did the possibility of China physically supplanting Soviet presence and influence in the Third World.[24]

Although the Chinese could boast of few demonstrable successes in the Third World, and Sino-American relations remained largely stagnant following the initial breakthrough, Soviet leaders continued their strong criticism of China through the 1970s. China, in turn, did not appear eager to mend ties with Moscow. Brezhnev's report to the 25th CPSU Congress, in February 1976, accused Beijing of trying to wreck detente and provoke a world war. China's foreign policy, he charged, was associated with the most extreme elements of reaction – Western militarists, South African racists, and Chilean fascists. The door to normalization remained open, Brezhnev suggested, but only if China was willing to make concessions.[25]

The period from 1977 to 1979 was an important turning point for Soviet policy toward Northeast Asia. China's relations with the United States began to improve more rapidly. As tensions between the United States and the Soviet Union mounted during the final years of the Carter administration, Washington accelerated the normalization of Sino-American ties at least partly in an attempt to put more pressure on Moscow. Former US National Security Advisor Zbigniew Brzezinski notes in his memoirs:

We were convinced that a genuinely cooperative relationship between Washington and Beijing would greatly enhance the stability of the Far East and that, more generally, it would be to US advantage in the global competition with the Soviet Union. Moreover, normalization was definitely in China's interest, especially in view of the increasingly threatening Soviet attitude toward the PRC.[26]

Meanwhile, China and Japan concluded a friendship treaty in 1978 incorporating a clause opposing attempts by any outside powers to establish "hegemony" in the region. Although Soviet public reactions to the treaty were only moderately critical, this development, together with the possibility of future developments in Sino-Japanese military cooperation, heightened Soviet unease about trends in Asia.[27] That same year China began implementing far-reaching agricultural reforms. Agriculture was the most important of Deng's Four Modernizations, the other three areas being industry, science and technology, and national defense. While Soviet leaders were encouraged by Beijing's clear rejection of Maoist practices, the dynamic capitalist principles on which Chinese reforms were based presented an unwelcome contrast to stagnant Soviet policies.

The Soviet response to this unexpected and discomforting confluence of events was typical for the Brezhnev leadership – to hunker down and augment Soviet military forces in the region. Starting in 1978, Soviet Far Eastern forces underwent both quantitative expansion and qualitative improvement. Deployment of the mobile, MIRVed SS-20s began in 1978, augmenting the capabilities of the long-range

Backfire bombers and greatly increasing the number of nuclear war-heads stationed in the Far Eastern theater. Modern conventional weapons replaced the less sophisticated aircraft, tanks and other equipment that had previously been positioned in the east. Approximately four divisions were forward-deployed in Mongolia, one in the contested Kurile islands, and in 1978 the Soviet Union established a naval presence at the former American facility at Cam Ranh Bay in Vietnam. Treaties of friendship and cooperation were signed with both Mongolia and Vietnam in 1978. A new high command, the Far Eastern Theater of Military Operations (TVD) was established in December 1978.[28] Not coincidentally, this development was made public two weeks after Washington announced the decision to establish full diplomatic relations with Beijing.

At the end of the decade, Soviet relations with China showed little promise of improvement. The euphoria and high expectations with which the Brezhnev leadership greeted the death of Mao in September 1976 were not borne out by subsequent events. Moscow had failed to make any significant progress in bilateral relations with the PRC in the latter half of the 1970s. Moreover, from Moscow's alarmist perspective there was now the disturbing possibility of a Washington–Beijing–Tokyo pact directed against Soviet interests in East Asia and the Pacific. The aging and infirm Politburo, led by the dogmatic Brezhnev, Suslov, and Gromyko, was unwilling to consider much less enact new and creative solutions to the domestic and foreign policy challenges confronting the USSR. Under these conditions, there was very little adaptation, and no discernible learning taking place in Sino-Soviet relations.

Japan

While China evolved from opportunity to ally to threat in the course of this century, Japan changed from a significant military threat in its own right to a potential threat as an ally of the United States after World War Two. China's disintegration in the first half of the twentieth century offered the new Soviet government significant opportunities for promoting revolutionary influence in the Far East. Japan's imperialistic ambitions arising from the Meiji Restoration, however, presented a distinct military challenge to Soviet interests in the region. The Russo-Japanese war, a series of clashes along the Manchurian border in the late 1930s, and the brief engagement at the end of World War Two left a legacy of mistrust and hostility between the two countries that persisted throughout the post-war period.

Soviet decision-makers continued to deal with Japan as a semi-sovereign nation well after the American occupation had ended. Japan had been defeated and disarmed, but still represented a potential security threat to the USSR, primarily through collaboration with and support for US military power in the region. Japan's intractable demand for return of the Kurile islands, viewed by Moscow as proof of aggressive, revanchist claims on Soviet territory, frustrated conclusion of a peace treaty and poisoned relations throughout the post-war era.[29]

A persistent concern with the possibility of a resurgent, militaristic Japan strongly influenced Soviet policy in the region. The Sino-Soviet agreement of 1950 and Soviet efforts toward concluding a peace treaty with Japan in 1955–56 were both oriented toward neutralizing Japan and weakening the links between Japan and the United States. Although Soviet policy toward Japan in the 1960s and 1970s centered primarily on economic ties, the tendency during the Brezhnev period to assess power according to military capability rather than economic strength reinforced the marginality of Soviet–Japanese relations for the Kremlin. Moscow resisted acknowledging Japan as an independent and, by the 1970s, increasingly powerful international actor in its own right.

Stalin's goals *vis-à-vis* Japan in the immediate post-war period were to consolidate Soviet control over territory lost in the Russo-Japanese war (southern Sakhalin); seize the Kurile islands, which had been ceded to Japan in the treaties of Shimoda (1855) and St. Petersburg (1875); establish and maintain a presence in formerly Japanese-controlled territories in Korea and Manchuria; and acquire a zone of occupation in Japan proper. Overall, the Soviet Union did not fare too badly. The first ambition was successfully realized, and the second at least partially through Soviet occupation of North Korea and the CCP victory in China. While the third aspiration – joint governance with US occupation forces – was not fulfilled, this did not appear to be a critical issue for Stalin. As one prominent historian notes, under MacArthur's trusteeship Japan was completely disarmed, the Japanese Communist Party was permitted to function openly, and the USSR was accorded some influence through the Allied Council.[30] These gains clearly improved the Soviet position by making a resurgence of Japanese militarism unlikely at any time in the near future.

One important Soviet objective of the Stalin period did not succeed: the withdrawal of American forces from Japan and the surrounding region. Kim Il-sung's invasion of South Korea in June 1950, sanctioned if not encouraged by Stalin, abruptly reversed official American policy toward the Korean peninsula and reinforced the US commitment to protect Japan's security from communist aggression.

In 1951 the United States pushed through the San Francisco peace treaty and shortly thereafter concluded a security pact with Japan. The USSR, which demanded but did not obtain the neutralization of Japan together with recognition of the PRC, refused to sign the treaty. Instead of intimidating Japan and encouraging the United States to retreat from East Asia, the Korean War strengthened US determination to maintain a military presence in the region. Soviet–Japanese relations remained hostile through the final years of Stalin's life.

The post-Stalin leadership, preoccupied with a succession struggle and willing to reassess some of the late dictator's more intractable positions, demonstrated new flexibility in pursuing "peaceful co-existence" with states having differing socio-economic systems. Foreign Minister Viacheslav Molotov first indicated Soviet willingness to normalize relations with Japan in September 1954. This was followed in January of the following year by a diplomatic note proposing negotiations. Formal talks opened in June. Initial Soviet demands for the complete military neutralization of Japan were soon dropped, and the USSR offered to return two smaller, less significant islands of the Kurile chain, the Habomais group and Shikotan, to Japanese control. Resolution of the territorial issue, however, fell victim to Japanese domestic political wrangling and American pressures.[31]

The Joint Declaration signed in October 1956 between the Soviet Union and Japan normalized diplomatic relations and provided for economic links, but left the territorial question unsettled. According to Article 9 of the Declaration, talks on a peace treaty would continue after normalized relations were resumed. The Soviet objective in pressing a peace treaty was to obtain international recognition of the post-war frontiers (that is, Soviet sovereignty over the Kuriles and Sakhalin), ensure Japan's political neutrality, and encourage the withdrawal of US military forces. Similarly, the development of Soviet–Japanese economic relations, addressed in articles 7 and 8, was viewed as a step toward reducing Japan's economic dependence on the United States. These expectations were frustrated in 1960 when Japan and the US concluded a new mutual security pact.[32]

Although Soviet policy failed to drive a wedge between Japan and the United States, Soviet–Japanese trade relations expanded from a miniscule $27 million in 1957, to $5.2 billion in 1981.[33] Geographic proximity and natural complementarity oriented the Soviet–Japanese economic relationship around exchanging Japanese finance and technology for Soviet raw materials in Siberia and the Soviet Far East. Coastal trade developed between Primorsk krai and the northern island of Hokkaido. Under a series of five-year agreements, Soviet round wood, pulp, and wood chips were traded for Japanese machinery, pipe, rolled steel, and extraction equipment. The Japanese provided further assistance in developing the South Yakutia coal fields, and supplied credits and equipment for expanding port facilities at Vostochnyi and Nakhodka. Vostochnyi since 1971 has served as the major port for Japanese container shipments to and from Europe on the trans-Siberian rail line.[34]

In the 1970s detente muted American opposition to Soviet–Japanese cooperation, while the energy crisis heightened Japanese interest in diversifying its supply of fossil fuels. Several major projects were undertaken between Soviet and Japanese firms, with occasional US participation. Exploration and development of the Tiumen' oilfield in north-central Siberia, for example, was organized through a joint US–Soviet–Japanese consortium. A similar project involved Japanese financial backing for joint exploration of the Sakhalin continental shelf by Gulf Petroleum and the USSR's Sakhalin Oil and Development Company (SODECO) in the latter half of the 1970s.[35]

Soviet trade and economic cooperation with Japan during the Brezhnev period reflected general Soviet foreign economic policies toward the developed capitalist nations. First, economic cooperation was designed to compensate for perceived marginal inadequacies of central planning. Japan could provide much-needed investment in Siberia and the Soviet Far East, and could supply technology and products such as high-quality steel pipe, mining and excavation equipment not efficiently produced by Soviet firms. Compensation in the form of oil and other raw materials conveniently bypassed the problem of ruble inconvertibility.

Second, expanding economic relations with Japan had clear political objectives. Moscow favored any weakening of Japan's close economic ties to America. An added benefit of developing Soviet–Japanese economic relations, then, was the prospect of undermining Japan's political dependence on the United States. As the political relationship deteriorated, so the reasoning went, the United States would come under increasing pressure to reduce or eliminate its military presence in the region. This would deprive the United States of its forward bases in Japan, and possibly weaken the US military commitment to South Korea and other allies in the region.

Third, economic interaction was carefully circumscribed to limit the possibility of Soviet workers and executives being "infected" by unacceptable capitalist ideas that might filter in through contacts with Japan. Economic ties were to remain compartmentalized; organic linkages that might call into question Soviet managerial practices or the fundamentals of central planning were avoided. From the Kremlin's point of view, Soviet–Japanese economic relations should be oriented toward preserving, rather than transforming, essential elements of the autarkic Soviet system. Carefully regulated trade could obviate the need for structural economic reforms which, as the Czechoslovak experience had suggested, could be politically destabilizing.

Of course, this highly restrictive form of interaction greatly limited the Soviet economy's ability to learn and benefit from the Japanese economic miracle. A closed system, as we have noted in chapter 2, is not conducive to learning. However, the "lessons" that interested the Brezhnev leadership in the late 1960s and through the 1970s related more to preserving political power than to stimulating economic growth and development. The positive example of Japan's economic progress was more than offset by the negative example of political instability in Eastern Europe. Domestically, the modest economic reform program sponsored by Premier Kosygin in 1965 was discredited by 1968, and as Brezhnev secured his ascendancy in the Politburo, his conservative influence came to dominate Soviet foreign economic policies during the 1970s.

Soviet–Japanese economic cooperation did not significantly affect political relations. Japan's close ties to the United States, the development of relations with China in the 1970s, and continuing disagreement over control of the Kurile islands constrained the potential for *rapprochement*. Moreover, the Soviet political leadership normally assigned Japan a place of secondary importance in foreign policy. Gromyko's influence in Soviet foreign policy, which increased following his 1973 elevation to full Politburo status, emphasized ties with the United States and Western Europe rather than with Asia or the Third World. One prominent former member of the Soviet Foreign Ministry has described a privileged caste in the Soviet diplomatic service consisting of the Americanists, Europeanists, and those involved in disarmament negotiations. Diplomatic personnel serving in the less desirable posts in Asia and Africa, by contrast, had more limited access to the foreign policy leadership and faced greater difficulties in advancing to senior positions.[36] Given the overriding Soviet preoccupation with military challenges, Asia was simply less important in Soviet calculations than either America or Europe.

The normalization of Sino-Japanese relations in 1972, the development of trade relations between these two Asian powers, and the conclusion of the Sino-Japanese friendship treaty in 1978 exacerbated Soviet fears of a possible Beijing–Tokyo–Washington axis in East Asia. Soviet commentators criticized anti-hegemony statements made when Japan and China established diplomatic relations, and expressed regret that Japan would allow itself to be "used" to further Chinese foreign policy ambitions.[37]

Satisfaction over the course of East–West detente, however, had muted Soviet concerns. But by 1978, US–Soviet relations had deteriorated sharply. The Sino-Japanese friendship treaty, when seen in the context of Washington's renewed overtures to China, raised the unsettling prospect of a US–China–Japan military alliance directed against Soviet interests in the Asian-Pacific region. Clearly, the possibility of a marriage of Japanese and American technology with limitless Chinese manpower profoundly disturbed Soviet military planners.[38]

In response to these developments, the Soviet leadership accelerated both quantitatively and qualitatively their military build-up in the Far East, begun in the 1960s. Specifically, the Soviet Union, concluding a friendship treaty with Vietnam that included port rights to Cam Ranh Bay, backed the Vietnamese in their 1979 border conflict with the Chinese, expanded Soviet forces in the Kurile islands to divisional strength, and announced the reestablishment of a Far Eastern Military District. The Soviet commitment to aid Afghan revolutionary forces, and the decision to invade Afghanistan in December 1979, become more comprehensible when placed in the context of what from the Soviet perspective was a rapidly deteriorating security environment in Asia.

By the end of the 1970s few if any of the major Soviet post-war goals *vis-à-vis* Japan had been realized. The Kurile dispute stymied negotiations on a peace treaty and prevented the full normalization of Soviet–Japanese relations. Although America had moved toward isolationism following its defeat in Vietnam, US security ties with Japan had not been significantly affected. Nor did Soviet policy impede the development of Sino-Japanese relations. Japanese military expenditures had remained below the self-imposed limit of 1.0 percent of GNP, but given the extraordinarily high growth rates of Japan's economy, absolute military spending grew at a substantial rate. There was no marked resurgence of Japanese nationalism, but neither did the pacifist movement effectively damage the Japanese–American security relationship.

Japanese assistance did provide the financial capital, technology, and equipment to undertake a number of major Siberian development projects, and Japan had risen to second place in Soviet trade with the capitalist world by the late 1970s. However, the overall trade balance had shifted in Japan's favor after 1974, reaching a deficit of $1.2 billion in 1981.[39] The energy crisis of the 1970s accelerated Japan's conservation efforts and the transformation of the Japanese economy toward less-energy-intensive industries, lowering interest in exploiting Soviet raw materials. In addition, Japanese businessmen had become disillusioned by a combination of having to operate in harsh natural environments, contending with a weak infrastructure and poorly motivated labor force, and dealing with the inflexible Soviet bureaucracy. The actual economic impact of a decade and a half of cooperation had been marginal; the hoped-for political benefits non-existent.

Korea

Korea clearly was less important to Soviet policy in Northeast Asia than either China or Japan, although the peninsula occupied a geographically strategic position in Soviet security calculations. Soviet goals toward the Korean peninsula in the post-war period included promoting friendly governments that would not threaten Soviet security interests in the Far East; a policy of general support for the North, which fluctuated after the deterioration of Sino-Soviet relations; non-recognition of South Korea, considered a vassal of the United States; formal albeit unenthusiastic support for North Korea's goal of reunifying Korea under the leadership of the Korean Workers' Party, in the expectation that the Soviet Union would exercise considerable influence over a unified communist Korea; weakening American presence on the peninsula and in the region more generally; frustrating any possible Japanese attempts to revive their imperial ambitions; and, following the Sino-Soviet split, competing with the Chinese for influence with Kim Il-sung's regime.

At the end of the war, the Soviet Red Army occupied Korea north of the 38th parallel, enabling Stalin to place in power a coalition of forces that at least initially was compliant with Soviet objectives. Soviet officers and advisors were installed at all levels of the North Korean government and economy, replicating the pattern established in the occupied states of Eastern Europe. A lopsided agreement signed in March 1949 granted the Soviet Union dominant control over North Korea's foreign policies and preferential treatment in trade relations. Soviet officials guided North Korean industrial development toward meeting the needs of the Soviet economy. Cultural penetration was attempted through exchange programs in the arts and the introduction of compulsory Russian language courses in Korean primary and secondary schools.[40]

Kim Il-sung's invasion of South Korea in June 1950 and the ensuing conflict greatly intensified the cold war. Analysts generally agree that Stalin approved Kim's venture as a relatively low cost, low-risk opportunity to secure communist control over the entire peninsula. The vigorous American response must have come as a surprise to both the Soviets and the North Koreans. Secretary of State Dean Acheson had clearly indicated that Korea was outside the region defined as crucial to US security interests. The attack revised America's perception of the Soviet threat in Asia, and enabled the Truman administration to mobilize public opinion in support of an activist foreign policy to contain communism worldwide. US defense spending more than tripled from 1950 to 1953, while military forces on both the Soviet and American sides expanded dramatically.

The Korean war also significantly reconfigured Soviet–North Korean relations. Although the USSR supplied equipment, food, fuel, medicine, military advisors and even pilots, Stalin refused to commit Soviet troops. China's military intervention in November 1950 was instrumental in preserving communist rule in the North, and left the favorable impression that, in contrast with the Soviet Union, the Chinese were willing to shed blood to defend their Korean allies.[41] China's troop presence in Korea also made it possible for Kim to consolidate his position by eliminating members of the competing "Soviet Korean" faction, and enabled the adoption of more radical domestic policies opposed by Soviet leaders.[42]

By the end of the war, North Korea had asserted a more independent position, accepting assistance from both China and the USSR to rebuild North Korea's devastated economy. North Korean policy was formalized in the *chuch'e* (self-reliance) doctrine announced in December 1955. As differences between the USSR and China emerged, Kim pursued an eclectic strategy of accepting aid from both communist giants, while trying to avoid alienating either power and preserving North Korea's freedom to maneuver. For example, North Korea voiced strong support for Khrushchev's notion of peaceful coexistence following the 20th Party Congress. Yet at the 3rd Congress of the Korean Workers' Party in April 1956, the Soviet representative to the meeting, Leonid Brezhnev, criticized the KWP's proposed five-year plan (which had been formulated without Soviet assistance or approval), and hinted that Korea would be wise to follow the Leninist policy of collective leadership.[43] Moreover, North Korea emulated China's disastrous Great Leap Forward, developing a similar plan for rapid economic development designated the "Flying Horse Movement."[44]

For Moscow, Kim's adherence to the Soviet line in domestic and international affairs became increasingly important as the Sino-Soviet split widened. The wily North Korean dictator carefully straddled the fence, however. In July 1961, North Korea concluded identical treaties of Friendship, Cooperation, and Mutual Assistance with the USSR and the PRC, designed to emphasize North Korea's neutrality in the conflict. Khrushchev's attempts to tighten Soviet control over the socialist camp by promoting an enhanced division of labor among CMEA members heightened tensions between the USSR and DPRK in 1962, resulting in the suspension of Soviet aid. Relations deteriorated through the remainder of Khrushchev's rule, as North Korea moved closer to the PRC. An editorial published in *Nodong Shinmun* (the Korean Workers' Party newspaper) on 31 August 1964 attacked Soviet efforts to convene a world conference of communist parties as an attempt to impose uniformity, supporting similar charges made in the Chinese press a day earlier.[45]

Relations with the USSR improved after Khrushchev's ouster. Chinese economic and military assistance had proved a poor substitute for Soviet aid, and North Korea's trade links to Japan foundered as Japan and South Korea signed a normalization treaty in June 1965. The USSR moved to fill the gap, sending Premier Kosygin to Pyongyang in February 1965. North Korea and the USSR signed several trade, technology, and military agreements in the period from 1965 to 1967. Despite an openly neutralist North Korean policy enunciated in 1966, relations with China deteriorated during the Cultural Revolution, and sporadic military clashes occured over disputed territory around Mt. Paektu.[46]

The USSR supplied the bulk of North Korea's military needs through the 1960s and early 1970s. Soviet military equipment accounted for approximately three-fourths of North Korea's arms imports during the period from 1964 to 1973. After 1973, Soviet military assistance diminished, with the Chinese providing T-59 tanks and jet fighter aircraft. The Soviet Union did furnish technology to help the

North Koreans produce the T-62 tank in the mid-1970s, but refused to supply the more advanced versions of Soviet armor or aircraft that were being delivered to India and several countries in the Middle East. Consequently, much of North Korea's military growth during the 1970s resulted from domestically produced weapons.[47]

Ties with China improved after the 9th CCP Congress in April 1969, as Zhou Enlai visited Pyongyang. In addition, China dropped its territorial demands by the end of 1970. As relations between North Korea and the Soviets cooled, and in the climate of better US–Soviet relations, the South Korean government sought an opening to Moscow. Tentative cultural contacts were explored between Moscow and Seoul following President Park Chung Hee's declaration that South Korea was ready to cooperate with any nation, irrespective of political system or ideology. Korean athletes, businessmen, and educators attended international meetings in the USSR during the 1970s, although no Soviet citizens were allowed to visit South Korea.[48] Predictably, North Korea complained loudly about these contacts.

Relations between Moscow and Pyongyang remained cool during much of the 1970s. In his introductory remarks to a conference celebrating the 40th anniversary of the 7th Comintern Congress, chief Party ideologue Mikhail Suslov stressed the importance for the CPSU of further strengthening the unity and solidarity of the international communist movement. He condemned the Chinese for the divisive influence of their opportunistic and nationalist ideas, and reminded communist parties that each had a responsibility to their people, and to world communism.[49] North Korea, however, continued to pursue a policy of careful neutrality and good relations with both communist giants. Trade with the USSR stayed at roughly $400–500 million from 1971 to 1977, and high-level political contacts were put on hold. By contrast, Kim Il-sung visited Beijing in 1975, and Vice-Premier Deng Xiaoping attended the thirtieth anniversary celebrations of the DPRK in September 1978. The pendulum shifted once again in the late 1970s, as Soviet–Korean trade expanded to $555 million in 1978 and $750 million in 1979.[50] North Korea, which initially criticized the Soviet Union over the invasion of Afghanistan, was by April 1980 voicing support for the Soviet-backed regime in Kabul.

While seeking to maintain a balance between the Soviet Union and the PRC, North Korea also attempted to develop trade links with Japan and other Western nations. One goal of developing such contacts was to limit North Korea's dependence on the two communist giants. In addition, North Korea's inability to produce exportable products resulted in regular trade imbalances with the Soviet Union, and the Soviets were apparently cautious about granting large credits.

North Korea also made overtures to the United States toward the end of the decade, but these tentative contacts failed to bear fruit. Congressman Stephen Solarz was invited to North Korea in July 1980, and was informed by Kim that North Korea was ready to establish cultural and other types of exchanges with the United States, even in the absence of diplomatic relations. The reversal of President Carter's decision to withdraw American troops from South Korea, combined with North Korea's large hard currency debt and poor export record, hindered North Korean attempts to diversify their economic ties.[51] By the close of the Brezhnev era, as strains developed in North Korea's relationship with China, Moscow and Pyongyang were once again moving closer.

Several "lessons" emerge from this brief review of Soviet–Korean relations. First, the Korean War demonstrated that armed conflict on the peninsula did not necessarily serve Soviet interests and could easily involve the United States or China, to Soviet disadvantage. The presence of American troops in South Korea following the war, and China's demonstrated willingness to commit forces in support of the North, may have made Soviet leaders more cautious about the potential for escalation. In this sense, Korea was different from regional conflicts in other parts of the world where superpower proxy competition could be more effectively regulated.

Second, Soviet efforts to secure North Korea's support for Soviet leadership of the world communist movement were at best only sporadically successful. Kim Il-sung's clever strategy of playing the communist superpowers against each other, together with his *chuch'e* policy of self-reliance, preserved the DPRK's independence and freedom of action. However, this same absence of control tempered Soviet and Chinese military and economic assistance to the mercurial dictator. The political and economic benefits derived from such largesse tended to be fairly modest.

Finally, tenuous as were the ties that bound the USSR to North Korea, they were sufficient to constrain Soviet efforts at normalizing relations with an increasingly independent and economically powerful Republic of Korea. By the beginning of the 1980s, South Korea's GNP was about four times that of the North, and was growing far more rapidly. In Europe, Germany's *Ostpolitik* provided from the Soviet perspective a model solution for the Korean stalemate – acceptance of the status quo by both states, normalization of relations between the principle actors and with each others' allies, and full acceptance into the international community. Kim, however, was not Walter Ulbricht, and could not be pressured out of office in order to facilitate a solution. But then Korea, unlike Germany in Europe, was not the key to regional politics in Northeast Asia.

Conclusion

This survey of post-war Soviet relations with Northeast Asia supports the premise that there has been more continuity than change in Soviet foreign policy from Stalin through Brezhnev.[52] Soviet "learning," which occurred in the immediate post-war period, consisted of Stalin adjusting to Soviet superpower status and the conditions of a newly bipolar world. Stalinist patterns of interaction developed from 1945 to 1953 were not substantially altered by the successor generation of leaders, who rose to positions of authority in the 1930s, had been thoroughly socialized into Stalinist thinking, and were not imaginative enough to challenge the central tenets of the dictator's foreign policies. A generational change was needed before the ideas behind new thinking could be formulated into policy.

The minor modifications in Stalin's foreign policies toward Northeast Asia by his successors are at best adaptive, and do not constitute genuine learning. Khrushchev repudiated Stalin's tactical errors (for example, in dealing with the Chinese), but none of his policy innovations questioned the Stalinist dichotomized world view, the heavy reliance on military power, or the messianic approach to international relations. The Brezhnev elite reversed many of Khrushchev's domestic experiments in agriculture and management, and toned down his rather blustery style of diplomacy, but they too pursued an essentially Stalinist path in foreign policy.

Ideology broadly defined stands out as a critical variable inhibiting Soviet learning in relations with Northeast Asia. Notwithstanding Soviet claims to the contrary, there could be no possibility of a fully equal socialist state coexisting with the USSR. Proletarian internationalism meant subordinating one's national interests to a Soviet-defined domestic and foreign policy agenda. It is revealing that Soviet criticisms of China routinely equated the terms "nationalist" and "anti-Soviet." Even when the country in question was small and/or occupied by Soviet troops, as in the case of Eastern Europe, strains were evident. China, a huge nation with a long and distinguished history, and a tradition of regarding outsiders as barbarians having little to offer the

Middle Kingdom, naturally resisted accepting a position subordinate to Soviet interests.

Japan was a different matter. As a defeated belligerent occupied by and later allied with the USSR's major competitor, a member of the capitalist world and, by the 1970s, an economic and technological giant, Japan posed an entirely different set of policy problems. Soviet diplomacy, however, was no more successful with Japan than with China. The major goals of legitimizing Soviet control over the occupied Kuriles and weakening the US–Japanese security relationship were not realized.

Soviet efforts to obtain substantial Japanese investment in Siberian development projects were only partially successful. The autarkic, centrally planned, and relatively inefficient Soviet system meshed poorly with Japan's dynamic export-oriented economy. The obvious contrast between the two economic systems was apparent by the 1970s, but ideological strictures and the closed nature of the Soviet system precluded any serious efforts to learn from the Japanese model.

The relationship with the two Koreas was likewise less than satisfactory. Because of the Sino-Soviet rift, North Korea maintained considerable freedom to maneuver politically. On the surface, relations with the Soviet Union were generally cordial to warm; in reality, considerable tensions existed between the two. Moreover, North Korea had little to offer the Soviet Union other than occasional diplomatic support. The USSR did not particularly benefit from the trade relationship, and Kim Il-sung's adventurist policies raised the possibility of the USSR being drawn into unwelcome confrontations on the peninsula.

Moscow's fixation on political-military questions in Northeast Asia constrained efforts to improve relations with a newly industrializing South Korea. As long as Soviet leaders viewed regional issues through the prism of Sino–Soviet or Soviet–American military competition, North Korea's strategic value outweighed the potential benefits to be derived from economic cooperation with the South. And finally, one should not discount the significant role bureaucratic inertia played in a static Korea policy.

4   The People's Republic of China

By the most modest calculations, the confrontation with China cost us 200 billion rubles.

Eduard Shevardnadze, *The Future Belongs to Freedom* (New York: The Free Press, 1991), p. 58.

As the 1970s drew to a close, one potentially bright spot in a dismal landscape of domestic crisis and foreign policy setbacks was the outlook for Sino-Soviet relations. The fanaticism and anti-Sovietism of the Cultural Revolution had been replaced by pragmatic, reformist approaches toward economic development and less strident proclamations on foreign policy. Frictions between Washington and Beijing in the early Reagan administration were a source of encouragement to Kremlin leaders seeking better relations, as China moved toward an "independent" position between the superpowers. The time seemed right for patching up a long and costly dispute.

Soviet overtures toward China at the end of the Brezhnev era and during the transition phase were directed toward this goal, but Moscow's strategy consisted of a series of marginal adjustments that did not challenge the basic premises on which Soviet foreign policy was based. However, intellectual ferment generated by domestic problems and foreign policy setbacks provided new concepts for an energetic Gorbachev leadership convinced that fundamental change was needed. These ideas percolated through the hierarchy as Gorbachev consolidated his position and learned the ropes in foreign policy.

On China, the lessons were fairly obvious to all but the most obtuse. The rupture had put the Communist Party on the defensive ideologically, undermined Moscow's standing in the world communist movement, and divided the allegiance of communists between Moscow and Beijing. The Kremlin's arrogant posture toward China had helped create a substantial threat from a country that had not presented any significant military challenge to its northern neighbor for centuries. The expense of two decades of confrontation, in direct military costs and foregone trade opportunities, was exorbitant. Moreover, the dispute provided America with considerable leverage in playing regional power politics.

By 1987–89, a reformist leadership was questioning the basic ideological premises on which Soviet aspirations toward hegemony in Northeast Asia rested. This learning process was now being reflected in foreign policy deeds, and paralleled the transformation of the domestic political system. A new China policy would be only one outcome of this learning process.

Soviet China policy, 1979–1985

As noted in chapter 3, relations between the Soviet Union and People's Republic of China remained hostile through the decade following the Ussuri border conflict in 1969. Mao's death in September 1976 encouraged Moscow to seek a reconciliation, but the Chinese were cool to these overtures. The events of 1978 – the Sino-Japanese friendship treaty; normalization of Sino-American relations; the signing of a Soviet–Vietnamese friendship treaty; Vietnam's invasion of Cambodia and the subsequent brief Sino-Vietnamese war; and the Soviet invasion of Afghanistan – combined to make any genuine improvement in relations problematic.[1]

Perhaps more importantly, Soviet approaches toward China were predicated on the same assumptions that had governed Soviet policies since the Khrushchev period. According to this view, Mao and his fellow radicals were responsible for the poor state of relations. With Mao gone, the Gang of Four under arrest, and the post-Mao leadership shifting away from the radicalist policies of the Cultural Revolution, Moscow could also hope for a concomitant shift toward greater "reason" in China's foreign policy. In other words, renewed efforts by Moscow to improve relations were based more on expectations of greater Chinese flexibility than on Soviet willingness to modify policies.

Despite their serious differences, the two sides conducted exploratory talks from the spring of 1979 through early 1982. The invasion of Afghanistan added a third Chinese precondition for normalization to the extant demand for reductions of Soviet forces in Mongolia and on the Sino-Soviet border, and for the Vietnamese withdrawal from Cambodia, and delayed progress for a year.[2] In March 1981 the

USSR proposed confidence building measures in Northeast Asia, and twice sent Mikhail Kapitsa, chief of the First Far Eastern Department of the Ministry of Foreign Affairs, to Beijing. In addition, Moscow made several proposals for border negotiations in late 1981 and early 1982.[3]

Two external developments appear to have prompted Moscow to undertake these initiatives in the late Brezhnev years: China's apparent deradicalization; and the deteriorating relationship with the United States in the early years of the Reagan administration. Domestically, the infirmity and eventual death of two of China's most hostile critics – Mikhail Suslov and Leonid Brezhnev – paved the way toward reconciliation.

China's willingness to abandon Mao's radicalism in favor of a more pragmatic style of governing raised the possibility of a similar re-evaluation of foreign policy. The arrest and trial of the Gang of Four symbolized China's rejection of the radical policies of the Cultural Revolution. However, while encouraged by China's shift toward moderation, Soviet hardliners viewed China's economic experiments with some suspicion. Oleg Rakhmanin, First Deputy Chief of the Central Committee Department for Liaison with Ruling Socialist Parties in charge of relations with Asian nations, commented on China's reforms in a lead article in *Problemy dal'nego vostoka* following a January 1982 Moscow conference of Soviet sinologists. While acknowledging that China's internal policies had in recent years moved away from the more discredited Maoist practices, Rakhmanin asserted that there was no discrepancy between China's domestic and foreign policies. Beijing's economic reforms, and its military and economic co-operation with the United States, Japan, and other NATO powers, were means of strengthening the basis for an hegemonistic, anti-Soviet foreign policy.[4]

Developments in China's rural areas, where market-oriented reforms had been in place since 1978, were criticized by other specialists for exacerbating social-economic contradictions and threatening the socialist achievements of the Chinese people.[5] Western scholars were assailed for attributing the weaknesses in Soviet and Chinese economies to Leninist and socialist practices, rather than the deformities of Maoism. American scholars, who gave a positive assessment of Chinese nationalism, were simply apologists who justified China's political and economic cooperation with imperialism.[6] Other observers disparaged the growth of privately owned businesses, the corrupting influence of bourgeois mentality, the flourishing black market, and worst of all, the Chinese Communist Party's willingness to allow businessmen into its ranks.[7]

Reformists, on the other hand, appeared to be interested in the potential application of China's economic experiments to the stagnating Soviet economy. Feodor Burlatskii, then head of the Central Committee's Institute of Social Sciences and a leading biographer of Mao Zedong, published a lengthy article in the April 1982 issue of *Novyi mir* assessing China's political and economic problems. Burlatskii presented an intelligent and fairly objective portrait of China's economic difficulties. However, the thrust of his article criticized the overlap of Party and state administrative functions in China, and the corruption, systematic falsehoods, and nepotism which led to moral degeneration.[8] Coming just four months after Burlatskii's former boss in the Central Committee Department for Liaison with Ruling Socialist Parties, Iurii Andropov, had launched his attack on the Brezhnevite corruption (with the arrest of Boris Buriatiia, a close friend of Brezhnev's daughter), this article was simultaneously an indictment of the stalinist tendencies and corrupt practices of the late Brezhnev regime.

It is also significant that following the death of long-time ideology guardian Mikhail Suslov, a major debate over the "crises of socialism" erupted in the academic journals and the mass media, and continued throughout the transition period. Although this debate focused primarily on the question of whether or not socialism in Eastern Europe was facing a fundamental crisis, the debate clearly had implications for internal Soviet reform efforts, and for Soviet relations with all socialist countries.[9] A central supporter of the reformist line in this debate was Oleg Bogomolov, Burlatskii's former colleague from the days when Andropov headed the Department for Liaison with Ruling Socialist Parties.

As personnel changes eased the way for a reassessment of the standard China line, international developments began to work in Moscow's favor. Washington's announcement in late December 1981 that it was resuming arms sales to Taiwan encouraged the trend in China toward a less anti-Soviet foreign policy. This approach was made public by CCP Chairman Hu Yaobang in fall 1981, and was formalized at the 12th Chinese Communist Party Congress, in September 1982. The essence of this policy, which criticized hegemonism, imperialism, and colonialism equally, indicated China's intention of following a policy of equidistance between the two superpowers. Hu expressed China's hope that relations with the United States and

Japan would continue to develop, but expressed displeasure with America's Taiwan policy.[10]

Soviet leaders recognized the opportunities for better relations, and responded with signals of their own. The Soviet digest of anti-Chinese articles *Opasnyi kurs* ("Dangerous Course"), published yearly since 1969, produced its final issue in 1981. Polemics against China in the Soviet press virtually ceased in 1982.[11] In addition, Moscow sought to portray the Soviet Union as a more reliable partner than either Japan or the United States. Brezhnev's March 1982 Tashkent speech supported the PRC's sovereignty over Taiwan, and acknowledged that China was a member of the socialist community.[12] An *Izvestiia* article in July criticized Japan and the United States for blatantly disregarding the sovereign interests of the Chinese people by maintaining close relations with Taiwan.[13] Shortly before his death, Brezhnev again reaffirmed Soviet willingness to move toward normalization and gradual improvement of relations.[14]

Deputy Foreign Minister L. Il'ychev was sent to Beijing in October to resume talks on normalization. When Brezhnev died in November, Chinese Foreign Minister Huang Hua praised him as an outstanding statesman, and expressed China's hopes for a genuine improvement in Sino-Soviet relations.[15] Hua met with Gromyko in Moscow, and the two sides agreed to continue discussions. Progress in negotiations proceeded slowly but steadily during Andropov's brief tenure. Andropov, who succeeded Brezhnev in November 1982, sent Aleksandr Bovin, *Izvestiia* commentator and a long-time Asia watcher, to Beijing as his unofficial representative early in 1983.[16] In February, then Deputy Foreign Minister Qian Qichen headed a delegation to Moscow for talks, and at the end of March Qian met with Gromyko.[17] However, this modest detente ended when Andropov died. Konstantin Chernenko, the sickly and incompetent Brezhnev protégé who assumed the post of General Secretary in February 1984, presided over a static and uninspired thirteen months during which little progress was made in Sino-Soviet relations.

Under Gorbachev, Sino-Soviet relations improved as new thinking changed longstanding assumptions about relations among socialist states. The development of new thinking as applied to China can be divided into economic, political-ideological, and military aspects of policy, although the three are of course interrelated. Each aspect, as we shall see, is linked both to Soviet domestic reform imperatives, and to changing Soviet conceptions of relations with other socialist states, above all Eastern Europe. The economic dimension is addressed first.

Economics: motivation and instrument

Perestroika in the early Gorbachev years (1985–87) was designed to reinvigorate the Soviet economy through modest domestic reforms and further integration into the world economy. During this period, however, relatively greater benefits were anticipated through cooperation with socialist countries than with capitalist nations. Soviet reformers initially envisioned enhanced economic cooperation and integration with the socialist countries of the Council for Mutual Economic Assistance (CMEA). China's experience with limited private enterprise in agriculture and industry, and the example of the special economic zones of the southern coastal areas, intrigued Moscow's economists.

For the first two years, however, economic practices that smacked of genuine capitalism were viewed with suspicion. Extensive privatization, the development of a convertible currency, and the shift to a market economy were not yet acceptable to most of the Soviet leadership. Radical experiments such as the special economic zones, analysts noted, opened the socialist economy to the outside world and introduced serious social, ideological, and political problems, including crime, corruption, and speculation.[18]

Sino-Soviet trade and economic cooperation accelerated shortly after Mikhail Gorbachev came to power in March 1985. In July, a breakthrough came in the conclusion of a major trade agreement between the USSR and the PRC. Deputy Premier Yao Yilin and First Deputy Premier Ivan Arkhipov signed a five-year pact for 1986–90 worth $14 billion, nearly doubling the level of bilateral trade. As might be expected for two nations with non-convertible currencies, this was a barter arrangement. China agreed to supply consumer goods, agricultural commodities, and some raw materials in exchange for Soviet machinery, machine tool equipment, automobiles, chemicals, and building materials. The USSR agreed to build seven new plants in China, and to assist in reconstructing some seventeen installations in energy, metal processing, machine building, coal, chemicals and transportation.[19]

Commerce between the Soviet Union and China grew steadily through the second half of the 1980s. Total trade turnover more than tripled from $110 million in 1981 to $363 million in 1982; this expanded to $960 million in 1983, $2.63 billion in 1986 and then to over $3.2 billion in 1988. In 1988, the Soviet Union ran a trade surplus of about 160 million rubles with the PRC, and exports to China in the following year significantly outpaced imports.[20] Trade with China grew to nearly $4 billion in 1989, but that figure was still well below the $6 billion in trade with Japan or the $5 billion with United States. In addition, trade with China made up only 4 percent of total Soviet trade for 1990. During 1990, Sino-Soviet trade dropped off to about $3.8 billion.[21]

Although the absolute level of trade was not very high, these exchanges filled significant gaps in each country's economy. Fertilizers comprised 22.7 percent of Soviet exports to China; iron and steel products 19.3 percent; wood products 10.9 percent; transportation equipment 10.1 percent; and non-ferrous metals 9.3 percent. China in turn exported to the USSR much-needed food products and consumer goods, of which meat comprised 7.9 percent, apparel 13.4 percent, yarns and fabrics 12.2 percent, edible oils 10.8 percent, and grains 9.5 percent.[22]

As Sino-Soviet relations improved, communities in Primorsk krai and the border regions of Central Asia welcomed the opportunity to trade with their Chinese neighbors. China's northeastern and western border regions, especially Heliongjiang, Jilin, and Xinjiang provinces, valued the rapid expansion of cross-border trade and agreements. These regions had not experienced the rapid growth of the special economic zones in the southeast. Provincial officials on both sides were eager to restore and expand transportation links and economic development projects suspended in the 1950s.

Agreements were concluded on completing a 100 mile rail link between Urumchi in Sinkiang province and Soviet Kazakhstan (December 1987), a major deal involving the sale of electric locomotives and rolling stock to the Chinese was struck, and joint ventures were proposed in non-ferrous metallurgy, power generation, geology, and the chemical industry. In May 1988 the Kazakh republic set up a foreign trade company to conduct business deals with the neighboring province of Xinjiang. Heilongjiang province alone had signed seventy-one contracts with Soviet firms by the beginning of 1991 in the fields of construction, labor cooperation, and urban drainage systems. A color duplicating center established jointly by the Chinese town of Suifenhe (located north of Vladivostok) and Soviet Pogranichnyi was con-structed on Soviet territory using Chinese building materials, equip-ment, and manpower. Chinese and Soviet banks in October 1988 concluded agreements to expedite financing and settle local barter arrangements for rapidly expanding cross-border trade.[23]

In many respects, the Soviet and Chinese economies were highly complementary. The Soviet Far East was a storehouse of land and

Map 4.1   Western border sector

natural resources – oil, natural gas, minerals, coal, timber, and river
water for hydropower – but a weak infrastructure and sparse population made effective utilization of these resources problematic. Building supplies were inadequate, with housing at a premium. Given the
enormous distances involved, transportation costs to ship equipment
to the east from the industrialized western zone were prohibitive.
Harsh living conditions and the lack of consumer goods in the Far
Eastern territories resulted in severe and continuing labor shortages.

Manpower for Soviet industry was frequently supplemented by North Korean and Vietnamese workers. As Soviet–Chinese ties improved, surplus rural laborers sought employment across the border. By late 1990, some 30,000 Chinese were working in Soviet agriculture, timber, and construction industries.[24]

Western press reports during the Gorbachev period did not appreciate the importance of Sino-Soviet trade for perestroika. Conversely, they often exaggerated the importance of attracting Japanese investment and technology for developing the Soviet Far East, and the national economy in general. Prospects for expanding economic relations with China in the late 1980s were more favorable for several reasons. Until the territorial dispute was resolved, full normalization of political and hence economic relations between Japan and the USSR was unlikely. Sino-Soviet economic cooperation, on the other hand, progressed steadily as the Soviets moved to address each of the three major obstacles long cited by the Chinese – Soviet military deployments and boundary disputes along the border areas, the occupation of Afghanistan, and support for Vietnamese occupation of Cambodia.

Soviet–Chinese *rapprochement* was based on more than just structural economic complementarity. Both countries were in the midst of restructuring their socialist, centrally planned economies. With close to a decade of experience in economic reform, China's record provided useful insights for Soviet economists. By the latter part of the 1980s, after Gorbachev had renounced Soviet claims to ideological orthodoxy, it became acceptable to discuss China's reforms objectively – in other words, to learn from the Chinese experience. China's special economic zones, for example, were studied and evaluated as potentially valuable strategies for attracting capital investment and advanced technology to the Soviet Union.[25] One of the two Soviet special economic zones first approved by Moscow was to be located in the area around Nakhodka.

Political and military considerations

Cultivating trade relations and other forms of economic cooperation with China was both a goal and a means to certain political ends. Perestroika's international component emphasized the need to develop more organic linkages with the world economy to bring Soviet industry up to international standards. China and the USSR were physically proximate, and their economies, while structurally similar, were at sufficiently different levels of development to take full advantage of the "international division of labor." However, Soviet leaders also sought to improve political ties with the Chinese through expanded trade and economic cooperation. Sino-Soviet reconciliation became more urgent in the mid-1980s, as the United States began providing the Chinese with limited military assistance.

Biannual discussions between Soviet and Chinese foreign ministers had been held regularly since 1982. In April 1985, the sixth scheduled round of talks was hosted in Moscow, with Deputy Foreign Minister Qian Qichen representing the Chinese side and Soviet Foreign Minister Andrei Gromyko heading the USSR delegation. The Chinese reiterated their usual three conditions for normalizing relations, demanding a reduction of Soviet forces in Mongolia and along the Sino-Soviet border, the withdrawal of Vietnamese forces from Cambodia, and an end to Soviet occupation of Afghanistan. While the Soviet Union would not agree to these conditions, a joint statement released at the conclusion of the discussions reaffirmed the commitment of both sides gradually to improve political ties.

Following two years of strained ties with the PRC, the Reagan administration moved to repair the damage caused by the flirtation with Taiwan. Defense Secretary Caspar Weinberger was sent to Beijing in 1983, and military cooperation between the United States and China expanded. General John Vessey, Chairman of the Joint Chiefs of Staff, held three days of talks with Chinese military and political officials in Beijing early in 1985. Subsequently, the United States agreed to sell modern anti-submarine warfare (ASW) equipment – submarine detection devices, sonar, and gas turbine engines – to the Chinese. China agreed to a port call by three US destroyers in April 1985, the first such visit since 1949. In addition, the US army and air force had discussed selling anti-tank and air defense systems to China. These developments must have been highly disturbing to Moscow.

In early January 1986 Soviet Deputy Minister of Foreign Affairs Mikhail Kapitsa revealed Soviet intentions to seek a non-aggression pact with the PRC. Kapitsa rejected China's three preconditions for normalization of relations, however. The following month, the aging Soviet ambassador to Beijing, Ilia Shcherbakov, was replaced by the USSR's chief delegate to the United Nations, Oleg A. Troianovskii. An Asian specialist and skilled diplomat, Troianovskii's appointment reflected the growing significance of the Sino-Soviet relationship in Moscow's calculations. In March, talks in Beijing between Soviet Deputy Premier Ivan Arkhipov and then Vice-Premier Li Peng resulted in an agreement to increase bilateral trade and for the Soviets to provide technical assistance to Chinese industry. On 14 April Shevardnadze and Qian conducted the eighth round of normalization talks. Despite these moves toward better relations, the Chinese foreign affairs ministry rejected as "unrealistic" Soviet proposals to fully normalize relations.

In April 1986 the Soviet government released a major pronouncement calling for better relations in the Asian-Pacific region. Falling between the 27th Party Congress and Gorbachev's Vladivostok address, this compromise statement embodied elements of both the new and old thinking. The United States and Japan were charged with trying to mold a "Pacific community" that could eventually be transformed into another militaristic bloc. In a more conciliatory vein, positive references were made to the growing interdependence of states. The document recommended enhancing the role of the United Nations Economic and Social Commission for Asia and the Pacific in addressing the region's economic and environmental problems. Many of the proposals Gorbachev would make in his July Vladivostok address – an all-Asian forum on security problems, implementation of confidence-building measures, reducing naval activities, and creating additional nuclear weapon-free zones in the Pacific – were set forth in this document. Developing Siberia and the Soviet Far East through trade, economic, scientific and technical cooperation was also declared to be a matter of paramount importance to the USSR.[26]

Addressing the 27th Congress of the CPSU, Gorbachev had expressed satisfaction with "a certain improvement" in relations with China. The two countries still had differences over international issues, he noted, but on the whole there was great potential for "acting together on the basis of principle and equal rights without prejudice to third countries," an allusion to Vietnam and the United States. Referring to relations within the socialist community, Gorbachev stressed that "a solicitous and respectful attitude to each other's experience" was "an enormous asset." One of the advantages of socialism, he observed, was its ability to learn, among other things, "to prevent clashes of interest between different socialist states."[27]

Gorbachev also invigorated the Soviet foreign ministry establishment through a number of personnel and organizational changes. A new Asian Division of the Socialist Countries Department was created, and career diplomat Igor Rogachev was appointed to head it in June 1986. Rogachev, whose father was also a sinologist, spent six years in China as a child and an additional nine years in the foreign ministry, where he developed complete fluency in Chinese. In late summer 1986 Rogachev was promoted to Deputy Foreign Minister, and in October replaced the aging Leonid Il'ychev as chief delegate to the Sino-Soviet negotiations.[28]

Gorbachev's highly-publicized Vladivostok speech of 28 July 1986 made additional, specific overtures toward China, Japan, and other Asian-Pacific nations. Gorbachev warned that the Pacific Ocean was turning into an arena of confrontation although, he conceded, the region had not yet become as militarized as Europe. The Soviet General Secretary criticized American, Japanese, and South Korean attempts to foment tensions in the region, asserting that the Soviet Union would do no more than the necessary minimum to ensure its security and that of its friends and allies. He voiced support for the concept of Asian non-alignment, praised the idea of peace and nuclear-free zones in the Pacific, and reiterated Soviet determination to help solve regional conflicts. In order to develop a comprehensive system of international security, Gorbachev proposed convening a Pacific Conference modeled on the Conference on Security and Cooperation in Europe.[29]

In his speech, Gorbachev stressed the importance of Sino-Soviet relations for the USSR. He spoke approvingly of the Chinese Communist Party's reformist objectives, and noted that Chinese and Soviet domestic priorities were similar. Gorbachev also praised the developing economic ties between the two countries. However, his only concessions to China's three preconditions were the proposal to resolve disputed areas of the Sino-Soviet border according to the thalweg principle (that is, along the main navigation channels), and vague promises that Soviet troops would withdraw from Afghanistan after a political settlement was reached.[30] As Gorbachev made his proposals in Vladivostok, Viktor Karpov, Moscow's chief arms control official, was visiting Beijing for discussions on the "arms race in space" and other disarmament questions.

Gorbachev's thinking at this time still had not broken free of traditional Soviet approaches toward Asia. For example, the proposal for an Asian conference on security and cooperation resurrected an idea initially floated in 1971 by Leonid Brezhnev as a means of isolating China and securing international acquiescence to the post-war boundaries. Gorbachev's aims may have been different than Brezhnev's, but this simplistic attempt to transplant a European regime into Asia disregarded the radically diverse security environments of the two regions. No major concessions were made toward meeting China's three preconditions, nor was there any indication of flexibility on the

Kurile islands. South Korea remained a non-issue. Perhaps the most significant aspect of the speech was the evident Soviet willingness to deal with China as an equal partner.

Beijing reacted cautiously to Gorbachev's Vladivostok initiatives. His speech was carried on the front page of the *People's Daily* on 29 July, and China's radio commentary welcomed the apparent new Soviet flexibility. However, the Chinese urged further movement on withdrawing Soviet troops from Afghanistan and Mongolia, and criticized Gorbachev's failure to address the Vietnamese–Cambodian issue. By this point, though, Sino-Soviet relations were considerably better than during the early 1980s. An exchange of fire between Soviet and Chinese border troops that took place in July, in which one Chinese soldier was reported killed, was downplayed by both sides. On 9 August China signed a consular treaty with Mongolia, signalling greater flexibility toward the Soviets.

Soviet new thinking toward the Asian-Pacific region was further elaborated in Gorbachev's November 1986 visit to New Delhi, and in his July 1987 interview with the Indonesian newspaper *Merdeka*. While in New Delhi, the General Secretary and Prime Minister Rajiv Gandhi signed a "Declaration of Principles for a Nuclear-Free and Nonviolent World," and concluded several new agreements on economic and technical cooperation. The two sides expressed concern over tensions in the South Asian and Asian-Pacific regions, urged political rather than military solutions to the area's conflicts, and called for dismantling all foreign military bases in the Indian Ocean, referring specifically to the American base at Diego Garcia.[31] In a press conference following the meeting between the two leaders, Gorbachev emphasized that better relations between China and the Soviet Union would not be at the expense of India, and expressed the hope that normalization among all nations in the region would be achieved.[32]

In the *Merdeka* interview, Gorbachev announced Soviet readiness to destroy the Asian SS-20s (the "global double zero"), reiterated the Soviet desire to limit superpower naval activities in the Pacific Ocean, pressed the idea of ending nuclear testing in the area, and urged new measures to strengthen security in the Indian Ocean.[33] In choosing an Indonesian newspaper as the medium for this major breakthrough, Gorbachev demonstrated a sensitivity to Asian, particularly Chinese, interests in the Intermediate-range Nuclear Forces (INF) negotiations. In contrast to the usual Soviet position that China had no legitimate interest in US–Soviet arms limitations talks, the Chinese had been briefed routinely by Moscow on INF from early 1986 through the

Washington summit in May 1988.[34] Following the *Merdeka* interview, Soviet diplomats energetically promoted the double-zero decision throughout Asia, in an attempt to take credit for what was originally an American proposal. This public relations campaign proved effective; opinion in both Asia and Europe appears to have credited Gorbachev with the initiative.

Moscow's decision-makers still did not demonstrate clear evidence of learning in Sino-Soviet relations as of mid-1987. From Beijing's perspective, the Soviet Union had granted few concessions on the issues that divided the two countries. Soviet material and political support for Vietnam's occupation of Cambodia continued to be the major impediment to improved relations between the two in late 1986 and early 1987. On a September 1986 broadcast of the American news program "60 Minutes," Deng Xiaoping offered to meet Gorbachev if the USSR was willing to persuade the Vietnamese to withdraw their forces. Deng called this issue the "main obstacle," to a Sino-Soviet *rapprochement*, and he suggested the USSR was still undecided on how best to conduct its China policy.

The Chinese evaluation of the Soviet position was basically accurate. The Soviet leadership appeared to be on the verge of learning, but could not yet bring itself to abandon longstanding practices or commitments. As a result, Moscow's positions often seemed poorly coordinated or somewhat contradictory. On Vietnam, for example, the Soviet Union urged their allies to pursue normalized relations with China as early as December 1986, yet continued to supply Vietnam with substantial economic and military assistance until 1991.[35] When Vietnam and China clashed in March 1988 over disputed claims to the Spratley and Paracel islands in the South China Sea, Moscow refused to criticize either nation. An article in *Pravda* encouraged the two sides to resolve their differences through negotiations, and praised Vietnam for its "constructive stand" in offering to settle the matter peaceably.[36]

Relations between several East European countries and China began to improve in late 1986. Tacit Soviet approval of this development indicated greater tolerance for an autonomous Eastern European role in world affairs, and a readiness to acknowledge China as a socialist power fully equal with the USSR. In Gorbachev's words:

the entire framework of political relations between the socialist countries must be strictly based on absolute independence. This is the view held by the leaders of all fraternal countries. The independence of each Party, its sovereign right to decide the issues facing its country and its responsibility to its nation are the unquestionable principles.[37]

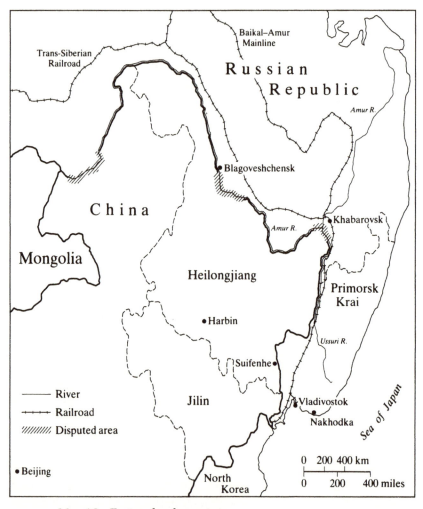

Map 4.2   Eastern border sector

Gorbachev's rhetoric about the sovereign authority of each party, however, was tempered by other statements emphasizing the importance of harmonizing the initiatives of each fraternal nation with a common international line.[38]

Starting in 1987, the Soviet Union initiated military force reductions in the Far East. In January, the Soviet Ministry of Defense announced plans to withdraw one motorized rifle division (about 10–13,000 soldiers) and several additional units from Mongolia, with reductions scheduled to begin in June. The Soviet Union had approximately

75,000 troops, or four divisions, deployed in Mongolia in 1985. These forces decreased to 55,000 in 1988 as readiness levels were reduced.[39] Planned reductions of Soviet forces coincided with the start of an attempted cease-fire in Afghanistan, and were directed primarily toward Beijing.

By 1987, a joint Soviet–Chinese commission had begun work on resolving the border dispute along the Amur and Ussuri rivers, predicated on Gorbachev's acceptance of the thalweg principle in his Vladivostok speech. At the beginning of March, Foreign Minister Shevardnadze made a well-publicized swing through Southeast Asia, visiting Australia, Thailand, Indonesia, Laos, Cambodia, and Vietnam. The major topic of Shevardnadze's discussions in Thailand and Indonesia was the Cambodian situation. In Vietnam, Foreign Minister Thach promised Shevardnadze his country would find a political solution to the conflict, and would seek consultations with China and the ASEAN countries to reach an acceptable compromise.

Sino-Soviet *rapprochement* was greatly aided by a fundamental change in Chinese attitudes. Buoyed by the success of their reform program, less dependent on US support for their security, the Chinese began to reexamine the nature of the Soviet threat. Chinese leaders were impressed with Gorbachev's conciliatory style, and by 1986 the preoccupation with Soviet "hegemonism" in East Asia was under critical review. At the 13th Party Congress, held in late 1987, Premier Zhao Ziyang pointedly dropped the reference to "antihegemonism" as a major principle of China's foreign policy. The Chinese expressed fulsome praise for the Soviet Union on the seventieth anniversary of the October Revolution, but continued to rebuff Gorbachev's repeated efforts to arrange a summit meeting with Deng Xiaoping.[40]

Major changes that would revolutionize the Soviet political system and Soviet foreign policy were instigated in 1988. New thinking moved from the realm of cautious official pronouncements to concrete actions and more open public discussion. The decision to leave Afghanistan, announced by Gorbachev on 8 February, was a significant turning point. Soviet troops were scheduled to begin their withdrawal on 15 May, and all forces would be out by 15 February of the following year. Admitting that Afghanistan was a mistake and deciding to withdraw was, as one expert has noted, a catalyst for a candid reappraisal of the Brezhnev regime's foreign policy.[41] Encouraged by the highest levels of officialdom, Soviet politicians, foreign ministry bureaucrats, international affairs specialists and journalists openly debated this previously taboo subject.

Parallel to the major institutional changes planned for the 19th Party Congress, proposals for reforming Soviet foreign policy were solicited from members of the foreign ministry. In a major address to ministry officials after the conference, Shevardnadze remarked that, in contrast to the uninspired foreign policy recommendations advanced after the April 1985 Central Committee Plenum, this time the results "exceeded all expectations." In relation to Asia, the working groups had suggested more attention should be paid to China's reform experience – China and the Soviet Union could build on shared interests in solving similar economic development problems. The section on military-political aspects of security, headed by arms control expert Iulii Vorontsov, devoted considerable attention to security issues and arms reductions in the Pacific. Finally, Shevardnadze remarked on the need to investigate whether the USSR had done all it could to avert the confrontation with China.[42]

Bold criticisms of Soviet foreign policy were finding their way into print by the middle of 1988. In May, Viacheslav Dashichev published his widely cited critique of Soviet foreign policy. In it, he attacked previous claims to infallibility in foreign affairs. Acknowledging that the USSR could make mistakes in foreign policy, just as it had in internal development, was an important and necessary step toward learning. The practice of basing relations among socialist states on a rigid, Stalinist version of democratic centralism, Dashichev argued, was counterproductive. The CPSU's overcentralized approach to domestic affairs seriously distorted foreign policy, leading to a hegemonistic, great-power mentality that contributed to the splits with Yugoslavia and China. In an interview the following month, Dashichev cited expansionist Soviet Third World policies as a central factor damaging relations with China and the West.[43]

Consistent with new Soviet efforts to present a non-threatening foreign policy, Gorbachev routinely insisted that any improvements in Sino-Soviet relations would not be at the expense of US security. On the contrary, Soviet strategy in East Asia was predicated on a strategy of removing sources of tension with the United States, while improving relations with the PRC. Finding a solution to the Afghanistan impasse, for example, removed a major stumbling block to *rapprochement* with both countries. The Geneva accords that negotiated an end to Soviet occupation of Afghanistan were concluded just one month prior to the Reagan–Gorbachev summit in Moscow. However, the Soviet decision to abandon their campaign in Afghanistan was brought about by the coincidence of several factors in addition to a desire to eliminate sources of tension with the US and PRC. The continuing expense of the war, the large number of casualties, growing disillusionment on the home front, the Politburo's preoccupation with internal reforms, and the extraordinary effectiveness of American-made Stinger surface-to-air missiles in downing Soviet aircraft all contributed to bring about a settlement.[44]

With the Sino-Soviet border talks progressing and a complete Soviet withdrawal from Afghanistan scheduled for 15 February 1989, Vietnam's occupation of Cambodia was the single most important obstacle dividing the two countries. In late August, Chinese Deputy Foreign Minister Tian Zengpei and Soviet Deputy Foreign Minister Igor Rogachev met in Beijing for several days of talks on the Cambodian conflict. Both sides praised the recent Jakarta conference as a positive development, although a concrete agreement had foundered on the timetable for Vietnamese withdrawal. The two sides concurred on the need to resolve regional conflicts through peaceful means, and agreed that the internal aspects of a settlement should be left to the Cambodian people. However, Moscow and Beijing had still not resolved all their differences over the terms of a Cambodian accord.[45]

As Sino-Soviet *rapprochement* progressed, the more relaxed atmosphere in East Asia contributed to easing longstanding tensions between the Indians and Chinese, and between the Indians and Pakistanis. In his November 1986 visit to New Delhi, Gorbachev had called for a conference on making the Indian Ocean a zone of peace, proposed establishing confidence-building measures in the Asian-Pacific region, and suggested that India and China mend relations. Gorbachev's peacemaking efforts led to a Chinese–Indian summit in December 1988, the first visit by an Indian leader to Beijing in thirty-four years. By working to relieve tensions in Asia, Gorbachev reinforced his claim that the Soviet Union was now a responsible, constructive actor entitled to a larger role in Asian-Pacific affairs.

At the beginning of December 1988, Chinese Foreign Minister Qian met with Gorbachev and Shevardnadze in Moscow. The two sides noted that border talks were proceeding satisfactorily, and agreed that their common tasks of reform and restructuring favored *rapprochement*. The time of competing power blocs and hegemonism, they concurred, was in the past; the economy, ecology, and other issues now commanded attention. Shevardnadze pointedly underlined Soviet fulfillment of its obligations toward Afghanistan under the Geneva accords. Qian spoke favorably of the prospects for border trade and other forms of economic cooperation in developing the Soviet Far East.

Finally, Shevardnadze was invited to visit China early in 1989 to prepare for a summit meeting between Gorbachev and Deng.[46]

The Soviet Foreign Minister met with Deng Xiaoping, Li Peng, and Qian Qichen at the beginning of February. According to an Eastern bloc diplomat, Shevardnadze brought with him a team of experts on the Cambodian question.[47] In a major breakthrough, China and the USSR concluded a nine-point agreement on Cambodia. Both sides acknowledged the need for an unspecified "effective control mechanism" to supervise the Vietnamese withdrawal, an end to all foreign military aid, maintenance of peace, and respect for free elections. The main point of disagreement was on the shape a future Cambodian administration would take following Vietnam's departure. Both parties noted Vietnam's decision to end its occupation by late September 1989.[48] With this last remaining obstacle resolved, Gorbachev's visit to China was scheduled for 15–18 May 1989.

The May summit

Gorbachev's visit to Beijing, the first Soviet–Chinese summit meeting in thirty years, was an event of great importance for both sides, marking as it did the normalization of diplomatic relations and the restoration of links between the two communist parties. In a speech to Chinese academics and international affairs specialists, Gorbachev commented on the common revolutionary heritage shared by the PRC and the USSR. He supported Deng's suggestion to "let the wind blow away what was, and look toward the future," putting hostilities behind them. Relations were to be "de-ideologized" – neither party would seek to assert ideological primacy, as in the past, and each would respect the experience and sovereign independence of the other.

Gorbachev praised the reduction in military tensions along the Sino-Soviet border, and specified that in addition to the 436 intermediate and shorter range missiles in Asia being eliminated under the INF treaty, Soviet land forces in Asia would be reduced by a total of 200,000 troops during 1989–90. Of these, 120,000 (or 12 divisions) would come from the Far East. In addition 11 air regiments would be disbanded and 16 warships withdrawn from the Pacific Ocean fleet. Finally, 3 full divisions, including 2 tank divisions, 1 motorized rifle division, and all aviation units, would be withdrawn from Soviet forces in Mongolia.[49] This constituted a reduction of approximately 75 percent in Soviet troops deployed in Mongolia, and all three divisions to be withdrawn were in a category 1 (highest) level of readiness.

Gorbachev also stressed the great potential for economic cooperation between the two countries, especially cross-border trade between the Soviet Far East and northeast China, and between Soviet Central Asia and the adjoining Chinese provinces. Two of the most promising areas of cooperation singled out were the rail line being constructed to connect Beijing and Moscow via Urumchi and Alma Ata (this line would also serve as China's link to Europe), and joint development of coal slurry pipelines. Gorbachev emphasized Soviet interest in the lessons to be drawn from China's economic reform efforts – specifically, its success in integrating into the world economy, and its experience with special economic zones. Deputy Premiers Masliukov and Tian held separate talks on exchanging reform experiences, and finalized cooperation in the priority areas of energy, transportation, heavy and light metallurgy, consumer goods, medicine and health care, and labor.[50]

Cambodia dominated the international agenda. In their joint communiqué, the two sides pledged support for a peaceful, independent, neutral and non-aligned Cambodia following a complete Vietnamese withdrawal. They also advocated convening an international conference, and a gradual end to all military assistance to the various Cambodian factions. Some differences remained, however. China favored the formation of a coalition government, consisting of representatives of all four parties and headed by Prince Norodom Sihanouk, during the transition period. The Soviet side advocated an internal solution allowing the Cambodian people to determine the electoral process and form of transitional government.[51] China's plan would ensure participation by the Khmer Rouge, while the arrangement promoted by the Soviets favored the Hun Sen government and the other two parties, who were united in opposition to the Khmer Rouge.

The student demonstrations taking place in Tiananmen Square during Gorbachev's visit deflected attention away from the summit, to the dismay of both leaders. The subsequent imposition of martial law and the massacre in early June was, from the Soviet perspective, cause for great concern. First, these events negated much of the public relations value Gorbachev hoped to reap from the summit. Given the disastrous record of perestroika domestically, the General Secretary needed a foreign relations triumph to enhance his image.

Second, Soviet commentaries faced the dilemma of either siding with the students, whose inspiration was in large part derived from Gorbachev's democratization campaign, or expressing support for the Chinese regime's bloody repression. The compromise arrived at was simply to report the events in China as dispassionately as possible, in an attempt to avoid imputing blame to either side. At least a handful of Soviet scholars, however, vigorously condemned their government for not taking a more principled stand against the violence.[52]

Third, the violence that took place in Tiananmen Square strengthened the position of Soviet conservatives wary of the potential for destabilization in Gorbachev's reforms.[53] The June events graphically illustrated the potential for instability in reforming communist systems. Soviet political observer Aleksandr Bovin's comments typified the "lessons" Soviet reformers have drawn from China. Bovin noted that in the PRC economic reform outpaced political reform – the reverse of what occurred in the Soviet Union. The results of this disparity, he warned, could be the same for both countries.[54]

For Soviet reformers the lesson to be drawn from Tiananmen was the need to accelerate the reform process in the economic sphere, in order to bring the level of material well-being up to the level of political consciousness. Soviet conservatives, by contrast, concluded political retrenchment was necessary to avoid comparable violence.

After the summit

Several factors dampened relations in the months following the summit. Moscow's China policy, once the twin goals of a Sino-Soviet summit and normalization of relations had been realized, was supplanted by more pressing domestic concerns. The first meeting of the new Congress of People's Deputies, the evolution of the Supreme Soviet as a functioning legislature, declarations of sovereignty and independence by union republics and smaller ethnic units, the worsening economic situation, crime, ethnic tensions, and a renewed power struggle between conservatives and reformers dominated the Soviet political agenda in the two years following the summit. Relations with China moved to the back of the Soviet policy agenda.

China's aging leaders, or at least the conservative faction that succeeded in ousting Zhao Ziyang after the June events, feared the impact of Soviet glasnost and democratization, and the resultant instability, on Chinese society. The downfall of communism in Eastern Europe and the Soviet government's decision in February 1990 to rescind article six of the Soviet Constitution, guaranteeing the "leading and guiding role" of the Communist Party, alarmed Chinese leaders. Another source of concern was the impact of decentralization and the growing demands for autonomy from Soviet border nationalities, which threatened to ignite separatist movements along China's northern border. Internal Chinese Communist Party documents circulating in winter 1989–90 criticized Gorbachev for undermining socialism, and none-too-subtly suggested a conservative takeover would be welcomed in Beijing.[55]

Soviet–American detente, however, significantly limited Beijing's ability to play the two superpowers off against each other. China's repressive policies jeopardized the crucial economic ties developed over the past decade with the West and Japan. In response to Tiananmen, for example, the US Congress attached a sanctions amendment to the State Department's authorization bill. Japan officially suspended a planned six-year development aid package worth US $5.9 billion, scheduled to begin in 1990, while $490 million in Asian Development Bank loans were put on hold. In addition, the World Bank delivered only $500 million of a projected $2.5 billion loan to China scheduled for fiscal year 1990.[56]

Soviet aid and trade could not effectively substitute for trade with the advanced industrialized nations, since the USSR did not have all the technology and capital China needed. Moreover, China's trade with the United States was four to five times greater than that with the Soviet Union. However, both Moscow and Beijing had a keen interest in preserving the advantages derived from normalization. These included not only the direct benefits of trade, but also the potential gain from scientific and technological cooperation, savings realized through reductions of military forces, mutual interest in preserving stability on the Korean peninsula and in the Asian-Pacific region more broadly, and the lessons derived from common reform experiences.

Chinese Premier Li Peng visited Moscow in April 1990 in an effort to expand cooperation and continue the dialogue. The Chinese leader was granted a warm, albeit low-key welcome. Agreements were concluded on economic and scientific-technological cooperation, space exploration, further reductions in armed forces and confidence-building measures along the Sino-Soviet border, and cooperation on building a nuclear power station in China. The two sides announced that approximately 90 percent of the disputed border area had been resolved. Military exchanges were planned, and the Chinese government agreed to extend the Soviet Union credits for the purchase of consumer goods.[57]

While Cambodia, Afghanistan, and Korea were discussed, these foreign policy issues did not dominate the agenda. The major source of disagreement during Li's visit appears to have been over ideological questions and the demise of communism in Eastern Europe. Gorbachev's ideological revisions and the Soviet democratization process, like Khrushchev's revelations at the 20th Party Congress, raised expectations and undermined the legitimacy of the Chinese system among intellectuals and students. Beijing welcomed Moscow's renunciation of the Brezhnev doctrine, but the instability and rapid transformation of Eastern Europe and the tenuous hold on power exercised by communist elites was troubling to Chinese leaders. However, the two sides agreed that each country was entitled to follow its unique path, and reiterated their commitment not to interfere in each other's internal affairs.

Traditional Soviet *realpolitik* led the government to avoid any criticism of Beijing that could jeopardize normalized Sino-Soviet relations. However, by 1989–90 glasnost had progressed to the point that public opinion became a significant factor in Soviet foreign policy. During Premier Li Peng's April visit several hundred citizens demonstrated in Moscow, carrying placards reading "Bloody Butcher Li Go Home." In addition, six members of the Supreme Soviet condemned his visit and repressive Chinese policies as immoral.[58] Treatment of Li's visit in the Soviet mass media was rather constrained, in contrast to what might be expected for an event of this significance.

By 1991, Soviet decline had progressed to the point that the Chinese, fearing the consequences of Soviet instability, decided to extend aid to their former enemy. A commodity loan was offered by General Secretary Jiang Zemin during a March visit to Beijing by V. Ivashko, deputy General Secretary of the CPSU, enabling the Soviet Union to purchase some 1 billion Swiss francs (US $730 million) worth of Chinese grain, meat, milk products, peanuts, tea, textiles, and cigarettes. The loan was repayable over a five-year period in manufactured goods and raw materials, according to Soviet reports.[59] Western sources, however, suggested that repayment might be in the form of Soviet fighter aircraft, including MiG-27s, MiG-29s, and Su-24s.[60] Soviet commentaries praised the loan as an example of the maturing of economic relations between the Soviet Union and the PRC.

Economic cooperation continued to expand as Sino-Soviet relations shed the constraints of ideological competition. The total volume of trade for 1989 was 18.7 percent higher than in 1988. The expectations for trade to expand to over $5.3 billion in 1990 were not realized, as the Soviet economy's free-fall accelerated.[61] In exchange for Chinese light industrial products, the Soviets contracted to sell China two nuclear power plants, two thermal power stations, a pulp and paper mill, and flax treating plants.

Barter arrangements, although convenient for evading the problem of hard currency shortages, proved cumbersome and hindered the further expansion of trade. Transportation bottlenecks and supply problems in the Soviet Union put Soviet deliveries of machinery behind schedule, and cross-border exchanges slackened after 1989. To facilitate Sino-Soviet trade, the two sides made provisions in 1990 for the mutual extension of credits and for shifting exclusively to hard currency trade.[62]

Continuing the process of high-level dialogue, China's Communist Party General Secretary Jiang Zemin visited Moscow in May 1991. The two sides discussed reform issues, inter-party relations, trade and scientific exchanges, and international issues including the Middle East, Cambodia, and Korea. Gorbachev stressed the importance of developing the potential of Sino-Soviet economic cooperation in the traditional spheres – energy, transportation, metallurgy, consumer goods, and agricultural products – and also in such new areas as nuclear energy, civil aviation, space exploration, and other scientific enterprises. The Russian republic, and other republics, he noted, were eager to develop direct economic links with China.[63]

Jiang supported Gorbachev's call for expanding economic co-operation, adding that China was interested in developing exchanges in medicine, culture, and sports. He expressed concern, however, over the possible consequences of tumultuous events taking place in the Soviet Union. Jiang emphasized that the main guarantee of success in the reform process, in the opinion of the Chinese leadership, was to ensure *socialist* direction of society's transformation. Both countries had the responsibility to strengthen internal stability, he stated, since events in these two large nations had a determining influence on Europe, Asia and therefore the entire world.[64]

As conditions in the Soviet Union deteriorated, some conservatives looked to China as an example of a reformist socialist system that had preserved the leading role of the Communist Party in society. Ivan Polozkov, First Secretary of the Russian Communist Party led a dele-gation to Beijing in June. Polozkov, who denied the CPSU was to blame for the crisis situation in the USSR, praised the Chinese Com-munist Party's experience as "very important and instructive."[65] Although many commentators adopted a more critical attitude toward China following the coup, praise for China's relatively stable reform record could be found on occasion.[66]

Several issues in Sino-Soviet relations complicated ties as the USSR moved toward its denouement. An agreement delineating the eastern border between the two countries was concluded in late June, but a few disputed areas remained.[67] Economic cooperation became more problematic as the Soviet economic crisis worsened. Interviewed shortly after the August coup, Premier Li Peng claimed Sino-Soviet relations would not be affected by upheavals in the Soviet Union. He asserted China's respect for the principle of non-interference in Soviet internal affairs, and rejected suggestions that Beijing was worried about possible turmoil among its national minorities in the border regions.[68] However, the Chinese leadership sent Vice-President Wang Zhen to Xinjiang province immediately after the coup. Wang, who conducted a military inspection tour of the region, stressed the need for building a "steel wall" to safeguard Chinese socialism and national unity.[69]

Official denials notwithstanding, Beijing was clearly troubled by the growing instability on its northern and western borders. As the Soviet Union collapsed, the successor Russian state under Boris Yeltsin promised to continue the progress achieved under Gorbachev. However, the potential for ideological infection from a democratizing Russia, the prospect of Muslim resurgence in Central Asia, the sudden emergence of newly independent republics, and the possible spillover of ethnic conflict into China's frontier regions profoundly disturbed the aged Chinese leadership.

Conclusion

Under Gorbachev, Soviet policy toward Northeast Asia focused on reversing the single greatest setback to Soviet foreign policy in the post-war era – the rift between China and the USSR. Convinced the Sino-Soviet relationship was the key to strengthening their position in the Asian-Pacific region, Soviet leaders addressed each of the three major obstacles cited by China as impediments to better relations – the border dispute and Soviet troop deployments first, then Afghanistan, and finally Cambodia. Of course, Soviet flexibility in these areas was motivated by factors other than a desire to improve relations with China. These three issues also constituted significant barriers to better East–West relations, and hindered Soviet initiatives toward Japan, South Korea, the ASEAN nations, Pakistan, and other regional states.

In addition, there were compelling domestic reasons for their accommodative behavior. The expense of supporting over 50 divisions on the Sino-Soviet border and up to 115,000 troops in Afghanistan, while subsidizing Vietnam's inefficient militarized economy, imposed a significant drain on the Soviet treasury. As glasnost made critical discussion of foreign affairs possible, public opposition to the Afghan conflict began to exert pressure for an end to the occupation. However, the strenuous diplomatic efforts evident from 1985 suggest a *rapprochement* with China was high on the list of Soviet priorities, and accounts for much of Soviet flexibility on these issues.

Sino-Soviet relations in the 1980s contributed to learning in Soviet foreign and domestic policy, although this learning process cannot be considered in isolation from other internal and external factors. For example, China's market-style economic reforms, which were originally rejected by Soviet commentators as bourgeois and unsuited to Soviet conditions, could be analyzed more objectively once Gorbachev had committed the Soviet Union to economic restructuring. China's example appealed to a Soviet leadership searching initially for adaptive solutions, that is, for models of economic transformation possible within the existing structures of the party-state system. China's special economic zones were studied by Soviet economists as promising arrangements for attracting foreign investment and technical and managerial expertise.[70]

By 1988, however, a growing consensus had developed among Soviet reformers on the need for fundamental political change to accompany economic restructuring, in distinct contrast to the Chinese model. Early in his tenure Gorbachev had turned to social scientists like Abel Aganbegian, Oleg Bogomolov, and Tat'iana Zaslavskaia, who argued that democratization of society and the workplace were necessary to overcome the stultifying influence of bureaucratic socialism and release the creative potential of Soviet workers. These were the negative lessons of the Soviet and Eastern Europe experience. The demonstrations and subsequent bloodbath in Tiananmen Square reinforced the reformers' conviction that genuine economic progress was inextricably linked to political reform.

The foreign policy lessons drawn from Soviet–Chinese relations are more readily discernable. First, Eduard Shevardnadze on several occasions had remarked that the Sino-Soviet conflict had proved very costly to both nations. There were direct economic costs involved in deploying large standing armies along their common border, and in competing for influence in the developing world. The Soviet Far East military build-up threatened Japanese and American interests in the Western Pacific, and led to compensatory measures that negatively impacted Soviet national security. Both countries experienced significant opportunity costs as hostile political relations interfered with normal trade and economic cooperation. Finally, the Soviet pre-occupation with a Chinese threat, which often bordered on racist irrationality, skewed decision-making and contributed to inflexible and ill-considered Asia policies.

In deideologizing Soviet foreign policy, Gorbachev eliminated a key factor underlying Sino-Soviet hostility. Competing claims to ideological primacy assured the two nations would follow a confrontational course. The Soviet shift from an ideologically based foreign policy toward a policy based on the concept of a "balance of interests" and acceptance of universal values – a tolerant, pluralist approach to international relations – made it possible to deal with China as a fully equal, sovereign nation rather than an apostate vassal.

China's internal politics also played a role. There is no basis for asserting that Soviet policies were entirely responsible for persistent hostilities. However, the Great Leap Forward, the Cultural Revolution, and other radical campaigns were in large part manifestations of competition for ideological and political dominance. Sino-Soviet *rapprochement* was possible in the 1980s because for the first time reformers in both countries had the upper hand. For both Soviet and Chinese reformers, ideology had become subordinate to economics. It was only in the Soviet Union, where political pluralism was allowed to emerge, that the reform process led to the complete discrediting of the official ideology. As of this writing, Deng and the aging Chinese leaders are still struggling to reconcile the contradictions in their country.

With the normalization of relations in 1989, Gorbachev's policy toward China could be considered a success. A return to the close, albeit unequal relationship of the 1950s was not to be expected. Nor was it likely that the hostile and violent clashes of the 1960s and 1970s would be repeated. Soviet reforms made a new relationship possible, one predicated on a fundamentally revised Soviet perspective toward the People's Republic.

It was a mark of the maturity of this new relationship that China and the Soviet Union openly acknowledged and accepted that their interests were not identical. Nonetheless, the two countries shared an interest in reducing military expenditures and the level of tension in East Asia; in continuing the process of internal reform, notwithstanding their widely disparate approaches; in further developing trade relations and economic cooperation; and in supporting naval arms control and nuclear-free zones in the Western Pacific. Both nations favored a reduction, but not the elimination, of America's military presence in the region. Both were concerned about the possibility of a resurgent Japan, and both were anxious to avoid becoming involved in any conflict on the Korean peninsula. Finally, as ideology diminished in importance, Sino-Soviet competition for influence in the developing world became virtually irrelevant.

Despite the collapse of the Soviet Union, there remains enough common ground between the new Russia and the old China to suggest relations will continue on an even keel, at least in the foreseeable future. Much depends on whether the reformers under the leadership of Boris Yeltsin remain in power. These are the individuals who learned the lessons of Moscow's failed policies. It is unlikely they would seek to reverse the substantial gains made under Gorbachev. Of course, over time a democratizing Russia will have progressively less in common with a repressive authoritarian Chinese regime, and tensions may arise over human rights issues. However, to the extent that imposing domestic problems continue to dominate the agendas in both Moscow and Beijing, neither is likely to grant much attention to issues of foreign policy.

5 Japan

> The Japanese seem to have proved that in today's world the status of a great power can be attained without relying on militarism.
>
> Mikhail Gorbachev, Krasnoiarsk speech (*Pravda*, 18 September 1988, p. 2).

Following the reestablishment of diplomatic relations between the USSR and Japan in 1956, Soviet policy toward its island neighbor combined elements of both threat and promise. Politically, Soviet leaders sought to conclude a peace treaty that would force the Japanese permanently to accept USSR sovereignty over the Kuriles. The absence of fully normalized ties, however, was not to preclude the development of fruitful economic cooperation in exploiting the vast potential of Siberia and the Soviet Far East. Soviet security interests found expression in attempts to prevent Japan from rearming, encouraging Japanese pacifist and anti-nuclear movements, and efforts to drive a wedge between Japan and the United States. The process by which these contradictory approaches came to be recognized as ill-considered and counterproductive is the subject of this chapter.

In the Brezhnev era, a unidimensional concept of power was in large measure responsible for Soviet indifference, arrogance, and inflexibility toward Japan. Brezhnev, Gromyko, Suslov – those select few who had decisive input into foreign policy – conceptualized power and influence almost exclusively in terms of military potential. This approach conditioned both their evaluation of Soviet capabilities, and their perception of other nations' power. Gromyko's triumphant 1972 declaration, that no international question of significance could be decided without Soviet participation, was grounded in the Soviet Union's achieving *military* parity with America. From this perspective Japan, its military capability limited by close association with the United States and by cultural and constitutional proscriptions against maintaining a large military force, did not merit serious Soviet attention.

Gorbachev's new thinking reversed this one-sided concept of power, and in so doing accorded far greater importance to Japan by virtue of its economic strength. Japan's technological prowess and its position as the world's second most powerful economy generated new respect from the Soviet Union. Japanese assistance could be instrumental in the Soviet reform process, but it would be wrong to assume that Soviet need for Japanese technology or investment would outweigh the fundamental differences separating the two countries.

Soviet policy toward Japan changed significantly in the 1980s, although developments in the relationship were far less spectacular than the breakthroughs achieved with the People's Republic of China or South Korea. In this chapter, I suggest that learning was clearly evident in Soviet policy toward Japan. The major lessons revolved around the relationship between international economic cooperation and the need for domestic structural reforms, and the utility of military power in guaranteeing Soviet national security interests. The Soviet experience with Japan in the 1980s contributed significantly to a new appreciation of the limits of Soviet power and influence in Asia, and accelerated the push for more complete integration into the world economic system.

The roots of hostility

Soviet–Japanese relations suffered from a legacy of three wars in this century alone, recurring territorial disputes, and major cultural differences. Soviet–Japanese relations were shaped by a general cultural disaffection, although the evidence suggests that negative feelings were stronger on the Japanese side. Opinion surveys conducted by the Soviet Academy of Sciences Institute of Sociological Studies and the Japanese newspaper *Yomiuri Shimbun*, for example, found that only 17.6 percent of Japanese considered their attitude toward the Soviet Union and its people as "sympathetic," while 47.4 percent described their attitude as "antipathetic." Soviet respondents, by comparison, were much more favorably inclined toward Japan and its people – 88 percent were "sympathetic, and only 2.4 percent "antipathetic."[1] One Soviet author, considering these data, has suggested that the discrepancy might be explained by the often distorted information conveyed to the Soviet population about the true state of relations.[2]

The war legacy is another source of discord. While Japanese may feel guilt over their actions in China and Korea, they continue to perceive the Soviets as aggressors toward them. From their perspective, the Soviet Union entered the war in the final days, in violation of the non-aggression pact, and proceeded to realize its irredentist goals in the Far East. The official Soviet position, which appeared to be supported by a large sector of the population, was that the USSR was fulfilling its allied obligations as stipulated at Yalta, and merely reclaiming territories lost to Japanese imperialism. Public opinion, especially among the Russian segment of the population, tends to link this territorial issue with emotive questions of nationalism, and is therefore averse to giving up the islands.[3]

International events have also inhibited *rapprochement* between the two countries. After marginal improvements in the late 1960s and 1970s based on limited economic cooperation and coincident with East–West detente, Soviet–Japanese ties deteriorated in the 1980s. The peace and friendship treaty signed in 1978 between Japan and the PRC, with its anti-hegemony clause directed at the USSR; Japan's harsh reaction to the invasion of Afghanistan; and trade sanctions enacted against the USSR after martial law was imposed in Poland significantly worsened relations between the two countries. Soviet commentaries typically claimed that Japan was responsible for the poor state of relations between the two, with its stubborn insistence on "unresolved territorial issues" and unwillingness to conclude a treaty on good-neighborliness and cooperation.[4]

Prior to new thinking, the Soviets refused to accept any responsibility for the poor state of Japanese–Soviet relations. The standard position was that relations had improved steadily, albeit slowly, since diplomatic ties were reestablished in October 1956. Soviet–Japanese relations deteriorated in the 1980s as a result of US and Chinese pressure on Japan to adopt hard-line policies, not as a rational response to aggressive Soviet behavior in the region. The Reagan administration, portrayed as intent on accelerating the arms race and achieving military superiority over the Soviet Union, was blamed for encouraging their Japanese allies to apply economic sanctions and issue anti-Soviet declarations on the territorial issue and the Soviet military threat.[5]

From cooperation to irrelevance?

While political relations could improve only minimally in the absence of a peace treaty and some movement on the Northern Territories issue, trade between the two countries had grown steadily since 1965. A series of projects to develop Soviet oil and natural gas industries, coal, forestry resources, wood processing plants, and ports were concluded, based on barter arrangements to avoid the problem of ruble inconvertibility. Joint committees on economic cooperation were established.[6] The two countries, which in many respects appeared to be natural trading partners, seemed willing to put aside political differences in order to develop mutually beneficial economic ties.

The oil shocks of the 1970s, and Japan's subsequent restructuring away from energy-intensive industries, eliminated much of the attraction of the USSR as an energy and raw materials supplier. Japan's technological lead over the USSR had widened to the point that Soviet finished goods held no attraction for the Japanese market. In addition, political relations soured with the invasion of Afghanistan and Soviet-supported repression in Poland. Pressed by the United States, Japan boycotted the 1980 Olympics and agreed to impose sanctions on the Soviet Union.

Consequently, the rate of growth in Soviet–Japanese trade slowed from 1975 to 1983, as Soviet exports stagnated and the Soviet deficit with Japan reached 9.1 billion foreign trade rubles.[7] Trade declined in absolute terms from a high of $5.5 billion in 1982 to $4.2 billion in 1983, a drop of 18 percent. This figure dropped even further in 1984, to $3.9 billion, before recovering somewhat in the second half of the 1980s. Prospects for Soviet–Japanese cooperation improved after late 1984, however, when sanctions over Poland and Afghanistan were eased, and the Soviet–Japanese Joint Committee for Economic Cooperation met after a five-year hiatus.

The total volume of trade between the two countries leveled out during 1988–90, reaching $5.9 billion in 1988, $6.0 billion in 1989, and $5.9 billion in 1990. However, all of the "growth" evident since the early 1980s can be accounted for by the stronger yen; in real terms, there was no improvement in Soviet–Japanese trade in the 1980s.[8]

The stagnation and decline in Soviet–Japanese economic relations coincided with the general Soviet economic crisis. The obvious contrast between the floundering and technologically backward Soviet economy, and the dynamic, high-technology-oriented Japanese growth machine, became readily apparent by the late 1970s. And yet Soviet writings on Japan through the early Gorbachev period continued to assert that economic ties benefited Japan as much as the USSR, argued that Japanese companies stood to lose billions from their shortsighted support for sanctions, and rejected claims that Japan's

evolution toward a high-tech, low-energy intensive economy undermined Soviet usefulness as a trade partner.[9]

The primary basis for Soviet–Japanese relations through the 1960s
and 1970s had been economic cooperation. While trade with the USSR
in the best of times had constituted only a miniscule portion of total
Japanese trade, the Soviet share declined even further in the early
1980s. In short, the USSR found itself increasingly marginal to Japanese
interests. By the mid-1980s, in what must have been a serious shock for
the new, reform-minded leadership, Japan's total gross national
product matched and then surpassed that of the USSR.

The interregnum

As suggested in chapter 4, circumstances associated with Andropov's
brief rule led to an early reassessment of Soviet–Chinese relations,
laying the foundation for an energetic push by Gorbachev to normalize relations with the Chinese government and Communist Party in
1987–89. Japan, a capitalist country and close ally of the United States,
offered a different challenge to the architects of new thinking.
Moreover, Japan had not undergone a substantive change in policy
comparable to that of China in the post-Mao period. And finally,
Japan's position in the Soviet foreign policy design was primarily that
of a plausible economic partner and a potential security threat. Japan,
unlike China, had never presented the sort of political-ideological
challenge that divided communism and struck at the fundamental
premises of Soviet foreign policy. In sum, Soviet–Japanese relations,
albeit very poor, were not a disaster on the scale of the Sino-Soviet
split, and consequently merited less attention from policy-makers and
foreign affairs intellectuals.[10]

Policy toward Japan under Andropov and Chernenko continued
the rather contradictory mix of threats over Japan's "military resurgence," charges that Japan was virtually a tool of the United States,
and offers to expand economic cooperation that had characterized the
late Brezhnev period. It is quite possible that the USSR's Japan policy
was reviewed upon Brezhnev's death. A prominent KGB defector has
claimed the First Chief Directorate of the agency for the first time
elevated Japan to a major priority in its operations plans for the period
of 1982 to 1985. However, Japan still ranked behind the United States,
China, India, West Germany, Great Britain, and France as an intelligence target.[11]

Additional evidence of a possible policy shift was the publication of an article in the March 1983 issue of the Party theoretical journal *Kommunist*. The article, which quoted Andropov's remarks to a November 1982 Central Committee plenum, held out a small olive branch among the rather dense foliage of anti-Japanese rhetoric. The General Secretary had rejected the possibility of the Soviet government making preliminary concessions in order to normalize relations. The author emphasized that Japan's economy faced serious problems, and rather defensively asserted that "History has repeatedly confirmed the groundlessness of the opinion that the Soviet Union cannot develop without foreign assistance." Full blame was placed on Japan for not acting on a 1978 Soviet proposal for a peace treaty. But, the author concluded, good-neighborly relations with the USSR were not out of the question, and would prove to be a far better security guarantee for Japan than any US "nuclear umbrella."[12]

One theme repeatedly attacked in Soviet publications during this period was Japan's attempt to "artificially link" the "complex international situation," namely, Soviet involvement in Afghanistan and Poland, to Soviet–Japanese economic relations.[13] Soviet commentators adamantly rejected the notion that Soviet behavior in Asia and elsewhere may have given the Japanese legitimate cause for concern about their security.[14] Soviet unwillingness to acknowledge linkage in international relations, of course, was a fundamental source of tension in Soviet–American relations. The poor state of Soviet–Japanese relations during this period was partly due to US pressure on Japan over these issues, and partly the result of genuine Japanese concerns over aggressive Soviet actions in the region.

A minor turnaround in the Soviet–Japanese dialogue was evident toward the end of 1984 and the beginning of 1985. Meetings and discussions at the governmental level increased, as did those between Soviet and Japanese non-governmental organizations. The first meeting of the Soviet–Japanese Committees on Economic Cooperation since 1979 was held in Tokyo in December 1984.[15] Foreign Ministers Andrei Gromyko and Shintaro Abe held talks at the United Nations, while Premiers Yasuhiro Nakasone and Nikolai Tikhonov met in New Delhi at Indira Gandhi's funeral. Nakasone also flew to Moscow for Chernenko's funeral in March 1985, and met briefly with the newly appointed General Secretary.

The Japanese were clearly not eager to make rapid improvements in either the political or economic sphere, barring tangible Soviet concessions. A Soviet offer to conclude a long-term economic pact, for example, was rejected by the Japanese in January 1985. At the same time, Gorbachev sought to convey the impression that the USSR was not desperately seeking better relations with Japan. "History has repeatedly shown that Japan and the USSR can manage without one another," he told Foreign Minister Abe, "although it is unseemly for neighbors to hold such a position."[16]

New faces in Soviet diplomacy

High-level personnel changes enacted shortly after Gorbachev was appointed General Secretary paved the way for a shift away from the Brezhnev regime's foreign policy priorities and perspectives. At the June 1985 plenum of the Party Central Committee Andrei Gromyko, the conservative who served as foreign affairs minister since 1957, was relieved of his position and elevated to the largely ceremonial post of Chairman of the Supreme Soviet Presidium. Gromyko had centered the operations of the foreign affairs ministry around relations with the United States and the larger West European nations. Japan, in Gromyko's view, was a minor player in international affairs, more an appendage to US foreign policy than a significant power in its own right.

Gromyko's neglect of Japan was illustrated by the fact that he had made only one trip to Japan in the last decade of his tenure as foreign minister. This was particularly insulting to the Japanese in light of the fact that four prime ministers had traveled to Moscow during the same time frame. Gromyko was uncompromising on the Northern Territories, refusing even to discuss the issue with his Japanese counterparts. Reportedly it was Ivan Kovalenko, Deputy Chief of the Central Committee's International Department and a firm proponent of dealing with Japan from a position of strength, who exercised considerable influence over Gromyko's view of Japan.[17]

In the early stages of new thinking, some of the more obstreperous aspects of Soviet foreign policy were discarded. One year after Gromyko's dismissal, in a speech delivered to a closed meeting of the Soviet foreign ministry, Gorbachev criticized past Soviet policy for ignoring other nations' interests. In a passage clearly directed at Gromyko, he stated "We must resolutely avoid a situation in which our delegation is called 'Mr. Nyet' because of its meaningless stubborness."[18] The new style of diplomacy would emphasize a more constructive, flexible approach to foreign relations than had prevailed under Brezhnev and Gromyko.

Eduard Shevardnadze's appointment signaled a shift away from

Gromyko's confrontational style of diplomacy, marked a reorientation of traditional Soviet preoccupation with America and Europe, and allowed Gorbachev to place his individual stamp on Soviet foreign policy. In addition, Shevardnadze was clearly more in touch with Soviet domestic realities than was his predecessor. As First Secretary of the Georgian republic he had established one of the first public opinion institutes in the USSR. Shevardnadze, unlike Gromyko, appreciated the links between domestic and foreign policy that Gorbachev claimed were critical to the success of perestroika.

Additional personnel changes during Gorbachev's tenure – notably, the demotion of conservative Ivan Kovalenko, and the appointment of Nikolai Solov'ev as ambassador in 1986 – signaled a more accommodative Soviet policy toward Japan. Kovalenko, a hardliner regarded by the Japanese as a symbol of Soviet arrogance and inflexibility, was for years the leading Japan specialist in the Communist Party Central Committee's International Department. Kovalenko was transferred to a less influential position in the Institute of Oriental Studies, although he continued to participate in various exchanges.

Nikolai Solov'ev, who replaced Petr Ambrasimov as ambassador, had spent a total of eight years in the Soviet embassy in Japan prior to receiving his portfolio. He had directed the Ministry of Foreign Affairs' Second Far East Department for some ten years, and spoke fluent Japanese. Solov'ev was an ideal choice to implement Gorbachev's new, more skillful diplomacy. One Japanese newspaper called him the most pro-Japanese official in the Soviet foreign service.[19]

Structural changes in the Soviet foreign policy apparatus after Gorbachev came to power also reflected changing perspectives toward the Asian-Pacific region. Within the Ministry of Foreign Affairs, Japan, Australia, New Zealand, and Papua New Guinea were regrouped into a new Pacific Ocean Department (New Zealand was formerly part of the Second European Department, which included English-speaking countries outside the Pacific region). Japanese affairs were accorded the status of a Division, in place of the previous Japan section within the ministry. Although the South Asian Department was not revamped, a new Southeast Asian Department was formed. The PRC, Vietnam, and other Southeast Asian countries were now to be included in the Asian Division of the Socialist Countries Department.

Broad Communist Party supervision of all foreign policies, following the central Party Secretariat transformations in September 1988, was vested in the new foreign relations department. Aleksandr Yakovlev, appointed secretary in charge of the department, had long argued for a more multipolar approach to world politics in place of the narrower Gromyko perspective. Yakovlev also deemphasized the military aspects of power, and argued for approaching Asia and Western Europe as entities increasingly independent of US tutelage. Finally, the Asia focus of the top leadership was further emphasized in late September 1989 when Evgenii Primakov, Director of IMEMO and head of the Soviet Committee on Pacific Economic Cooperation, was elevated to candidate membership in the Politburo.

Evolving perspectives under Gorbachev

Despite these changes in the foreign policy establishment, Soviet–Japanese relations improved only marginally in Gorbachev's early years. This process, which consisted of a series of incremental steps culminating in Gorbachev's disappointing Tokyo summit, began with the Geneva summit in November 1985. At Geneva, the Soviet Union, the United States, and Japan announced cooperative measures to assure the safety of passenger aircraft flying near Soviet territory in the north Pacific, to reduce the possibility of another tragic disaster like the KAL 007 shoot-down in 1983. Tokyo and Khabarovsk would in the future be directly linked by phone line, replacing an indirect line channeled through Sapporo. The agreement also called for the Soviets to place a navigational beacon on Kamchatka peninsula as an auxiliary reference aid for pilots.

Shevardnadze's January 1986 trip to Japan was the first by a Soviet foreign minister in ten years, and was viewed by the Japanese as the first solid indicator of a change in Soviet policy. The object of his trip was to resume peace treaty negotiations broken off in 1976, when talks foundered on Soviet resistance to discussing the territorial question. Apparently, the outcome of the US–Soviet Geneva summit encouraged Soviet leaders to intensify their efforts toward normalization with the Japanese.

Military issues proved to be especially contentious during Shevardnadze's visit. The Soviet Foreign Minister warned that Japanese participation in America's Strategic Defense Initiative was an obstacle to better Soviet–Japanese relations. Japanese officials, however, rejected Soviet attempts to pressure Japan toward a more conciliatory defense policy. Foreign Minister Abe urged a reduction of Soviet military presence in Asia, and requested the removal of those SS-20s targeted eastward. According to Japanese reports, Shevardnadze reiterated Moscow's longstanding position that the status of the Kurile islands was non-negotiable. Peace treaty negotiations based on the joint communiqué of 1973 were to continue, however, and the two countries signed a set of accords on trade, technological cooperation, and cultural exchanges. High-level contacts were to increase over the next two years, and the possibility of a summit was mentioned.[20]

Improved ties with Japan and other Asian nations could serve Gorbachev's primary goal of reinvigorating the failing Soviet economy. A revised approach to international economic cooperation designed to reinforce domestic reform programs was reflected in the leadership's pronouncements on the Asia-Pacific region. In Gorbachev's address to the 27th Party Congress he noted the growing importance of Asia and the Pacific in world affairs. These remarks were amplified in a Soviet government statement released in April 1986, which stressed the economic potential of the area, the priority attached to developing Siberia and the Soviet Far East, and the need to address security questions connected with the Pacific basin.[21] Gorbachev's July Vladivostok speech elaborated on plans to develop the eastern regions of the USSR and, in this context, described Japan as "a power of paramount importance" which had "demonstrated striking achievements in industry, trade, education, science and technology."[22]

Plans for utilizing the natural wealth of Siberia and the Far East were formalized with the promulgation of a long-range development program for the Soviet Far Eastern Economic Region, in July 1987. This ambitious scheme, which would have invested 232 billion rubles in the region by the end of the century, never got off the ground. It appears to have been an early component of perestroika aimed at gauging the potential for Japanese investment and assistance in developing these neglected Soviet territories.[23] The legalization of joint ventures early in 1987 relaxed longstanding provisions against close cooperation between Soviet and capitalist firms. In an indication of Moscow's interest in developing the Soviet Far East, major enterprises in that economic region were given preferential treatment over their counterparts in the western USSR in their dealings with foreign businesses.

The arrest of two executives of the Toshiba corporation in May 1987 for selling a sophisticated computer program, which enabled the Soviet defense industry to produce quieter submarine propellors, soured Soviet–Japanese relations. In return for technologically advanced milling equipment, delivered in violation of COCOM (Coordinating Council for Multilateral Export Control) regulations, Toshiba had received some $23 million for a series of deals dating back to December 1982. Relations deteriorated further in the same month as

Japan announced it had broken a Soviet spy ring in Tokyo, and expelled four Soviet diplomats. In August the two countries traded expulsions, with the Japanese accusing the USSR of industrial and military espionage. In December Japanese fighter planes fired on a Soviet bomber that had strayed into Japanese air space. Moscow later apologized to Japan over the incident.[24]

The Toshiba affair renewed pressures in the United States for Japan to assume a greater share of the military burden in the Pacific. In January 1988 Premier Noboru Takeshita announced Japan would pay a higher share of the costs of US military bases on Japanese territory. Under previous arrangements Japan had paid half the cost of benefits granted to Japanese workers – retirement pay, bonuses, housing and commuting allowances. The United States covered the other 50 percent of these benefits and bore the entire cost of workers' base salaries. These salaries, paid in yen, had doubled in cost since 1985. Japan agreed to pay the total cost of fringe benefits by 1990, a move it was estimated would save the United States $165 million per year.[25] Later that month Prime Minister Takeshita, in a major policy speech, urged Japan to open its economic markets and assume a broader role in global affairs.

Overall, the period 1988–89 was a turning point in discussions on Soviet–Japanese relations, as glasnost gained a foothold in foreign affairs. However, there were no policy changes comparable to the rapid developments that made possible the normalization of Sino-Soviet relations, the rejection of communist governments in Eastern Europe, and the end of the Cold War with the United States. The reasons for this lack of progress in relations do not indicate a gap in Soviet foreign policy learning, but more the increasing political constraints associated with democratization and decentralization.

While Japan and the United States quarreled over trade issues and the Toshiba affair, Gorbachev continued to search for some formula that would boost perestroika by strengthening links to the world economy. His trip to Krasnoiarsk in September 1988 stressed the importance of obtaining Asian assistance in developing Siberia and the Soviet Far East. In a clear reversal of past attempts to deny linkage, Gorbachev cited the agreement to withdraw from Afghanistan as proof of Soviet sincerity in attempting to remove the obstacles to solving other regional conflicts and promoting a better political atmosphere in the Asia-Pacific. Through meetings with prominent Japanese politicians, public organizations, and cultural figures, Gorbachev stated, he had come to a better appreciation of the problems and possibilities in Soviet–Japanese relations. Yet it was unfortunate that the Japanese, who "seem to have proved that in today's world the status of a great power can be attained without relying on militarism," would accede so readily to American burden-sharing demands.[26]

Gorbachev's Krasnoiarsk address had been preceded by various political overtures toward Japan, including a meeting with the Socialist Party's chair Takako Doi in May. Soviet–Japanese relations were, Gorbachev emphasized at that meeting, completely abnormal, and the time had come to open a new chapter. He reiterated Soviet willingness to improve the relationship "on the basis of post-war realities" (that is, ignoring Japan's territorial demands), and on the good nature of Soviet intentions toward Japan. Gorbachev expressed his willingness to visit Japan, but only under circumstances in which a summit could yield visible results and the two sides could achieve a clearer understanding of their differences.[27]

The new Soviet willingness to admit a problem existed, in the form of the Northern Territories dispute, gave rise to considerable speculation in Japan and elsewhere about a possible compromise, although Soviet officials clearly refused to yield any ground on substance. Japanese press reports asserted that Soviet government sources had floated the possibility of transferring to Japan tenant rights over the four Kurile islands and Sakhalin, a claim vigorously denied by the deputy director of the Soviet foreign ministry's information section in September 1988.[28]

The dialogue continued with former Prime Minister Nakasone's visit to Moscow for three days of unofficial talks in July 1988. Although cordial, the meeting clearly illustrated the wide gap between Soviet and Japanese positions. Referring to the 1956 Soviet–Japanese joint declaration, Nakasone reminded his guests that any negotiations for a peace treaty were to take into account the disputed islands. Gorbachev stubbornly insisted that "in discussing Soviet–Japanese relations one must start not from the moment when diplomatic relations were restored but from the outcome of the war." The USSR had suffered 20 million dead in the Second World War, Gorbachev stated, and he implied that since any revision of Europe's borders was out of the question, so was any revision of Asian boundaries. In spite of their differences, the two leaders did agree that Japan and the Soviet Union should expand economic, cultural, sports, and tourist exchanges. Nakasone also conveyed South Korean President Roh Tae Woo's request for Soviet cooperation in reducing tensions on the Korean

Map 5.1 Kurile islands

peninsula. Gorbachev promised Nakasone that Foreign Minister Shevardnadze would visit Japan by the end of the year.[29]

Early in the fall of 1988 Keidanren, the Japanese business association, sent a technical mission to inspect Soviet factories, with a top-level business delegation to visit Moscow later in 1989. The Japanese delegation not surprisingly found levels of productivity, infrastructure, and managerial expertise in Soviet factories to be very low compared with Japan. Of the 191 joint ventures Soviet firms had set up with foreign concerns by the beginning of 1989, only 6 were with the Japanese. Moreover, the planned ventures were not the sort that would significantly benefit Soviet technological development – half of the firms were to process marine products. None of the Soviet–Japanese enterprises could be considered on the cutting edge technologically. One Soviet–Japanese venture formed to process timber in Central Siberia had experienced a myriad of difficulties. After a full year of operation, the firm was still waiting for an access road to be constructed. Soviet workers at the plant did not have a strong work ethic by Japanese standards, and the firm was producing poor quality timber.[30]

One potentially lucrative deal that would move beyond simple exploitation of raw materials toward higher value-added processing was concluded toward the end of 1988. The USSR Ministry of Chemical Industry signed an agreement with Mitsubishi Corporation, reportedly worth close to $5 billion, to build a chemical complex in Nizhnevartovsk, in Western Siberia. This project was part of a joint enterprise with several Western firms to produce polymers, with plans to export some 30 percent of the output for hard currency.[31]

Foreign Minister Shevardnadze arrived in Tokyo in late December 1988 for three days of consultations. Once again the Kuriles were the major item of contention. This time, however, the two sides created a permanent commission to negotiate a solution, while discussions for a peace treaty would continue at a reduced level. The two countries' foreign ministers were to meet at least twice in the next six months to review progress toward resolution of the issue.

At the December meeting, Japan's Foreign Minister Sosuke Uno voiced the official Japanese position that an improvement in political relations, hinging on resolution of the territorial question, was necessary before there could be any significant expansion of economic cooperation (the "entrance theory"). Shervardnadze advanced a plan to appeal to Japanese adherents of the "exit theory": critics of the government's policy who believed that economic, cultural, and other exchanges should build a better relationship between the two countries, paving the way for later resolution of the Kuriles issue.[32] The Soviet Foreign Minister proposed reaching agreement on five specific issues prior to a Soviet–Japanese summit: environmental protection; peaceful uses of outer space (to preclude Japanese participation in SDI); mutual protection of investments (to ease fears of expropriation for Japanese companies contemplating investments in the USSR); the establishment of bank offices in both countries; and developing principles to govern general economic cooperation.[33]

Soviet proposals for better economic relations contrasted sharply with an intransigent stand on military and security issues. In January 1989 Gorbachev told a visiting delegation of the Trilateral Commission that of the 500,000 cut in troop strength announced at the United Nations in December, 200,000 were to be withdrawn from the East Asian region of the USSR. Soviet troop strength in Mongolia was to be reduced by 75 percent (from a total of some 75,000), and the Soviet air group stationed there would be removed. However, Gorbachev hinted to Nakasone, a member of the delegation, that no troops would be removed from the Far Eastern coastline because of the continuing threat from US naval deployments in Okinawa, South Korea, and the Philippines, and Japan's military support for US forward deployment.[34] Japanese and American reciprocity, comparable to China's force reductions of one million, was expected in exchange for major adjustments in Soviet Far Eastern forces.

Strains in US–Japanese ties during this period may have encouraged the drive toward normalization in Soviet–Japanese relations. Japanese nationalism, at least in mild form, was beginning to reemerge, and Japan was seeking an expanded role in world affairs. Displeasure with American heavy-handedness was growing in some quarters, as indicated in Akio Morita and Shintaro Ishihara's much-publicized monograph "The Japan That Can Say No." This short book criticized America's arrogance and racial prejudice toward Japan, its lack of business creativity, American shortsightedness in economic planning, Congressional "bluster" and "hysteria" in dealing with Japan, and the unequal nature of the 1960 security treaty. The authors argued that their country had evolved into a technological powerhouse that should stand up to unreasonable American demands. Some of their suggestions – for example, threatening to sell advanced semiconductor chips to the USSR, or to buy Soviet jet engines for the FSX fighter aircraft – must have encouraged those in the Soviet leadership eager to establish warmer relations with Japan.[35]

Political reforms in 1988–90 dramatically altered the conduct of Soviet diplomacy, opening up the foreign policy process to new institutions and individuals. Historian and USSR People's Deputy Iurii Afanas'ev visited Tokyo in 1989 and proposed returning the Kuriles, a position that was immediately and widely assailed in the Soviet press. Moscow mayor Gavril Popov, during an October 1990 visit to Japan, also suggested a phased return of the islands. Popov, like Afanas'ev, was vigorously criticized for being duped by scheming Japanese politicians.[36]

Boris Yeltsin had toured Japan in January 1990, meeting Prime Minister Kaifu, Foreign Minister Nakayama, Abe, Doi, and other prominent Japanese scholars and politicians. During his trip Yeltsin put forward a five-point plan for solving the Kurile impasse, consisting of a two to three year period of conditioning Soviet public opinion, declaration of the islands as a free enterprise zone open to Japanese business, demilitarization of the islands, and long-term negotiations toward a peace treaty. The final phase of Yeltsin's plan would come perhaps thirty years after the first stage, when an entirely new political generation might find a solution amenable to both nations.[37]

Top Soviet leaders, however, proved more intractable than the emerging reformist elites. In an end-of-the-year newspaper interview, Gorbachev insisted that Soviet–Japanese difficulties could not all be reduced to the territorial question. He expressed his hopes for a substantial expansion of economic cooperation, and suggested that Japan's post-war transition from a totalitarian system to a parliamentary democracy was instructive for the Soviet reform program. Japan's evolution into a non-military power, Gorbachev observed, conferred an indisputed advantage over other countries.[38]

The April 1991 summit

In the weeks preceding Gorbachev's arrival in Tokyo, the Japanese and Western media speculated about the possibility of a "grand deal" trading the four islands for large-scale Japanese investment in the ailing Soviet economy. Japan had endorsed the Soviet reform process by supporting Soviet membership in the International Monetary Fund and World Bank, and had provided $100 million in emergency food and medical aid to the USSR. Analysts reasoned that after the revolutionary shift in Soviet policy on Eastern Europe, a settlement on the Kuriles would be a small price to pay in exchange for massive Japanese aid. A careful reading of Soviet domestic politics, however, explains why Gorbachev granted no significant concessions.

First, popular opinion, especially in the Russian republic (which has legal jurisdiction over the islands), was strongly averse to "selling" part of the homeland, no matter how small. The Soviet media produced a spate of articles defending Soviet claims to the islands. *Izvestiia*, for example, in March ran a series of articles entitled "Our Kuriles, Which the Japanese Consider Theirs." An opinion poll conducted in late 1990 by the Kyodo and TASS news services indicated a wide gap between Soviet and Japanese preferences for resolving the dispute. Only

9.8 percent of Soviet respondents were willing to return all four islands immediately; 2.5 percent thought they should be returned in phases with two islands returned first, and another 2.4 percent would return only two. By contrast, 46 percent of Japanese respondents favored the immediate return of all four islands, with 26 percent agreeing to a phased return.[39] Not surprisingly, a March 1990 poll of Soviet citizens living in the Kuriles found 88 percent were opposed to returning the islands to Japan; only 8 percent favored this solution.[40]

Second, by early fall 1990 the Soviet Union was experiencing a resurgence of conservative influence, which would continue through the spring of 1991. Hardliners in the military, Communist Party, and KGB were frustrated with social anarchy, moves toward independence or decentralization among Soviet nationalities, Gorbachev's acquiescence in the liberalization of Eastern Europe, and what they considered to be excessive concessions in the Conventional Forces in Europe negotiations. These conservative forces, whose leading members staged the August 1991 coup against Gorbachev, were strongly opposed to further compromises in foreign policy. Conceding the Kuriles would have called into question the status of other territories (the Baltic states, Moldavia, western parts of Ukraine) incorporated into the USSR following the Second World War.

Third, the legal authority of Moscow to transfer sovereignty of the islands was challenged by Russian republic President Boris Yeltsin. Yeltsin on several occasions asserted that any agreement negotiated by Gorbachev would not be acceptable without the participation of the Russian republic government. The Soviet President accepted Yeltsin's argument – Russian republic Foreign Minister Andrei Kozyrev and four other Russian republic officials accompanied Gorbachev to Tokyo in April.[41]

Given Japanese confidence in the strength of their bargaining position, and the monumental political obstacles constraining Gorbachev's options, the results of the summit were not unexpected.[42] Gorbachev urged Japan's business leaders to participate in Soviet economic projects. In turn, the President was informed that further progress toward building a market economy and ensuring internal stability was needed before major investments would be forthcoming. Negotiations on terms of a peace treaty, which included the territorial question, were protracted and inconclusive. A marathon final session produced a joint statement in which the two sides attached top priority to accelerating work on a peace treaty. General statements were issued on cooperation in fishing, trade, environmental protection, peaceful uses of nuclear energy, scientific and technical development, and cultural exchanges.

The summit was generally depicted in the Western media as a foreign policy failure for Gorbachev. This was in part based on a misunderstanding of the political constraints under which he was working, and on an overestimation of the importance of obtaining Japanese investment for Soviet economic development. An attempt to "trade" the Kuriles for Japanese aid, regardless of scale, would have been perceived across the political spectrum as a betrayal of Soviet interests and an affront to national pride. Moreover, Japanese criticisms were accurate – aid to the USSR would not benefit either side in the absence of greater progress toward a market economy.

It would be a mistake to suggest that the disappointing outcome of the summit and the continuing impasse over the Kurile islands indicated a failure to learn in Soviet policy toward Japan. Clearly, changes in the Soviet foreign policy structure and in analyses of Soviet–Japanese relations under Gorbachev demonstrated a reevaluation and rejection of past policies. Gorbachev and the reformers recognized the necessity of compromise, although the legacy of Soviet–Japanese hostility, domestic pressures within both countries, and Japan's unwillingness to contemplate significant concessions made compromise difficult.

The proposition that political factors rather than an inability to learn accounted for Soviet intransigence is confirmed by the course of Soviet–Japanese relations after the abortive August coup. Tokyo welcomed the defeat of Soviet hardliners and the subsequent turmoil, sensing an opportunity to conclude an agreement on the territorial issue favorable to Japan. In October, just prior to Foreign Minister Taro Nakayama's visit to Moscow, the Japanese government offered the Soviet Union an aid package worth $2.5 billion. Russian nationalists quickly condemned Japan's motives. Valentin Fedorov, newly elected governor of Sakhalin, condemned Russian Deputy Foreign Minister Georgii Kunadze's willingness to relinquish the Kuriles. Fedorov stressed the economic value of the southern Kurile fisheries, and declared his intention to mobilize a Russian protest movement against returning the islands.[43]

Japan's economic lessons

While conditions in Soviet–Japanese relations may not have been favorable for political learning, Japan's experience did provide concrete lessons for Soviet economic reformers. Japan had successfully put into practice many of the elusive goals advanced in the late Brezhnev era. The Japanese demonstrated that a resource-poor country which had suffered total defeat could, through a strategy of conservation, pursuing intensive development, maximizing exports, producing high value-added goods, and utilizing a motivated and disciplined work-force, become an economic powerhouse in a few decades. The Soviet Union, by contrast, had struggled since the 1960s in a futile attempt to keep pace with the technological and information revolutions sweeping the world.

Logically, the Japanese model would seem worthy of Soviet emulation. However, Soviet writings on Japan during the 1980s generally did not present that system as a realistic model for the USSR to follow. Japan was admired for its technological prowess and work ethic, but it was so different culturally from the Soviet experience that neither Soviet intellectuals nor government officials could reasonably expect to adapt Japanese practices to the Soviet system. As one Soviet scholar has observed "The Soviets are not going to take the Japanese as a pattern. Rationally, the Japanese experience is recognized as superior, but emotionally it is rejected as absolutely alien."[44]

There are some lessons of the Japanese experience, however, that Soviet reformers utilized in advancing economic reform. First was the demonstrated importance of integration into the world economy, in the expectation that competition would force firms to pay more attention to quality. Japan's national obsession with quality control conferred a distinct advantage over its European and North American competitors. While the Soviet economy could not hope to match Japanese quality any time in the foreseeable future, Japan's record supported those who argued for greater Soviet integration into the world economy as a necessary component of perestroika. Japan's economic growth was fueled by extraordinarily rapid growth in labor productivity, which was in turn related to imports of modern technology. Low growth rates in Soviet labor productivity, by contrast, have been a key element in economic stagnation. Finally, Japan illustrated the economic potential of a system in which a strong state cooperated with a few large monopolies and numerous small firms, a scenario that became increasingly plausible for the Soviet Union in the late 1980s.[45]

Conclusion

The original goals of Soviet policy toward Japan under Gorbachev included enlisting Japanese technology and capital investment to help modernize the Soviet economy; enhancing Soviet security by undermining US–Japanese military cooperation; and slowing or halting Japan's military build-up, in part a response to American demands for burden sharing. Additional goals during this period included weakening Japanese support for the American military presence in the western Pacific, and convincing the Japanese to refrain from lending their technical expertise to the American strategic defense initiative.

Soviet policy toward Japan abandoned the confrontational approach followed by Brezhnev and Gromyko, and attempted to convey a more reasonable image. However, while the level of dialogue improved, the Soviet Union made few tangible concessions to the Japanese. The territorial issue remained the major obstacle to better relations, and neither side seemed disposed to yield to the other. For reasons of national pride, Gorbachev made it clear that while the USSR would welcome normalized relations, Japan was not critical to Soviet reform efforts. In scheduling the Tokyo summit two years in advance, the two sides recognized that complete normalization of relations would be an extended process.

Political obstacles to returning the disputed territories consistently proved to be more significant than military considerations in frustrating progress toward normalization, although military factors were far from insignificant. As long as the Soviet Union remained a viable union, returning the islands would have set a dangerous precedent for further irredentist demands on the USSR. Gorbachev's proposal for an Asian security conference aspired to formal recognition of the post-war boundaries in the region, a goal realized by the Conference on Security and Cooperation in Europe. With the massive transformations that have taken place in Eastern Europe and in the USSR, the "chink in the armor" argument against returning the islands no longer had much validity. The islands still had some strategic value for Soviet forces in the Far East, but with the end of the Cold War protection of the Sea of Okhotsk missile bastion is far less significant. After the August coup, the military's opposition to relinquishing the Kuriles is much less a factor than it was during Gorbachev's April 1991 visit to Tokyo. The decision would now seem to rest with the newly empowered Russian republic rather than the emasculated center, in which case a version of Yeltsin's plan for resolving the territorial dispute may be adopted.

Japanese technology, investment, and managerial assistance could make significant contributions toward developing the Soviet Far Eastern economy. How *effectively* such assistance could be utilized is another question. Throughout the 1980s territorial concessions appeared to be too high a price to pay. Under the more relaxed conditions of glasnost, Soviet officials feared a backlash of public opinion were they to trade Soviet territory for Japanese investment.[46] Moreover, economic opportunities in the USSR remained unattractive to the Japanese as long as oil prices remained low, energy supplies from the Persian Gulf and Indonesia appeared secure, and, most importantly, the volatile situation within the country was unresolved. Japanese companies have had a quarter-century of experience in Siberian development, and are well aware of the past difficulties of doing business with the Soviets. Until the Russian state stabilizes and begins to make real progress toward a healthy market system, Japanese business will remain cautious.

The lessons of Soviet–Japanese interaction that emerged during the 1980s relate primarily to the utility of military power, and the role of economic strength in international affairs. Soviet policy toward Japan through the Brezhnev period and into the mid-1980s was conditioned by great-power arrogance, based on the USSR's military superiority. However, flexing Soviet military muscle in Asia and the Pacific did not intimidate Japan to be more accommodative to Soviet goals. Rather, threatening Soviet actions prompted Japan to expand its military forces and develop closer defense ties to the United States.

Complementing the lesson about the limited effectiveness of military power, comparisons between the Soviet Union and Japan demonstrated that even a country as large and potentially rich as the USSR would remain a marginal international player in the absence of significant structural reforms to the centrally planned economy, combined with full integration into the competitive world economy. The supposed superpower status of the USSR, based almost entirely on military might, did not translate into mutually beneficial forms of economic cooperation. Japan's interest in securing the return of the Kuriles led it to imply that investment and other forms of economic assistance would be forthcoming were the Soviet government more accommodating. In terms of genuine economic interests, however, Japan's fast-paced technological growth in the 1970s and 1980s had made the Soviet Union virtually irrelevant as a viable economic partner.

Finally, the major remaining impediment to better Soviet–Japanese relations – the Kurile islands issue – was found to be more a political problem than an inability to learn. A gradual improvement in relations has occurred, and will probably continue as the old Soviet Union is transformed into a more decentralized, less threatening, and more market-oriented Russia. However, the sensitive territorial question, a history of conflict between the two countries throughout the twentieth century, and serious structural impediments to close economic co-operation will very likely continue to plague Russian-Japanese relations.

6   The Korean peninsula

In developing relations with South Korea, we will proceed first of all from the interests of the Soviet Union.

Eduard Shevardnadze, *Izvestiia*, 11 September 1990, trans. in *Current Digest of the Soviet Press*, vol. 42, no. 37, 17 October 1990, p. 22.

For over four decades, the Soviet Union consistently if not enthusiastically supported the Democratic People's Republic of Korea (DPRK) politically and economically, even though the two countries could not be considered the closest of allies. The USSR also served as a major provider of weaponry for the DPRK, and refused to criticize the country's periodic violations of international norms. South Korea, in contrast, was officially vilified as a repressive dictatorship and a puppet of the United States. Contacts with the Republic of Korea were proscribed, and any objective information that might portray the South in a favorable light was withheld from public dissemination until well into the Gorbachev period.[1]

Were they not at the vortex of superpower confrontation, the two Koreas would have merited little interest from Soviet policy-makers. However, the interests of four major powers – China, Japan, the United States, and the Soviet Union – converged on the Korean peninsula. The struggle for power and influence in East Asia reached its apogee during the Korean conflict, and the division of Korea carried over into the 1990s as the last major vestige of the Cold War. For the Soviet Union, the potential for conflict on the peninsula throughout the post-war period conferred on Korea a position of strategic significance. Prior to the implementation of new thinking, Soviet relations with the two Koreas were almost solely a function of ensuring military security and strengthening the USSR's political position in the region.[2] Soviet policy on the Korean question, as one prominent South

Korean observer agreed, had been more a means of accomplishing global objectives than an end in itself.[3]

For Joseph Stalin, Korea presented an opportunity for projecting Soviet influence in East Asia. However, as noted in chapter 3, Stalin was not very enthusiastic about Kim Il-sung's invasion of the South, and was careful to avoid being drawn into direct conflict with the United States. The war liberated North Korea from Soviet tutelage, heightened China's prestige as a communist power in its own right, strengthened America's presence in South Korea, accelerated the US military build-up, and intensified the Cold War. These developments of course heightened Soviet determination to preserve some influence on the peninsula.

North Korea's status in Soviet foreign policy was enhanced following the Sino-Soviet break. Rivalry between the two communist giants enabled Kim Il-sung to maintain an independent stance throughout the Khrushchev and Brezhnev eras, although the North Koreans had a far greater affinity toward the Chinese. While formal ties between the USSR and North Korea at times appeared cordial and even close, the relationship was frequently strained by Pyongyang's leanings toward China, North Korea's stubborn insistence on complete independence of action, and Kim's unpredictable behavior. Still, Moscow carefully refrained from any public interaction with Seoul, despite indications in the late 1970s that Moscow would be willing to consider a cross-recognition solution comparable to that worked out for East and West Germany.

By the time Gorbachev came to power, the policy of refusing to grant South Korea diplomatic recognition had become increasingly untenable. South Korea had emerged as a leader among the so-called newly industrializing countries (NICs). Out of the devastation of the Korean war, Seoul's export-driven economic strategy had by the middle of the 1980s generated a gross domestic product some four to five times that of the North. South Korea's economic accomplishments were a source of pride for the Korean people. This pride translated into a stronger national identity, growing pressures for democratic reform, and a determination to achieve greater independence from Washington.[4]

South Korea's economic dynamism was arguably the single most important factor prompting a reevaluation of that country's standing in Soviet foreign policy priorities. The international component of Gorbachev's perestroika program, which emphasized developing new economic relations with the capitalist world, could draw on South

Korean technology and investment for developing Siberia and the Soviet Far East. Besides, South Korea was seeking to diversify its export market, and needed new sources of energy and raw materials. South Korea's weaker currency and marginally less advanced industrial structure made it in some respects a more attractive trading partner than Japan. Soviet domestic reform could be accelerated through integration into the Asian-Pacific economy, but this goal could not be accomplished without restructuring political relations with the more important states of the region.

From Moscow's perspective, a revised Soviet policy toward the Korean peninsula could also enhance Soviet security. Since the Korean war, the peninsula had been considered a potential flashpoint that could inadvertently draw the superpowers into a direct confrontation. A more cooperative Soviet approach toward South Korea would reduce the level of tension in the region, lower the probability of a direct Soviet–American clash in the event of a crisis, and generate pressures for a reduction of America's military presence. A lower level of tension between the two Koreas would also impede North Korea's ability to play off the two communist giants, a concern as Moscow moved toward normalizing relations with Beijing.

As in the case of China and Japan, Soviet policy toward the two Korean states was transformed in conjunction with the process of political and economic reform in the 1980s. This learning process involved a fundamental reassessment of Soviet interests on the peninsula, and the shift from a military-oriented posture toward a position based far more on economic considerations. Although Korea was clearly less important than China or Japan in Gorbachev's Asia policy, normalization of relations with the South proved to be one of the prominent success stories of Soviet new thinking.

Business as usual: 1979–1984

Soviet relations with North Korea were frequently strained during the later years of Brezhnev's rule, although relations began to improve gradually after 1978. The Sino-Japanese treaty signed in that year, and the *rapprochement* between the United States and the PRC, raised questions for North Korea about China's reliability as an ally. For Moscow too, these unsettling developments enhanced North Korea's status as a counterweight to the threat of a Washington–Beijing–Tokyo–Seoul alliance. In June 1979 Foreign Minister Kim Young-nam visited Moscow for consultations with Central Committee Secretary

Konstantin Rusakov, and in May 1980 Kim Il-sung and Leonid Brezhnev met during Josif Tito's funeral in Belgrade. Rusakov and Politburo member Viktor Grishin were sent to Pyongyang in October 1980 for talks with the North Korean leader.

Premier Yi Ching-ok was sent to Moscow as North Korea's representative to the 26th Party Congress in February 1981. In his speech to the Congress, Yi praised the Soviet Union and stressed Pyongyang's determination to be a valuable "eastern outpost" of socialism.[5] This positive assessment was prompted by Pyongyang's need for economic and military assistance. Similar considerations led to a reversal of Kim's initially critical position on the Soviet invasion of Afghanistan. Soviet–North Korean trade expanded from $789 million in 1979 to $925 million in 1980, slipped back to $774 million in 1981, and rebounded to $984 million in 1982.[6]

According to Soviet sources, trade with the USSR constituted nearly one-third of North Korea's total turnover during this period. However, Kim's pride and policy of self-reliance (*juche*) made North Korea reluctant to credit the Soviet Union for its help. This aversion to openly acknowledging the extent of Soviet assistance was a constant irritant to Moscow. Soviet publications and official statements prominently emphasized the extent of Soviet aid furnished to Kim's regime. For example, through cooperation agreements signed in the 1970s the USSR helped build or reconstruct a significant share of North Korea's energy, cast iron and steel, metallurgical, oil refining, ore extraction, and chemical fertilizer industries. The Soviet Union also provided extensive scientific-technical assistance to North Korea in geology, machine building, metallurgy, food processing, and energy. All told, some 3000 advisors were working in various sectors of the North Korean economy in the early 1980s. Finally, economic assistance was reportedly granted to Pyongyang on very favorable credit terms. North Korea accumulated large debts which frequently had to be written off or rolled over by Soviet lenders.[7]

North Korea, consonant with Kim's policy of trying to balance the communist superpowers, did not neglect efforts to preserve ties with the People's Republic of China in the early 1980s. Both Kim Il-sung and his son Kim Jong-il visited Beijing in June 1983, obtaining some 20 to 40 A-5 jet fighter aircraft for North Korea's military.[8] In turn, Kim's contacts with China encouraged Moscow to be more accommodating – an invitation for an official visit was extended to Kim Il-sung shortly after his trip to Beijing. At the same time, Moscow indicated its displeasure with Pyongyang's ties to China by periodically sounding out the South Koreans.[9] Reportedly, unofficial trade between the USSR and South Korea, conducted through Japan and involving an exchange of Korean clothing for Soviet timber, was inaugurated in late 1982.[10]

Despite these tensions, the two countries continued to voice solid diplomatic support for each other. North Korea defended Soviet actions over the downing of the Korean airliner in September 1983. In turn, the Soviet press derided Burmese and Western accusations that North Korea was responsible for the Rangoon bombing that killed seventeen South Korean officials, including four cabinet ministers, in October 1983. The Soviet leadership had in the past displayed caution regarding Kim's unpredictable nature and tendency toward violence and terrorist adventures. However, at this point in time the transitional regime was hunkered down, under pressure from the downing of Korean Airlines flight 007, the war in Afghanistan, the stalemate in Geneva over intermediate-range nuclear forces, and a massive US military build-up. Even a troublesome North Korean ally was better than no ally in the region.

Pyongyang itself was facing a revitalized American–South Korean alliance, and needed Moscow's assistance. The Reagan administration halted the troop withdrawals begun by President Carter, and eventually expanded the total number of US forces to over 43,000. Reagan met with President Chun Doo Hwan three times from 1981 to 1985, and the United States agreed to provide South Korea with a squadron of modern F-16 fighters. Since China could not supply North Korea with aircraft of comparable sophistication, Pyongyang sought to purchase fighter jets from the Soviet Union.

Moscow consistently supported Kim's initiatives on reunification, although they were clearly less than happy about his proposal for talks among the two Koreas and the United States. Although the substance of Kim's plan – the withdrawal of American forces from the South, and the transformation of the peninsula into a nuclear weapons-free zone – unquestionably coincided with Soviet security interests, Moscow clearly resented being excluded from the process. Brezhnev's 1981 proposal for a Helsinki-style Asian security conference and for multilateral confidence-building measures was periodically held up as an alternative to Kim's tripartite proposal. Likewise, Moscow's support for Mongolia's peace program, which called for signing multilateral non-aggression pacts, was a means of insinuating Soviet presence into any negotiations.

Kim Il-sung's visit to Moscow in May 1984, his first in seventeen

years, symbolized a distinct warming in Soviet–North Korean relations.[11] In his official statements, General Secretary Chernenko emphasized the Soviet commitment to strengthening both state and party ties
with North Korea, and noted recent trends toward improving Sino-
Soviet relations as a factor for stability on the Asian mainland. He
noted that ties between North Korea and the Soviet Union were
developing successfully, but emphasized that the possibilities for
cooperation were far from exhausted. Chernenko reiterated the Soviet
position that reunification of the Korean peninsula should be accomplished by peaceful means. He warned against a revival of Japanese
militarism, and American efforts to establish a Washington–Tokyo–
Seoul military bloc.

In response, Kim expressed gratitude for Soviet assistance in establishing and preserving Korean socialism, and assured his hosts that
North Korea sought reunification through peaceful means.[12] From this
meeting North Korea obtained, in addition to Soviet support for Kim's
reunification plans, promises of military and economic assistance. For
the first time, the Soviet Union agreed to deliver modern MiG-23
fighters to Pyongyang to compensate for American deliveries of F-16
fighters to Seoul. In return, the USSR obtained overflight rights for air
traffic to Vietnam. And trade turnover between the two countries in
1984 reached a new high of 712 million rubles ($1.14 billion).[13]

The early Gorbachev period

During Gorbachev's first two years in office, few changes were evident
in Soviet–North Korean relations. Moscow continued the policy of
closer military and economic cooperation with Pyongyang, with the
first MiG-23s delivered during 1985. Gorbachev, however, appeared
determined to extract a quid pro quo from Kim, in the form of lowered
tensions with the US and South Korea, in exchange for Soviet assistance. This was consistent with the Soviet leader's goal of creating a
more favorable international environment for domestic reforms.
Finally, Moscow continued the competition with Beijing for influence
in North Korea.

North Korean Foreign Affairs Minister and Politburo member Kim
Young-nam visited Moscow in April 1985 to discuss security issues,
and signed a frontier treaty. In August Politburo member Geidar Aliev
and first Deputy Minister of Defense Marshal V.I. Petrov headed a
large Soviet delegation to Pyongyang to commemorate the fortieth
anniversary of Korean liberation. Three Soviet naval warships

accompanied the group, calling on the east coast port of Wonsan. This visit came only three months after Chinese Party General Secretary Hu Yaobong had traveled to North Korea.[14]

In December, the Soviet foreign ministry informed Washington that North Korea had formally acceded to the 1968 Nuclear Non-Proliferation Treaty (NPT). In signing the treaty, Pyongyang pledged neither to make nor to receive nuclear explosives, and agreed to inspections of its facilities by the International Atomic Energy Agency. The United States had long urged the Soviet Union to help persuade North Korea to sign the NPT.[15] Apparently, Moscow had insisted on Pyongyang's adherence to the treaty before agreeing to help construct a 30 megawatt nuclear power reactor. North Korea and the Soviet Union concluded a five-year economic and technological agreement, including the deal on the nuclear power station, in late December 1985.

In comparison with Gorbachev's goals of normalizing relations with China and Japan, Korea remained secondary to Soviet interests. There were no references to the peninsula either in Gorbachev's February 1986 address to the 27th Party Congress, or in the April 1986 Soviet government statement on Asian-Pacific relations. At Vladivostok, Gorbachev merely reiterated Soviet support for the DPRK's reunification and security proposals, making no new overtures toward the South Korean regime. Consistent with the longstanding Soviet policy of avoiding alienating Pyongyang, South Korea was excluded from the long list of regional nations with which the Soviet Union planned to expand ties.

There are at least three reasons which account for the absence of significant change in Soviet thinking on the Koreas in the first years of the Gorbachev regime. As noted above, Korea was a relatively low priority, and simply did not merit the critical review accorded Soviet–Chinese and Soviet–Japanese relations. The central issue was to ensure that instability on the peninsula did not interfere with the goals of Soviet–Chinese and Soviet–American *rapprochement*. Second, the conservative advisors who shaped Soviet Korean policy remained in place until relatively late in the reform process. These members of the old guard strenuously resisted abandoning Pyongyang in order to strike a deal with Seoul. Finally, Roh Tae Woo's election to the presidency, his new policy of *nordpolitik*, Soviet–Korean interaction during the Olympic games, and the improved climate in East–West relations all combined to create a more congenial international atmosphere in 1988. These conditions had been absent in the preceding three years.

Through 1986 the Soviet press continued to condemn the United

States and South Korea for Team Spirit joint maneuvers and for attempts to militarize the peninsula.[16] North Korea's proposal to make the Korean peninsula a nuclear-free zone received strong official support from the Soviet government.[17] In October Kim Il-sung met with Gorbachev in Moscow to discuss Party and governmental co-operation, and security questions in East Asia. The 1986 summit resulted in a Soviet agreement to deliver forty-six MiG-23 fighter aircraft to Pyongyang in exchange for overflight rights and commercial access to the port of Najin, and assurances that North Korea would not become a base for attacks against the USSR.[18]

On the surface, Soviet relations with the two Koreas changed little during 1987. Politburo member V.I. Dolgikh headed a delegation of members of the Supreme Soviet to North Korea in May 1987.[19] Throughout 1987 the Soviet press was sharply critical of Seoul, down-playing the South Korean economic miracle and censuring the Chun Doo Hwan regime for its repressive actions against political demon-strators.[20]

However, indications began to surface that suggested officials at the top level were rethinking Soviet policy toward the two Koreas. In March 1988 a Soviet foreign ministry official indicated that there were no formal restrictions preventing Sakhalin's ethnic Koreans from visiting South Korea, as long as they did not fly direct to Seoul.[21] Indirect trade between the Soviet Union and the Republic of Korea continued to expand slowly; according to South Korean sources, the total volume was approximately $185 million in 1987.[22] Meanwhile, dissatisfaction over the state of economic relations with North Korea had begun to surface in mass publications and official statements.[23]

Soviet behavior leading up to the 1988 Olympics also hinted that a policy reevaluation was taking place. The USSR publicly supported Pyongyang's proposals for jointly hosting the 1988 Olympics, but never seriously considered boycotting the games as a statement of support for the North. Soviet Olympic attaché Nikolai Lents, in Seoul making last minute preparations for Soviet participation in the games, indicated that Soviet athletes would participate regardless of the final venue.[24] And apparently Moscow was concerned about potential North Korean terrorism. Japan's news service reported that KGB chief Viktor Chebrikov, who had been dispatched to Pyongyang ostensibly to help celebrate the fortieth anniversary of the DPRK, was actually sent to discourage Kim from attempting to disrupt the games.[25]

By 1988, Moscow was seeking to balance the imperatives of economic reform with the need to maintain its reputation as a reliable political ally. This explains Soviet efforts to develop trade links with South Korea, while expending considerable effort to preserve ties to the North. North Korea had little it could offer Moscow economically, although Pyongyang did provide cheap labor for several Soviet Far Eastern economic projects. When Pyongyang was accused of sabotaging a Korean airliner in November 1987, Moscow ridiculed the charges as unjust. Military deliveries continued, with the Soviet Union reportedly supplying North Korea with some 10 SU-25 attack bombers, 30 MiG-29 advanced fighters, and modern SA-3 and SA-5 surface-to-air missiles. In addition, a squadron of Soviet naval warships made an official visit to the North Korean port of Wonson in May 1988.[26]

Kim Il-sung, suspicious of Soviet reform efforts, continued his efforts to maintain equidistance between China and the Soviet Union. The North Korean dictator arranged his first visit to Beijing in five years, in May 1987. A year later, Kim stopped over in Khabarovsk en route to Mongolia for a three-day briefing on Soviet economic development plans for the Far East.[27] However, as South Korea began to move away from its authoritarian past, the similarities in Roh's and Gorbachev's political reform programs highlighted the contrast between new Soviet goals and North Korea's continued adherence to totali-tarianism.

Olympic and trade diplomacy: toward normalization

Soviet–South Korean relations received a boost in 1988 with the Olympics, Gorbachev's Krasnoiarsk address, and the growing openness of trade links. Reporting on South Korea had begun to change in late 1987 and early 1988. Criticism of the December presidential elections was considerably toned down from the previously harsh commentaries on Korean politics. A January 1988 *Pravda* article, in marked contrast to previous commentaries, praised the Koreans for their efficiency, hard work, successful exporting strategies, and ultra-modern production, observing "It wouldn't hurt to learn from all of those things."[28]

South Korea's government, seizing the opportunity to press its initiatives on an increasingly isolated North Korea, quickly acknowledged these signals. In a major televised speech in July 1988, ROK President Roh Tae Woo announced a major new policy of *nordpolitik*, calling for an end to confrontation between North and South Korea. Roh urged cultural exchanges, direct trade and improved diplomatic contacts. He also asked the international community, specifically Japan and the United States, to establish better ties with the North. South Korea, Roh stated, would pursue improved relations with the Soviet Union, the PRC, and other socialist countries. By offering to normalize relations with the DPRK's supporters, Roh intensified the pressure on Pyongyang to respond constructively to his efforts to reduce tensions on the peninsula.

Mikhail Gorbachev's Krasnoiarsk address, delivered in September 1988, responded positively to Roh's initiative and signaled a shift in the official Soviet position on South Korea. In general, the thrust of the speech emphasized the importance of linking the eastern regions of the Soviet Union into the Asian economies. Gorbachev noted that with the general improvement in relations on the Korean peninsula, the possibility now existed for open economic collaboration between the USSR and South Korea. However, the Soviet leader was still careful not to imply that political normalization might follow economic developments.[29]

This new Soviet flexibility provided South Korean President Roh Tae Woo with additional leverage over the North. In his October 1988 address to the United Nations, Roh responded to Gorbachev's Krasnoiarsk proposals by suggesting convening a consultative peace conference including the Soviet Union, United States, China, Japan, and the two Koreas, to address issues of reunification and Pacific economic cooperation. This proposal was acceptable to all parties except the North Koreans.

The White House lent its support to Roh's initiatives by easing some restrictions on diplomatic contact and trade with North Korea, and agreeing to work toward lower tensions on the peninsula. Although Washington refused to drop North Korea's designation as a terrorist country, US and North Korean officials met in Beijing four times from mid-1988 to mid-1989 in an effort to reduce tensions on the Korean peninsula. Moscow, seeking to effect a reconciliation between North and South, and interested in establishing closer ties with Seoul, encouraged the process by arranging a meeting between opposition leader Kim Young Sam and North Korean politburo member Ho Dam, in mid-1989.[30]

Even prior to Gorbachev's address, Soviet ministries and institutes had begun to develop ties with their South Korean counterparts. The Soviet Merchant Marine and Fishing Industry ministries both established links with South Korean businesses in early 1988. Discussions were held on the repair of Soviet ships at South Korean ports, and on cooperation in harvesting and processing seafood. An agreement was reached allowing free access to ports in each country, and several Soviet ships were overhauled at Hyundai shipyards.[31]

The possibilities for trade were further enhanced when Moscow formally eliminated the closed border status of the territory around Vladivostok, in September. (Foot-dragging by the military would continue to make access to Vladivostok difficult for outsiders until the beginning of 1992, but the symbolism of this move was important). In September 1988 Hangyang University's Institute for Sino-Soviet Studies invited Mikhail Titarenko, director of the Institute for Far Eastern Studies, to visit Seoul for a series of discussions with Korean businessmen and scholars. This encounter resulted in an unprecedented agreement on scientific cooperation between the two institutions.[32]

The Olympics provided a convenient opening for Moscow to pursue normalized relations with Seoul. Soviet athletes were something of a novelty for the South Koreans. Their deportment at the games was far more respectful of Korean sensitivities than that of the Americans, whose athletes and television crews behaved crassly by Korean standards and aggravated an already strong current of anti-American sentiment. The Soviet Olympic committee put together an elaborate cultural program involving ethnic Korean artists to impress the South Koreans. During the Olympics Seoul allowed port visits by Soviet tourist ships in Pusan and Inchon, and permitted Aeroflot to fly into the capital.[33]

Opportunities for trade, commercial, and cultural exchanges were also enhanced through Soviet–South Korean Olympic contacts. A delegation from the USSR Chamber of Commerce and Industry visited Seoul shortly after the Olympics to negotiate preliminary economic links. Official, direct economic ties were finally established in April 1989, when the Chamber of Commerce established a mission in the South Korean capital. The mission, headed by V. Nazarov, was tasked with organizing business, tourist, and cultural exchanges between the two countries. The Chamber of Commerce and Industry, Nazarov stated, would work to shift Soviet trade away from its traditional emphasis on exporting unprocessed raw materials, one of the central goals of the new Soviet economic strategy.[34]

The potential in Soviet–South Korean economic cooperation was viewed optimistically by Soviet scholars. V. Shipaev, a senior staff member of the Academy of Sciences' Oriental Studies Institute, suggested South Korea could resolve one of the key problems the Soviets faced in developing their Far Eastern territory – the shortage of suitable, permanent housing for the expected influx of Soviet and foreign workers. South Korean firms could be tapped to build industrial enterprises, roads, port facilities, hotels, and leisure centers. Although this would require large Soviet contributions, payment could be arranged through joint ventures (the first South Korean–Soviet joint venture, to produce fur garments, was announced in September 1988), in providing Korea with coking coal from south Yakutia, by giving forestry concessions to Korean firms, or by using revenue from hotels and other tourist attractions. Shipaev concluded that prospects for trade with South Korea looked promising.[35]

Economic relations with South Korea in the past had been limited by the absence of diplomatic relations between the two countries, and by Moscow's consistent political and military support for North Korea. The new Soviet East Asian policy, predicated more on economic considerations, substantially altered Soviet approaches toward both Koreas. By 1989, Soviet commentators and officials frequently complained that South Korea was far too cautious in developing economic relations with the USSR. USA and Canada Institute director Georgii Arbatov and Institute of Oriental Studies head Mikhail Kapitsa stressed this point during a visit to Seoul in September 1989. However, Korean business interests were understandably reluctant to invest heavily in the USSR given the formidable bureaucratic obstacles and absence of formal diplomatic relations.[36]

Soviet overtures toward Seoul during this period remained complicated by Moscow's determination to preserve cordial relations with the Democratic People's Republic of Korea. Initially, Gorbachev appeared determined to preserve the Soviet–North Korean relationship within the broader framework of his initiatives toward other countries in the region.[37] Foreign Minister Shevardnadze was sent to Pyongyang in December 1988 to reiterate Moscow's commitment to North Korea. Shevardnadze stated explicitly that the Soviet Union would honor its obligations under the 1961 treaty of friendship, and had no intentions of granting diplomatic recognition to Seoul.[38] These assurances were repeated on several subsequent occasions by Soviet commentators, including such high-level officials as Deputy Foreign Minister Igor Rogachev.

Economic links between the Soviet Union and ROK continued to develop during 1989, although progress on political normalization appeared to have stalled. The honorary chairman of the Hyundai business group, Chung Ju-yung, was invited to Moscow in January to discuss his company's participation in Siberian development projects with Vladislav Malkevich, chairman of the Soviet Chamber of Commerce and Industry. Later that month Hyundai signed a letter of intent with the Chamber of Commerce to establish a Soviet–South Korean cooperation committee. Trade between the two countries soared in the first quarter of 1989. First quarter trade was up nearly 150 percent to $132 million, with imports from the USSR far exceeding exports ($122 million to $10 million).[39] The total volume of trade for 1989 expanded to $600 million, more than double the figure for the preceeding year.[40]

South Korea's growing trade links with the Soviet Union raised the prospect of strategically significant technologies finding their way to Moscow. Washington had outlined a major initiative on revitalizing the Coordinating Committee for Multilateral Export Controls (COCOM) in October 1987, following the Toshiba–Kongsberg illegal sale of milling equipment. A Soviet report claimed that in a 1987 confidential memorandum the United States had persuaded Seoul to abide by COCOM directives, even though South Korea was not technically a member. Beginning in 1990, the article charged, South Korea would assume the formal obligations of COCOM membership. By 1990, however, the Commerce Department was eliminating a range of items from its list of products and technologies exportable to the USSR.[41]

The Korean Trade Promotion Corporation (KOTRA) and the Soviet Chamber of Trade and Commerce organized a "South Korea Week," held in Moscow in early July. Designed to commemorate the opening of KOTRA's Moscow office and to promote Korean products, the trade show included Samsung, Hyundai, and twelve other major firms exhibiting automobiles, textiles, construction equipment, and electronics. In all, Korea sent a delegation of over 200 businessmen, legislators, and officials from various foreign affairs, trade, industry, finance and fisheries ministries, in addition to musicians and taekwondo experts, to participate in the event.

The Korean government proposed setting up four consulates in the USSR – in Moscow, Vladivostok, Leningrad, and Tashkent. The two countries established permanent trade missions in each other's capitals, and Aeroflot scheduled regular flights to Seoul. President of the Reunification Democratic Party Kim Young Sam traveled to Moscow in June 1989 at the invitation of the Institute of World Economic and International Relations, and IMEMO director Vladilen Martinov reciprocated with a visit to Seoul in October. During Kim's visit, the Soviet government announced that it would allow Soviet–

Koreans living on Sakhalin, about 300,000 in all, to return to South Korea should they choose to do so.[42] Shortly after Kim Young Sam's visit, Seoul demonstrated its goodwill by sending an air cargo plane loaded with relief supplies for victims of the Armenian earthquake.

Recognizing the Republic of Korea

Buoyed by the prospects for diversifying its trading partners and optimistic that closer ties with Moscow would lower tensions on the peninsula, South Korea stepped up its efforts to secure formal diplomatic relations with the Soviet Union. During the latter half of 1989, however, Moscow's attention was diverted from Asia by the spectacle of emerging participatory democracy in its own country, and by the rapid collapse of communist governments in Eastern Europe. In addition, the Soviet foreign ministry, well aware of North Korea's hostile reaction to the establishment of Hungarian–ROK relations in February, approached diplomatic recognition of the South with caution.[43]

Developments in Soviet–South Korean political relations accelerated in early 1990. In March, following his inauguration as the new President of the Soviet Union, Gorbachev told Kim Young Sam, who was in Moscow as the head of an official South Korean delegation, that diplomatic relations would very likely be established before the end of the year.[44]

Gorbachev's meeting with Roh Tae Woo in June, at the conclusion of his trip to the United States, generated considerable publicity worldwide. China and the United States openly welcomed the prospect of normalizing relations. Japanese officials, noted one Soviet commentator with evident satisfaction, were sufficiently surprised to undertake a review of their Asian-Pacific policy.[45] Predictably, North Korea harshly condemned the meeting as leading to the recognition of two Koreas and the permanent division of the peninsula, warning that serious consequences could be expected from the encounter. In an attempt to minimize damage to Soviet–North Korean relations, the Soviet government refused to acknowledge that a meeting had been scheduled until after the fact.

Gorbachev described the meeting as a natural consequence of the two nations' developing commercial ties, asserting Soviet intent to improve ties with all countries in the Asian-Pacific region. In addition, Gorbachev was hoping to secure economic assistance – the South Korean news media speculated that Seoul was considering an aid package to the Soviet Union worth some $3–5 billion. President Roh in turn admitted his primary consideration was to exert pressure on Pyongyang in order to ease tensions with South Korea. Afterward, Roh told reporters he expected formal diplomatic relations to be established by the end of the year.[46]

Moscow, still seeking a means to avoid worsening ties to the North, postponed the decision on normalization for several months. In late July TASS released a statement by a foreign ministry spokesman welcoming North Korea's proposals for North–South relations. However, several other questions impinged on Moscow's efforts to prevent a deterioration in ties with Pyongyang. One factor was trade. Starting in 1991, Soviet exports to all former socialist allies were to be paid for in convertible currency at world prices. In 1990 North Korea imported over half of its oil from the Soviet Union on favorable terms. The new pricing structure effectively doubled the cost of oil imported from the Soviet Union, and Soviet officials signaled their intention to seek repayment of Pyongyang's debt to the USSR, some 2.2 billion rubles, through hard currency trade. In the first six months of 1991, North Korean imports from the Soviet Union dropped to $11 million, compared with $887 million for January through July 1990.[47]

Another issue straining relations between Moscow and Pyongyang was the latter's apparent determination to develop a nuclear weapons capability. During a visit to Tokyo in September, Foreign Minister Shevardnadze stated that the Soviet Union was urging North Korea to sign a safeguard agreement with the International Atomic Energy Agency. Under pressure from Moscow, Pyongyang had become a signatory to the nuclear Non-Proliferation Treaty (NPT) in 1985, but had consistently refused to allow International Atomic Energy Agency (IAEA) inspectors to visit North Korean nuclear facilities. Both Tokyo and Washington had expressed concern over the DPRK's nuclear program. Reportedly, the Soviet Union halted nuclear technology transfer and withdrew Soviet technicians working on the North Korean reactor program at Yongbyon following the San Francisco summit, in an attempt to encourage Pyongyang to accede to international controls.[48]

Moscow appeared determined to follow through on establishing diplomatic ties with the South. Foreign Minister Shevardnadze went to Pyongyang in the middle of September to explain the Soviet plans. Kim Il-sung refused to meet him, and Shevardnadze left the North Korean capital claiming that his talks with Foreign Minister Kim Young-nam had been possibly the most difficult in his career. The Soviet Ministry of Foreign Affairs issued a terse statement asserting that Moscow did not need Pyongyang's "permission" to conduct its foreign policy.[49] The official announcement on normalization of relations between Moscow and Seoul was then released on 30 September 1990. Oleg Sokolov, the Soviet ambassador to the Philippines, was appointed ambassador to Seoul, and Kong No Myong, head of the South Korean consular department in Moscow, was named ambassador to the Soviet Union.

Pyongyang's response to Soviet acceptance of two Koreas was predictably harsh. Moscow was accused of caving in to the forces of reaction and militarism on the peninsula, and of abetting US imperialist ambitions. North Korea also railed against Roh Tae Woo's December visit to Moscow. The South Korean leader, accompanied by a prominent delegation of industrialists representing Samsung, Lucky Goldstar, Daewoo, the Hanjin Group, and Jindo Fur Company, signed agreements on trade, scientific and technical cooperation, and taxation, in addition to a joint declaration on the general principles governing bilateral relations. During Roh's visit, Gorbachev emphasized the Soviet desire for the Korean peninsula to become a nuclear-free zone, and for the two Koreas to move toward reunification.[50]

Pyongyang's response to Soviet–South Korean *rapprochement* expressed bitter disappointment, but in a measured style that left the door open to further Soviet–North Korean cooperation. Under pressure from the North Korean government, the Novosti press agency and *Komsomolskaia pravda* closed their Pyongyang bureaus. In March 1991 the *Izvestiia* correspondent was expelled from Pyongyang, and the newspaper was forced to close its office for publishing articles critical of North Korea.[51] But North Korea's severe economic difficulties forced Pyongyang to moderate its criticism and continue to deal with Moscow and with the increasingly independent republics. In April 1991 the South Korean news agency reported that the Soviet Union had granted Pyongyang a moratorium on paying for 500,000 tons of oil to be delivered in 1991, in light of North Korea's poor financial position.[52] The DPRK signed economic agreements with the Turkmen, Tadzhik, Kazakh, and Kirgiz republics in spring 1991. Finally, an agreement was signed between Moscow and Pyongyang in April providing for the expansion of light industrial trade, limited Soviet credits, and the repayment of North Korea's debt in convertible currency.[53]

In May, following Gorbachev's disappointing visit to Tokyo, the Soviet leader met President Roh Tae Woo on Cheju Island off South Korea's southern coastline. In contrast to the tense and fruitless discussions in Tokyo, the Gorbachev–Roh meeting was amicable. Gorbachev stressed his intention to visit Pyongyang in an attempt to broker an agreement between the two Koreas. The two leaders agreed to begin work on a Treaty of Good-Neighborliness and Cooperation, and estimated that trade would increase to about $10 billion per year by the mid-1990s.[54]

The meeting in Cheju, and Gorbachev's implicit snub to Kim, emphasized the growing isolationism of North Korea. In an abrupt reversal of a longstanding policy, the North Korean declared his intention to seek an independent seat in the United Nations, and the two Koreas were admitted in September. Roh had indicated in December that South Korea would prefer that the Soviet Union maintain contacts with the North, and continue to exert its influence in favor of peaceful reunification. Although trade and economic cooperation between Moscow and Pyongyang had declined dramatically, the two countries maintained political, cultural, and some military ties.[55]

A major Soviet concern in the final months of 1991 was North Korea's failure to allow IAEA inspections of the nuclear reactor at Yongbyon. Official and press commentary welcomed President Bush's September announcement that all US nuclear weapons would be withdrawn from the peninsula.[56] In removing these short-range systems before the end of the year, the United States removed Kim's last excuse for refusing IAEA inspection, and raised the real possibility of denuclearizing the peninsula. Ironically, Soviet and American interests on the Korean peninsula had converged just as the USSR disintegrated.

Soviet learning and the Korean peninsula

It would be misleading to suggest that Soviet experience with the two Koreas was itself a critical factor contributing to Soviet learning in foreign policy. Soviet policy prior to Gorbachev, like policy toward China and Japan, was significantly conditioned by the ideological prism through which the Kremlin leadership viewed world affairs. North Korea, as a member of the socialist world, was viewed as a natural ally of the Soviet Union. Conversely, the Soviet leadership appeared to believe much of its own propaganda in claiming South Korea was merely a puppet of Washington.

But ideology only partially explains Soviet inflexibility in refusing to deal with the South. More importantly, the Korean peninsula was a

potential arena for conflict with the USSR's two major competitors in
the Asian-Pacific region. One Soviet scholar has described Soviet
policy toward Korea after the war as characterized by a kind of
paralysis, in which Moscow refused to acknowledge South Korea's
existence, and yet was unable to maintain truly cordial relations with
the North. This state of affairs existed because Soviet policy was in
essence a prisoner of relations with the United States and the People's
Republic of China.[57] Given the hostile state of Sino-Soviet and Sino-
American relations, strategic considerations naturally dominated
Soviet thinking into the middle of the 1980s. Once the strategic
environment had been transformed, the serious obstacles to recognition of South Korea were removed.

This does not diminish the impact of a new Soviet perspective
governed more by economics than by military considerations. The
fundamental rationale underlying new thinking was to improve the
international atmosphere in order to devote more resources to internal
reform. This meant devoting considerable effort to normalizing relations with the United States and with China. As the Cold War diminished, and Sino-Soviet ties improved, Moscow's perception of the
Korean peninsula changed fundamentally. North Korea's value as an
ally, which had always been problematic given Kim's insistence on
self-reliance and complete independence, declined for both the Soviet
Union and the PRC. The North Korean link had in the past contributed little to the Soviet Union economically – the prime reason
behind Soviet efforts to increase trade was political, and intended to
bind Pyongyang more closely to Moscow. South Korea, by contrast,
could offer substantial investment, technological, and managerial
assistance for Soviet economic development plans. Once the primary
objective of *rapprochement* with China and the United States had been
achieved, secondary benefits – in this case, greater flexibility allowing
for a reoriented policy toward the Korean peninsula – could be more
easily realized.

Conclusion

Through much of the decade under review, Soviet policy toward the
Korean peninsula followed the Khrushchev and Brezhnev pattern.
North Korea could not be considered a pliant ally of the Soviet Union,
but until the strategic environment in the region changed, Moscow
remained committed to its conservative policy of strong vocal support
and limited military and economic assistance for Pyongyang, together

with non-recognition of the South. Soviet journals and the official media continued to publish hardline, dogmatic articles on Korea long after glasnost had liberated discussion of other sensitive topics. As we have seen, articles favorable to South Korea did not appear in the Soviet press until late in 1987. Critical commentary on North Korea did not find its way into print until spring 1990.

Soviet policy on Korea moved slowly for several reasons. First, the conservative view predominated throughout most of the 1980s because of simple bureaucratic inertia and the failure of the top leadership to signal intentions toward a reevaluation of Soviet Korean policy. With China, and to a lesser extent Japan, Gorbachev was committed to improving relations; consequently, these policy areas generated the best critical thinking in Soviet Asian strategy among analysts and policy-makers. Learning occurs most readily on issues designated as significant problem areas and clearly accorded a high salience by political leaders. Conversely, less critical objectives naturally receive less attention, and the tendency is to follow established patterns.

This generalization is upheld by contrasting Soviet policy toward Korea, which remained frozen for over forty years, with that toward the People's Republic of China, which displayed considerably greater flexibility. China, as a hostile challenger to Soviet communist primacy, stimulated considerable thought and discussion within the Soviet intellectual establishment, even if the more innovative ideas derived from this process could not always be publicly disseminated. Once the leadership made a commitment to greater flexibility in their China policy, the "raw materials" (that is, the intellectual tools) for learning were readily available. The same could not be said of Soviet Korean studies. Korea was important as a geographic nexus of great power conflict, but in its own right did not warrant the intellectual attention granted to either China or Japan.

Secondly, the Soviet leadership had not reevaluated policy toward Korea until very late in the 1980s in part because opportunities for applying new thinking appeared only after relations with China and the United States had improved. By 1989, following the Sino-Soviet summit, the likelihood of the Soviet Union being drawn into a conflict with the major powers on the Korean peninsula was remote. The overall improvement in the international climate made possible greater flexibility in Soviet policy toward the two Koreas, as Soviet fear of "losing" North Korea diminished.

Thirdly, economics played an increasing role in prodding Moscow toward normalization with Seoul. In some respects, Soviet–South Korean economic cooperation held greater promise than did cooperation with the Japanese. South Korea's relatively less advanced technological infrastructure made for a better fit with the backward Soviet economy. South Korean businessmen had virtually no experience in dealing with the Soviets, and were initially less disillusioned about the prospects for economic cooperation than were their Japanese counterparts, who had dealt with Soviet firms for a quarter of a century. Soviet–Japanese relations were negatively affected by an antagonistic history not shared by the Soviet Union and the Republic of Korea. Finally, the German example in Europe suggested that the Soviet Union could preserve good relations with North Korea while substantially expanding economic relations with the South.

7   Learning and Soviet security in the Asian-Pacific region

> Did the world admire Soviet forces when they "brought order" to Hungary? Or when they crushed the "Prague Spring"? Was the world delighted when we entered Afghanistan to fulfill our "international duty"? It is time to recognize that neither socialism nor friendship, neither neighborliness nor respect can be founded on bayonets, tanks, and blood.
>
> Eduard Shevardnadze, *The Future Belongs to Freedom* (New York: Free Press, 1991), p. 125.

The rapid collapse of Eastern Europe's communist systems, the dissolution of the Warsaw Treaty Organization, and the decentralization of the Soviet Union fundamentally transformed the post-war European security order in the late 1980s and early 1990s. The Soviet security regime in East Asia and the Pacific was also changing during this period, albeit more gradually than that in Europe. Gorbachev proclaimed a new, less aggressive role for the Soviet Union in Asia and initiated limited reductions in personnel and equipment assigned to the region. Yet the modernization of Soviet land, air, and naval forces continued unabated throughout the 1980s. These contradictory signals derived from the Soviet leadership's inability to design a comprehensive new security plan for the Far East, poorly conceived attempts to transplant European security mechanisms to the Asian context, and the low priority accorded Asia relative to Europe.

During Gorbachev's six years in office, Soviet policy toward the Asian-Pacific region repaired much of the egregious damage to Soviet interests incurred during the Brezhnev period. The withdrawal from Afghanistan, successful *rapprochement* with China, normalization of relations with South Korea, some progress toward thawing relations with Japan, and highly publicized reductions in strategic and conventional forces altered the Soviet Union's threaten-

128

ing image in Asia. As Moscow's control over the union slipped and domestic problems worsened, security issues in East Asia became increasingly peripheral.

This chapter examines changes in Soviet security policies in Northeast Asia, and the Asian-Pacific region more broadly, in the 1980s. During Brezhnev's tenure, a massive build-up of conventional and nuclear weaponry in the Soviet Far East and the Western Pacific was oriented toward restraining the People's Republic of China, intimidating Japan into abrogating its military alliance with the United States, and challenging US military presence in the region. As the United States reduced its forces in the Western Pacific after Vietnam, the Soviet Union expanded its naval presence in an attempt to fill the vacuum. However, Soviet military expansion provoked the US, China, Japan and other Asian-Pacific nations to undertake measures to contain this perceived threat. The USSR displayed sufficient military force and aggressiveness to alarm its neighbors in the Far East, but possessed neither the political nor the economic power to establish significant influence in the region.

The learning process in Soviet security policy toward the Asian-Pacific region was one aspect of the larger process of reassessing the utility of force in foreign policy, and recognizing the growing import-ance of economic strength in foreign affairs. Soviet reformers recog-nized their reliance on raw military power in East Asia had been counterproductive, leading to collusion among putative enemies and a reciprocal military build-up that had undermined Soviet security. The new approach to regional security sought to reduce tensions with China through political reconciliation and mutual military reductions, to challenge the United States to accept asymmetrical cutbacks in the Pacific similar to those the Soviet Union acceded to in Europe, con-strain US freedom of maneuver in the region through active use of more sophisticated diplomacy, and to integrate the Soviet Far East into the Asian economic miracle.[1]

By late 1991 the threatening image of the Soviet Union in East Asia had disappeared, albeit more from the collapse of Soviet power than from consciously administered policies. Although it was possible to speak of Soviet "success" in lowering regional tensions, and in estab-lishing friendlier relations with Asian-Pacific nations, the conjunctive goal of integrating the Soviet economy with the Pacific economic system remained elusive. Little had come of Gorbachev's grand plans to replace Soviet military muscle with economic presence and influ-ence in this critical region of the world.

The Soviet military build-up in Asia

Soviet military forces in the Far East and the Pacific region underwent dramatic quantitative expansion and modernization throughout the Brezhnev period. The Soviet build-up started in 1965, and can be divided into roughly four phases: gradual expansion from 1965 to 1969; rapid growth of Soviet ground forces between 1969 and 1972; a period of consolidation from 1972 until 1977; followed by a qualitative and quantitative improvement of air, ground, and naval forces from 1978 to about 1985.[2] Under Gorbachev, modernization of Soviet military forces in the Far East continued, but at a reduced pace. Starting in 1988, the Soviet Union began cutbacks that, while not inconsequential, were far less impressive than the reductions implemented in Europe.

Soviet military forces in the Far East were organized into two primary groups, according to task. The first and marginally larger grouping was to counter US forces positioned in the Western Pacific, in Alaska, and on the Western coast of the United States, along with Japanese forces, and consisted of the Pacific Fleet together with ground forces deployed in the Soviet Far East. The second group, consisting largely of heavy tank divisions, was deployed against China in the Trans-Baikal military district, in Mongolia, and along the Sino-Soviet border areas of the Far East.[3]

Soviet ground forces deployed along the Sino-Soviet border and in the Far East constituted some seventeen to twenty divisions, or approximately 180,000 to 200,000 troops, in 1965. These numbers increased steadily over the next fifteen years, largely to address the perceived threat from China. Soviet troop strength peaked at some fifty-five divisions by the early 1980s, with approximately 110,000 to 120,000 occupying troops stationed in Afghanistan. Following reductions in the level of readiness along the Soviet–Chinese border, the number of Soviet ground forces remained fairly stable until cutbacks were initiated in the late 1980s. However, these forces experienced qualitative improvements with the addition of upgraded T-72 tanks, armored infantry fighting vehicles, surface-to-surface missiles, rocket launchers, and other categories of equipment.

From the late 1970s through the 1980s, the Soviets significantly upgraded their air forces in the Far East. In 1989, 215 strategic bombers were based in the Far East – 60 Tu-26 Backfire supersonic bombers with a range of approximately 4000 kilometers, 45 Tu-95 Bear G, 60 Tu-22 Blinder, and 50 Tu-16 Badger bombers. In the event of a conflict, these aircraft could deliver conventional or nuclear strikes against Chinese,

American, Japanese, and Korean forces in the region. Of approximately 1700 total Soviet combat aircraft (strategic, tactical, and naval) based in the Far Eastern region in the late 1980s, over half were modern fighter aircraft, many of which had been added during the 1980s. Air capability was enhanced through the deployment of MiG-23 and MiG-27 Flogger, and SU-27 Flanker fighters. Prior to the 1980s, advanced military aircraft were introduced to the Far East well after deployment on the European front. In the last decade, however, this deployment lag disappeared.

The Soviet Union maintained substantial nuclear capabilities deployed in or directed toward the Far Eastern theater of military operations (TVD). In the late 1980s, strategic and theater nuclear ballistic missiles in the Far East consisted of the following: a total of 408 ICBMs, including 250 SS-11s (which could be retargeted to a theater role); 38 SS-17s; and 120 SS-18s. In 1978, one year after deployment began in Europe, intermediate range SS-20s were introduced in Soviet Asia and the Far East. Eventually, 171 of these MIRVed missiles were based in central Siberia and the area around Lake Baikal, presumably targeted at China and US installations in Japan, South Korea, and the Western Pacific. Under the 1987 Intermediate-range Nuclear Forces (INF) Treaty, all these intermediate and shorter-range missiles were. destroyed by the end of May 1991.

Expansion of the Soviet Pacific Fleet, headquartered at Vladivostok, roughly paralleled that of Soviet ground forces in the Far East. Under the direction of Admiral Sergei Gorshkov, chief of the Soviet Navy from 1956 to 1985, the Pacific Fleet grew steadily during the 1960s, leveled off during 1972–78, and then underwent rapid expansion beginning in 1978. In addition to significant qualitative improvements, no less than five cruisers and the carrier *Minsk* were added to the Pacific Fleet from 1978 to 1981. Soviet naval presence, as measured by total ship-days per year, increased from 2500 ship-days in 1965 to 15,000 in 1983.[4] From 1986 to 1989, this naval activity was scaled back by some 30–35 percent as older ships in the fleet were retired.

In 1978 the Soviets enhanced their naval presence in the Pacific by moving into and expanding the former American facilities at Cam Ranh Bay, in Vietnam. For a decade this base supported some twenty-five to thirty-five vessels, including two to four submarines, sixteen Tu-16 Badger bombers, a squadron of fourteen MiG-23 fighter aircraft, and twenty-two other anti-submarine warfare and reconnaisance aircraft. In the early 1980s, the Soviets built five additional piers beyond the two constructed by the United States. Facilities at Kompongsong, in Cambodia, were also upgraded in conjunction with the Cam Ranh Bay expansion.[5]

While important, Cam Ranh Bay had limited utility given the generally weak Soviet position in the Pacific, and would have been vulnerable in the event of a major conflict. The recognition that Soviet forces in Cam Ranh Bay threatened US and Asian interests in the South Pacific, without providing the USSR with an effective power projection capability, was presumably a factor in the Soviet decision to withdraw all the MiGs and half the bombers in late 1989.[6] In April 1990, Vietnamese officials informed a US Congressional delegation that all Soviet troops, including the forces at Cam Ranh Bay, would leave their country by 1992.[7]

The year 1978 also witnessed the introduction of Soviet forces in the disputed Kurile islands, or Northern Territories. Approximately one division, or 10,000 to 13,000 troops were stationed on Etorofu, supplied with tanks, artillery, armored personnel carriers (APCs), anti-aircraft missiles, 130mm cannons, and Mi–24 Hind helicopters. In addition, some forty MiG-23 Flogger fighters were stationed on Etorofu. Politically, these deployments demonstrated Soviet commitment to maintaining control over the islands. Militarily, these forces were supposed to ensure free passage for Soviet naval forces through the Soya Straits between Hokkaido and Sakhalin.[8]

Organizational changes in the command structure of the region also revealed growing Soviet attention to enhancing their military capabilities in the late 1970s and early 1980s. A unified command reappeared as the Far Eastern theater of military operations (TVD) in 1978. Soviet TVDs were designed to centralize control over wartime theater operations by the General Staff of the Supreme High Command; they served as the level of command between the General Staff and the fronts. Soviet officials first leaked news of the Far Eastern TVD's existence in late December 1978, about two weeks after the United States and People's Republic of China announced their intentions to establish full diplomatic relations.[9]

The Far Eastern TVD incorporated the following military districts: the Siberian, with headquarters at Novosibirsk; the Transbaikal (HQ Chita); the Far Eastern (HQ Khabarovsk) the Central Asian (HQ Tashkent); and the Soviet Pacific Fleet headquartered at Vladivostok. In June 1989 it was announced that the Central Asian military district would be dissolved, presumably in conjunction with the planned 60,000 troop reduction along the southern border. Part of the territory of this military district, and those troops not reduced or disbanded, were to be transferred to the Turkestan military district under the Southern TVD.[10]

This brief survey of Soviet military developments during the Brezhnev period suggests the scope and pace of the build-up was influenced by the growing threat from an estranged and radical China, US deployments in the Western Pacific and Southeast Asia, and varying political alignments within the region. Underlying the military rationale was a stubborn political motivation, to match America's military presence and thereby demonstrate that Moscow was entitled to an equal role as regional superpower.[11] To the dismay of the reform-minded leaders who succeeded Brezhnev, Soviet military expansion in the Asia-Pacific had prompted an aggressive military response by the United States, interfered with Soviet efforts to normalize relations with the People's Republic of China, precluded significant progress in stalemated Soviet–Japanese relations, and in general relegated the Soviet Union to marginal political and economic status in the region.

Soviet expansionism and the US maritime strategy

For the Soviet Union, the 1970s proved to be a decade of optimism, opportunities, and some pitfalls in East Asia and the Pacific. Detente temporarily reduced tensions between the US and USSR, leaving the Soviets in a more favorable position to deal with a hostile China. One major Soviet objective in pursuing East–West detente was to isolate the PRC, thereby raising the costs of any potential Chinese aggression in the Far East. The American threat diminished further during the 1970s as, weary from the Vietnam débâcle, the country drifted toward a more isolationist position. America's reluctance to become involved in regional conflicts contributed to a lower military profile in the Pacific. In 1969, at the height of the Vietnam war, the US Navy deployed more than 200 ships in the Pacific and logged 62,400 out-of-area ship days. By the late 1970s the United States fielded only 55 ships for a total of 18,000 out-of-area ship days in the Pacific.[12]

As the American military presence in East Asia diminished following the withdrawal from Vietnam, US military doctrine adjusted to compensate for a reduced presence. Soviet aggression in Europe was to be deterred by a "swing strategy," predicated on shifting forces from the Pacific to Atlantic theaters in the event of a conflict. This strategy compensated for reduced US military expenditures in the Ford and Carter years, but it also lowered the costs of Soviet forces having to resist balanced attacks on two fronts. Soviet military planners, who held conventional war in the European theater to be the primary strategic threat, must have welcomed the prospect of not having to fight a full contingent of American air and naval forces in the Pacific should a conflict break out in Europe. America's retreat in the Pacific vindicated Soviet theorists' contention that the "correlation of forces" was shifting in favor of socialism, and encouraged the Kremlin to pursue a more provocative strategy in the region.

By the 1980s, this relatively favorable situation had changed dramatically. Soviet–American detente had foundered on Soviet Third-World adventurism, human rights abuses, and the Brezhnev leadership's generally inept foreign policies. The sizeable US military build-up, initiated in 1978 under the Carter administration but pursued with considerably greater vigor by the Reagan White House, together with the Reagan doctrine of supporting opposition forces in Soviet client states, reversed the environment for Soviet expansionism that existed in the 1970s. In place of the relatively passive swing strategy, US naval doctrine moved toward a policy of more aggressive forward deployment known as the maritime strategy. America's forces in the Pacific comprised an essential element of this new, more confrontational approach.

The maritime strategy, supported primarily by Navy Secretary John Lehman and Chief of Naval Operations Admiral James T. Watkins, was not recognized as official strategy and proved controversial even within the US Navy.[13] However loosely defined, this naval doctrine played a significant role in the Reagan administration's determination to challenge an expansionist Soviet Union around the globe.

In brief, the maritime strategy incorporated the following principles.[14] First was a recognition that America's strong point was naval power. This was especially true in the Pacific. In dealing with the Soviet Union, the reasoning went, the United States should utilize its naval capabilities to the fullest extent. This would include maintaining an impressive naval force at a high state of readiness in peacetime. In wartime, the United States would immediately take the offensive at sea, not merely accepting a sea-denial role. The maritime strategy assigned critical importance to protecting the vulnerable sea lanes of communication (SLOCs) in the southern Pacific, a task that became more difficult as US and allied naval forces were withdrawn from the region.[15]

Protecting the SLOCs in the Western Pacific was a major priority, both to ensure the continued supply of raw materials to US allies, and to prevent Soviet attempts to interdict strategic trade between the

United States and its major Asian partners. Approximately three-fourths of Japanese oil imports transit the Malacca Straits, and the waters around the Indonesian archipelago are similarly critical for ASEAN trade. Moreover, in the event of an extended conflict in Europe, preserving resupply lines between the US and its Asian-Pacific allies would be a top priority. Since the USSR had a significant disadvantage at sea, the maritime strategy called for the US to exploit that weakness in the event of a conflict to ensure that the Soviets remained landlocked and vulnerable to US control of the SLOCs.

Second, in the event of war in Europe, United States actions in the Pacific would force the Soviet Union to divert considerable military effort toward defending their distant frontiers in the Far East. Since the maritime strategy was predicated on forward deployment, the extensive network of allied bases and support facilities in the Pacific were critical to US plans. Soviet military planners, by contrast, had only the modest Cam Ranh Bay facilities outside their territory. The Soviet Far East was particularly vulnerable to interdictment of supply lines, even when the recently finished Baikal–Amur Mainline (BAM) railway was factored in. Rail transport from the industrial western regions of the Soviet Union takes two weeks or longer to reach Vladivostok.

The maritime strategy recognized that the primary focus of a possible war would be in Europe, but raised the stakes for Soviet decision-makers by forcing them to consider the likelihood that a conflict would be extended into the Pacific, where they were clearly disadvantaged. Geopolitical realities restricted Soviet military options in the Pacific. In the event of war, Soviet naval forces at Vladivostok could be trapped in the seas of Japan and Okhotsk by US, Japanese, and South Korean forces at the three chokepoints. Control of the straits would block the reentry of Soviet ships into their ports for repair and resupply, and would allow the US and its allies to take a heavy toll on ships and submarines attempting to transit the straits.[16] If Soviet security interests in the region depended heavily on maintaining open SLOCs to guarantee supply deliveries to the Far East, or to preserve access to an extensive network of military bases in the Pacific, the situation would be even more disadvantageous. Troops and *matériel* could be reinforced from the Far Eastern reserves, or resupplied overland through the BAM, but supplying the Far Eastern forces would become more problematic as conflict dragged on.

By prolonging a conventional war, the maritime strategy was designed to make it more difficult for Soviet forces to consolidate their control over Europe in the event of a conflict, despite their conven-

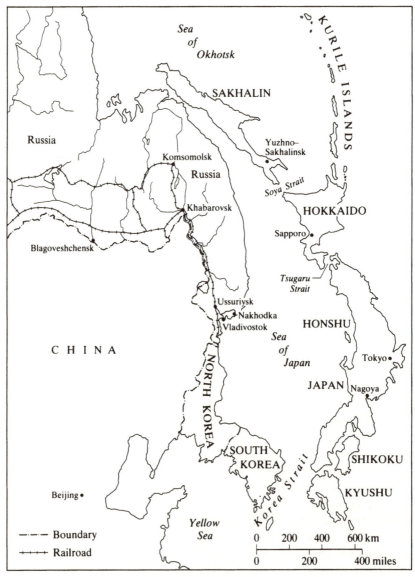

Map 7.1   Russian Far Eastern region

tional superiority in the European theater. The intent was to seriously complicate Soviet war planning. Finally, the emphasis on American naval dominance in the Pacific recognized that East Asia's growing economic might, including Japan's high-technology capabilities, enhanced the region's strategic significance. Defending Asia became more critical in Allied calculations as Europe's (and America's) relative world importance declined.

The United States and its Asian-Pacific allies

Soviet military planners have faced a security environment in the Far East and Western Pacific radically different from that in Europe. There is no collective security arrangement in the Asian-Pacific region resembling NATO. Consequently, the United States has relied on a web of bilateral security treaties with Japan, South Korea, Taiwan (until 1978), the Philippines, Thailand, Australia, and New Zealand (security commitments to New Zealand through the ANZUS organization were suspended in 1986). Following the normalization of Sino-American relations in 1979, China has from time to time cooperated with the United States militarily, complicating Soviet security planning in the region. Although structurally dissimilar, the European and Asian security regimes have been molded by a common perceived threat – Soviet military power.

Washington's official policy has consistently asserted a major role for the United States in Asia and the Pacific. This is predicated on the recognition that the two largest military conflicts in which the United States participated in the post-war period have been in Asia. Currently, close to 40 percent of US trade is with the dynamic economies of the region, and East Asian countries account for three-fourths of the US trade deficit. These factors led the United States to assume a role as primary security guarantor for its regional allies.

The number of US personnel assigned to the Pacific region has fluctuated considerably since 1945. From the post-war highs of 650,000 at the end of the Korean war, and 855,000 at the height of the Vietnam conflict, US forces declined to 140,000 by early 1979.[17] As of March 1991, a total of about 383,000 personnel were assigned to the Pacific command; of these, 60,000 were stationed in Japan, 40,000 in Korea, 7200 in Guam, and about 6000 in the Philippines. Approximately 115,000 US personnel were deployed aboard ship in the Western Pacific and the Indian Ocean. Following the eruption of Mount Pinatubo, Clark Air Force Base was returned to the Philippine government in late November 1991 and the associated personnel transferred to Guam.[18]

At sea, the USSR could not effectively challenge the technologically more sophisticated American forces, reinforced by the network of allied bases and defense commitments in the Pacific. The United States currently maintains one carrier battle group, the Midway, homeported at Yokosuka, Japan. Four additional carriers are homeported in California. Total US forces in 1991 comprised ninety-three additional major surface combatants, forty-three attack submarines, and eight ballistic missile submarines in the Pacific. Long-range (2500 kilometer) conventional and nuclear Tomahawk land-attack missiles (TLAM-C and TLAM-N) capable of striking targets along the eastern USSR have been deployed on ships and aircraft in the Pacific. With President Bush's October 1991 announced reductions in tactical nuclear weapons, the TLAM-Ns will be eliminated along with the nuclear-armed Lance missiles in South Korea.

American military strength in the Pacific has been augmented by Japan's Defense Forces, and by the Australian and South Korean militaries.[19] Japan's 1981 defense commitment, to protect the sea lanes and air space to a distance of 1000 nautical miles, marked a new stage in US–Japanese military cooperation. Prime Minister Nakasone's 1983 statement that Japan was in effect an "unsinkable aircraft carrier," and Japan's 1986 decision to participate in Strategic Defense Initiative research and development, represented a commitment to play a more active role in regional security. Under burden-sharing pressures from the United States, Japan accelerated its defense build-up in the late 1980s. In 1991, the Japanese budgeted approximately $32.9 billion for defense, roughly equivalent to the military budgets of the United Kingdom or the Federal Republic of Germany.[20]

Japan currently has only 246,400 armed forces personnel, but fields some very modern equipment. Upon completion of the National Defense Program Outline in 1991, Japan substantially upgraded its Ground, Maritime, and Air Self-Defense Forces. Overall, the US Department of Defense has been satisfied with Japan's expanding role in preserving regional security.[21] Secretary of State James Baker had described the US–Japan security alliance as "the foundation of our relationship," even in the post-Cold War era, and had called for this union to be strengthened.[22]

America's other major ally in Northeast Asia, the Republic of Korea, has also contributed substantially to US security interests in the region. South Korea maintains armed forces of some 750,000 personnel, facing over 1 million troops, a developing nuclear capability, and a highly unpredictable regime in the DPRK. However, South Korea's economic dynamism has yielded a gross national product nearly ten times that of North Korea. Consequently, South Korea's defense spending of 4.7 to

5.5 percent of GNP is in absolute terms larger than North Korea's 20–25 percent of GNP. South Korea modernized its forces in the 1980s with the addition of American F-16 fighters (facing Soviet-supplied MiG-23s and MiG-29s), and the planned development of the controversial FSX. South Korea's defense spending for 1991 totaled about $11 billion.[23]

Soviet security concerns in East Asia and the Pacific also had to take into account China, both as a land power in its own right, and as a potential military partner of the United States. Although Sino-Soviet relations improved markedly in the 1980s, especially under Mikhail Gorbachev's more accommodative diplomacy, China still represented an important factor in Soviet strategic calculations. First, China had developed a small nuclear deterrent force consisting of 8 ICBMs, 60 IRBMs, and one SSBN. At present the PRC fields approximately 3 million military personnel, equipped with 7500–8000 main battle tanks, 5000 combat aircraft, 92 tactical submarines, and an additional 56 principle surface combatants. Roughly half of China's forces have been concentrated to the north along the Soviet border.

In 1983–86 the United States and China initiated a series of high-level military exchanges, and the US agreed to supply China with advanced dual-use technology. Voicing official Reagan administration policy during his 1983 visit to Beijing, Secretary of Defense Caspar Weinberger claimed that efforts to build an enduring relationship with the PRC was one of "five pillars" of US defense policy in East Asia and the Pacific.[24] For its part, Beijing was eager to enlist US assistance in its modernization program and to counterbalance Soviet power in the region, although China was by this time observing a policy of equidistance from both superpowers.

In sum, the growing threat from Soviet military expansionism in the late 1970s and early 1980s was countered by a more aggressive US forward deployment strategy and enhanced security ties among the United States and its Asian friends and allies. Washington was determined to persuade Moscow that military adventurism in the Asian-Pacific region would be costly, calling forth a response from both the United States and its allies. Given the geostrategic limitations on Soviet operations in the Asian-Pacific region, the Soviet military build-up was sufficient to raise the level of insecurity among the regional powers, but could not guarantee the USSR concrete improvements in national security or an effective power projection capability.

Geostrategic factors in Soviet regional security

Geography had imposed significant constraints on Soviet security options in the Far East. Although the Pacific Fleet became the largest of the four Soviet fleets under Admiral Gorshkov, the Soviet Navy still did not have the capability effectively to challenge the United States in the Western Pacific. As a land power, the bulk of Soviet population and industrial resources were concentrated on the Western side of the Urals mountains. The Russian Pacific littoral (Primorsk and Khabarovsk krais, Sakhalin, Kamchatka, and the Chukotskii autonomous okrug), a territory four times the size of France, has fewer than 5 million inhabitants. Transportation and communication links between European Russia and the Far East are inadequate, even after completion of the Baikal–Amur Mainline. Finally, the Soviet Union was disadvantaged by the absence of any truly reliable allies in Northeast Asia.

The Soviet Navy's inability to achieve significant power projection capabilities led to the adoption of a defensive strategic posture in the Pacific. To counter the threat of America's forward deployed forces, assigned to bottle up and destroy Soviet forces close to home, the central Soviet naval missions were to defend Soviet Far Eastern territory from attacks by cruise missiles and carrier-based strike aircraft, and to protect the SSBNs deployed in the Sea of Okhotsk bastion. These two principal missions created a strong emphasis on locating and destroying Western sea-based nuclear assets – ballistic missile submarines, aircraft carriers, and platforms capable of launching cruise missiles.[25] Soviet naval deployments were concentrated near the coastal USSR to ensure the survivability of their Delta-III class strategic submarines. Soviet naval aircraft based at Sovetskaia Gavan, Vladivostok, Petropavlovsk (facing the open Pacific), and on the Kuriles were to provide reconnaissance, anti-submarine warfare, and strike capabilities against US naval forces and bases in the region.

In opting for the bastion strategy, Soviet planners sought to make the best of an unfavorable geostrategic situation in the Asia-Pacific. Soviet ballistic missile submarines were less vulnerable to enemy attack in Okhotsk than in the open ocean, since the sea is a relatively shallow body of water, and the presence of noisy ice floes makes submarine detection difficult.[26] By retreating into the Sea of Okhotsk, mining entrances to the three straits, and utilizing surface ships to protect the SSBNs in the event of a conflict, the Soviet military stood a good chance to preserve their second strike capability. The relative invulnerability of these systems would deter an American preemptive attack on Soviet Far Eastern territory.

Michael MccGwire has suggested that Soviet naval expansion in the Pacific during the late 1970s resulted in part from transferring SSBN forces from the Arctic Ocean to the more secure Okhotsk bastion. The inability of the Soviet Navy to deny US submarines access to the Arctic, the costliness of gaining and maintaining command of the Norwegian Sea, and the security of East–West detente, MccGwire argued, resulted in a shift in priority to the Pacific bastion. Prior to this realignment, which began in 1976–77, some 70 percent of Soviet SSBNs were based in the Northern Fleet, and 30 percent in the Pacific Fleet. By 1985, the proportions were 55 and 45 percent respectively, although the balance shifted to 60/40 by 1987. According to this argument, basing a larger proportion of strategic submarines in the Sea of Okhotsk necessitated augmenting Soviet forces on the Kurile islands, and reinforcing the Pacific Fleet, and should not be interpreted strictly as an attempt to intimidate Japan.[27]

From the perspective of the Soviet military, the absence of an extensive network of Pacific basing facilities, the withdrawal of all significant forces from Cam Ranh Bay, and North Korea's hostility toward the Moscow-Seoul normalization heightened the importance of maintaining a military presence on the Japanese-claimed Kurile islands in the late 1980s. Control over the Kuriles was claimed to be vital to Soviet defensive strategy, primarily in order to protect strategic submarines in the Sea of Okhotsk. Once control over the islands was lost, combined US and Japanese forces could seal off the straits and isolate the major bases at Vladivostok and Petropavlovsk.[28] For this reason, the Soviet military establishment was strongly opposed to returning the Kurile islands to Japan.

The Kuriles issue proved to be the major impediment to normalization of Soviet–Japanese relations during Gorbachev's historic visit to Tokyo, in April 1991. The weakening of the Soviet central government encouraged Japan to "hang tough" on the issue – Prime Minister Kaifu asserted that the Soviet Union must return all four islands before there could be an improvement in bilateral relations. The issue was further complicated as the Russian republic and Primorsk krai governments asserted their right to participate in deciding the fate of the islands. Although no agreement was reached on the disposition of the islands, Gorbachev did announce Soviet readiness to reduce military forces on the islands. During a visit to Japan in May, the commander of the Far Eastern Military District, Viktor Novozhilov, announced that Soviet military units in the Kuriles would be reduced 30 percent by the end of the year.[29]

The Korean peninsula's geographic position, political configuration, and history have accorded it a disproportionate weight in Northeast Asian relations. Korea represents, as one analyst has noted, "the only place in the Asian-Pacific region where the interests of the four major powers come into direct conflict; the only territory on the Asian continent where US military forces are deployed; and the only over-land bridgehead for the United States to the Soviet Far East."[30] The existence of an unpopular authoritarian regime in the South and an irrational totalitarian dictatorship in the North, a heavy concentration of modern weaponry on both sides, and the intersection of great power interests created a volatile situation that survived the end of the Cold War.

Throughout most of the post-war period, Moscow followed a policy of vocal support for North Korea, conditional on Soviet forces not being drawn into any potential conflict. During the Korean War, Stalin carefully avoided commitments that might lead to direct clashes with US forces, although a number of Soviet pilots did engage in direct combat during the war. His successors were even less inclined to risk Soviet interests to defend an independent and unpredictable regime in Pyongyang.

Soviet–North Korean relations had reached their nadir in the early 1980s. By 1984, however, strains were developing between Beijing and Pyongyang, and Soviet efforts to cultivate Kim Il-sung resulted in his 1984 and 1986 visits to Moscow and the agreement on MiG-23 fighters; as of late 1988, the Soviets had delivered forty-six of these advanced aircraft to North Korea. In the summer of 1988, some twenty-four MiG-29s were delivered to Pyongyang, at the same time that modern SA-5 surface-to-air missiles were being deployed along the de-militarized zone.[31] In exchange for these deliveries the Soviets were granted overflight rights valuable in transit to Vietnam and in gathering intelligence on the Chinese border, and secured the use of bases at Najin on North Korea's east coast, and Nam'po on the west. Access to facilities on either side of the peninsula improved Soviet prospects for keeping the Tsushima straits open, or at a minimum strengthened Soviet ability to mine the straits in order to deny hostile forces entry. It also strengthened their position for defending the southern Primorsk territory from a possible land attack.

Under Gorbachev, avoiding conflict and preserving stability on the Korean peninsula became even more important as Moscow sought *rapprochement* with China and the United States. As suggested in the previous chapter, there was little in the way of fresh thinking on Korea prior to 1989. Both Gorbachev and the conservative elements in the leadership attempted to preserve ties to the North, while developing enhanced trade relations with the South. It became increasingly apparent, however, that Soviet political and military support for the North was incompatible with new thinking toward the South and the Asian-Pacific region more broadly.

Soviet–North Korean relations continued to deteriorate as the reform process within the USSR accelerated, and as contacts with Seoul expanded. In April 1990 North Korean commentaries expressed outrage at critical articles printed in the Soviet media; the reporting on Gorbachev's meeting with Roh Tae Woo in San Francisco was even more hysterical. As Sino-Soviet relations improved in the second half of the 1980s, North Korea's ability to play off the two major powers declined. Pyongyang's isolation grew after diplomatic relations between the USSR and the Republic of Korea were established in September 1990.

China's reactionary policies following the Tiananmen events of June 1989 and the subsequent international criticism of the PRC provided some reassurance to the beleagured North Korean regime. Yet China and the USSR retained a shared interest in discouraging North Korean adventurism, nuclear weapons development, terrorism, or other actions that could destabilize the peninsula, weaken the new Sino-Soviet *rapprochement*, or reverse the trends toward lower tensions in Northeast Asia. The normalization of Sino-Soviet relations, together with Soviet reform politics, in turn pressured North Korea to adopt a more accomodationist stance toward the South. A new Soviet approach to security had altered key aspects of the regional power balance.

Changing security policy under Gorbachev

The new approach toward Soviet security policy in the Asian-Pacific region revolved around two major goals. The first goal was to end two decades of hostile relations with China, enabling Moscow to transform the Soviet Far East from a military outpost to a center of trade and economic cooperation. China and the Soviet Union were preoccupied with domestic reforms, and needed stability in foreign relations. Their common perspectives and priorities enhanced mutual understanding, and led to substantive agreements within a relatively short time frame.

The second major goal of new thinking in the Asian-Pacific region was to restrain the aggressive forward-based US military strategy, discourage military growth and if possible encourage reductions', and develop collective security arrangements in Asia patterned on the European CSCE experience. Washington would be encouraged to accept Soviet ideas about reasonable sufficiency. Since the US clearly had the military advantage in the Pacific, this implied asymmetrical reductions of American forces. In contrast to Soviet security goals *vis-à-vis* China, however, the United States and the Soviet Union held starkly contrasting perspectives on regional security that did not augur well for communication between the two powers.

The concepts of reasonable sufficiency and mutual security were formalized in Party policy at the 27th Congress, in 1986, and were elaborated over the next three years. In brief, these concepts were predicated on rejecting the use of military force in favor of political means to resolve conflicts, supplemented by the idea that Soviet security could best be achieved through cooperative rather than uni-lateral efforts. The Brezhnev approach to national defense, which equated greater security with the steady expansion of military power, was subjected to critical scrutiny. Mutual security was to substitute for previous efforts to attain absolute security, whereby military power would be at least equal to all possible combinations of forces arrayed against the USSR. The new nomenclature for a non-threatening mili-tary stance, "reasonable sufficiency" (*razumnaia dostatochnost'*), was defined as maintaining enough military power to rebuff any potential aggressor, but with forces structured so as to make offensive Soviet operations unfeasible.

The doctrine of reasonable sufficiency was subject to considerable debate among Soviet military and civilian analysts.[32] The essential thrust of reasonable sufficiency, however, was to halt the Soviet mili-tary build-up in both strategic nuclear and conventional weaponry, and then reduce down to levels consistent with new budgetary restraints. Arms reductions would be combined with a move toward a strictly defensive, non-threatening force posture. Deterrence would be preserved, although military and strategic conditions were to be estab-lished that would deny any state the opportunity to conduct sudden offensive actions. In effect, Soviet military doctrine abandoned the longstanding commitment to maintain sufficient forces to pursue a military advantage in the event deterrence failed.

Consonant with the principles of new thinking, several major Soviet initiatives toward halting and reducing military expansion in the Far

East were advanced under Gorbachev. The most significant of these were the decision to include all Asian intermediate and shorter-range missiles in the Intermediate-range Nuclear Forces (INF) agreement; Gorbachev's unilateral reductions in the European, Southern, and Far Eastern theaters, announced in December 1988 at the United Nations; the Soviet withdrawal from Afghanistan; a reduction in Soviet naval activity in the Pacific; and the decision to remove all Soviet fighters and half the bombers from Cam Ranh Bay.

Gorbachev's July 1986 Vladivostok speech stressed the importance of reducing tensions and of entering into a new dialogue with the Chinese. Over the course of the next three years, the Soviet Union addressed each of the three preconditions the Chinese had stipulated for normalized relations: reductions of Soviet forces on the Sino-Soviet border and in Mongolia; withdrawal of Soviet troops from Afghanistan; and a Vietnamese pullout from Cambodia. Soviet military cutbacks in the region were portrayed as a reciprocal action in response to Chinese planned reductions of 1 million troops, announced in 1985. This approach was designed to encourage further reductions by the Chinese, and indeed the two sides signed an agreement on principles of joint reductions following Li Peng's visit to Moscow in April 1990. Soviet statements also hinted that little movement could be expected regarding Soviet forces deployed against Japan – on Sakhalin, the Kuriles, and in the Far East – until Japan and the United States showed greater flexibility.[33]

Gorbachev's visit to Krasnoiarsk in September 1988 announced several foreign policy initiatives targeted at the Pacific region. Gorbachev proposed a multilateral freeze on the deployment of nuclear weapons in the Asian-Pacific region; consultations on limiting naval deployments; freezing and commensurately lowering naval and air force activity along coastal areas; elimination of the Soviet base at Cam Ranh Bay in exchange for the Clark and Subic bases in the Philippines; measures to prevent incidents on the open seas and in the air; holding an international conference to discuss making the Indian Ocean a zone of peace; and consultations toward creating a negotiating mechanism to consider Soviet and other proposals on the security of the Asian-Pacific region. Gorbachev also suggested transforming the Krasnoiarsk radar station into a center of international cooperation for the peaceful uses of outer space.[34]

Soviet military deployments in Siberia, Mongolia, and the Soviet Far East had, in addition to their primary mission of constraining Chinese activities along the border, and defending the homeland against possible attack by Chinese or American forces, a secondary mission to deter Chinese military actions against Soviet client states to the south.[35] Soviet troop movements on the Sino-Soviet border, in conjunction with naval visits to Cam Ranh Bay, obliged the Chinese to exercise restraint in their punitive war with Vietnam in 1979. The result was a humiliating defeat for China's army. By withdrawing 200,000 troops, a force reduction of approximately 40 percent, the Soviets signaled a perceived diminution of threat along the Sino-Soviet border. In addition, a cutback in troop deployments along the border indicated Sino-Soviet *rapprochement* would take precedence over Soviet commitments to Vietnamese ambitions in Indochina. This point must have become apparent to the Vietnamese when their Soviet allies declined to provide support during the 1988 conflict with China over the disputed Spratley and Paracel islands.[36]

While Gorbachev's announced troop reductions in Europe were essentially unilateral actions, Soviet reductions in Asia constituted reciprocal actions "rewarding" China's cutback of 1 million men in the mid-1980s. Beijing reacted favorably to Soviet force reductions in Asia, and at the May 1989 summit the two sides announced further reductions in their armed forces. However, the Chinese continued to be wary of Soviet intentions in the Asian-Pacific region. To demonstrate Chinese impartiality toward the superpowers, the US Navy was invited to make its second port call to China immediately following Gorbachev's visit. Moreover, although Beijing valued Moscow's political support, particularly after the storm of international criticism that followed Tiananmen, the Soviet Union could not provide the technology and investment China needed to pursue its economic modernization program.

If the Soviet Union could not match Japanese, American or West European assistance in developing China's civilian economy, at least they were competitive in the military field. Soviet and Chinese military delegations were exchanged in 1990, the first in thirty years, following the reestablishment of formal military ties in April. By early 1991, stung over the suspension of US–Chinese military cooperation, Beijing was considering purchasing Soviet hardware. In May, during Party Secretary Jiang Zemin's visit to Moscow, the two countries reached an agreement by which China would purchase a limited number of Su-27 jet fighter aircraft, along with the services of Soviet flight instructors.[37]

Although the Moscow-Beijing *rapprochement* clearly did not signal a return to the close security cooperation arrangements of the 1950s, the two nations did have compatible security goals. The same could not be said for Washington and Moscow, at least not until the virtual end of the Soviet Union. Conservative US defense analysts viewed Gorbachev's proposals for military reductions in the Asian-Pacific region with suspicion, as one-sided propaganda designed to undermine ties between the United States and its Pacific allies.[38]

The US and the Soviet Union approached Pacific security from highly divergent perspectives, and neither fully understood the other's reasoning or motives. Official Washington during the Reagan administration was determined to restore America's undisputed ascendancy in the Pacific. Proposals that would have hindered America's freedom to maneuver in the Pacific were automatically rejected, since any agreement to reduce naval forces or activities would have impacted disproportionately on the American strategy of forward deployment. Washington resisted Gorbachev's attempt to apply lessons learned from the European process of dialogue, confidence-building measures, and multilateral agreements as inapplicable to the culturally diverse, politically multipolar Pacific region.

In contrast to American satisfaction with the regional status quo, Moscow was intent on reducing and reconfiguring its military forces into a less threatening posture. The goal was to gain acceptance as a legitimate regional player, albeit one that could continue to effectively defend the population, territory, and strategic forces in the Far East. Gorbachev and the reformers expected the United States to reciprocate by accepting the Soviet concept of reasonable sufficiency, and shifting American forces to a more defensive posture in the Pacific. Washington, in turn, insisted that new thinking had to be accompanied by concrete measures to match Soviet words.

Arms reductions in the Gorbachev era

The initial evidence for a lower Soviet military profile in the Asian-Pacific region was suggested by changes in Soviet naval deployments. In his unusual testimony to the US House Armed Services Committee, USA and Canada Institute deputy director Andrei Kokoshin outlined Soviet efforts to present a more defensive posture in the Pacific Ocean. Kokoshin stated that from 1984 to 1988 the Soviet Pacific fleet had been reduced by forty ships. In addition, he noted, fleet maneuvers were being carried out closer to Soviet shores, in a more defense-oriented posture, with less emphasis on long-range, blue water naval operations.[39] However, some Western and Japanese analysts asserted that these quantitative reductions involved the retirement of obsolete ships, and were carried out in conjunction with the addition of more modern vessels which upgraded the overall effectiveness of the Soviet Pacific fleet.

Reduced Soviet naval activity coincided with an apparent decision early in the Gorbachev period to curtail surface shipbuilding, both for budgetary reasons and as a result of political pressure from rival services. Admiral Vladimir Chernavin, who replaced Sergei Gorshkov as Commander-in-Chief of the Soviet Navy in December 1985, had supported expansion and modernization of the submarine force over the surface fleet. These developments reinforced the impression of a process of consolidating and refining Soviet naval missions in the Pacific region, focusing on defense of the Soviet homeland over more problematic attempts at power projection.

In accepting the US proposal to eliminate all intermediate and shorter-range nuclear missiles exclusive of British and French systems, Gorbachev relinquished a significant military advantage. These missiles conferred an edge in firepower to compensate for superior Chinese manpower in the Far Eastern theater.[40] While China had initially assumed the position of an interested observer when NATO adopted the dual-track policy, no distinct position on INF was adopted until 1983. The Chinese and Japanese vigorously opposed any INF agreement that would allow Soviet intermediate-range missiles to be transferred to Asia. Specifically, China criticized the proposal advanced by Gorbachev at Reykjavik that would allow each superpower to keep 100 warheads deployed outside the European theater, in Soviet Asia and in the western United States. Under this compromise arrangement, Soviet missiles would not constitute a threat to Europe or the American homeland, but could be utilized against the PRC and Japan.

The INF Treaty of December 1987, which provided for the dismantling of 162 intermediate-range MIRVed SS-20s, 36 shorter range SS-12s, and 22 shorter range SS-23s deployed in the eastern USSR, was welcomed by all countries in the region.[41] Even with these significant reductions, the USSR still maintained a considerable nuclear force in the area, in the form of retargetable ICBMs, IRBMs, and strategic bombers. Six Golf II-class submarines based at Vladivostok, each armed with three SS-N-5 intermediate-range missiles, were available to cover targets in China, Japan, South Korea, and American forces in the Western Pacific.[42]

By the end of the 1980s, it was apparent that the Soviet Union was undertaking significant reductions in its Far Eastern forces. The International Institute for Strategic Studies estimated that forty-two divisions were deployed in the Far Eastern Theater of Military Operations (TVD) as of mid-1991 – seven tank and thirty-five motorized rifle divisions, together with three heavy machine gun-artillery and four artillery divisions. This constituted a reduction of twelve motorized rifle divisions over the past four years. The bulk of these reductions was concentrated in those units deployed against China. By comparison, forces arrayed against Japan and the United States experienced only marginal cutbacks.[43]

In addition, levels of firepower and readiness were substantially reduced. According to the Soviet Ministry of Defense, the motorized rifle divisions along the Chinese border as of early 1991 had only 150 tanks per division, compared with 250 tanks previously.[44] The machine gun–artillery divisions are believed to be smaller and less mobile than the motorized rifle division, and therefore more in keeping with the concept of a less threatening, defensive force structure. The US Department of Defense has estimated that as many as ten motorized rifle divisions may be converted to machine gun–artillery divisions by the mid-1990s.[45]

Of the fifty-six divisions fielded at the height of the Soviet Far East build-up, three were deployed in Sakhalin and the Kamchatka peninsula, one in the disputed Kurile islands, and three in Mongolia; the remainder were deployed along the Sino-Soviet frontier. Of the half-million troops stationed in the region, 200,000 or 40 percent were withdrawn by January 1991 under Gorbachev's United Nations proposals of December 1988. Three-fourths of Soviet troops in Mongolia were withdrawn by 1990, and were repositioned in the Transbaikal military district. The remaining 3000 troops in Mongolia were scheduled to be removed by the end of 1992.

In 1991, the Soviet Navy had a total of 98 submarines deployed in the Pacific Ocean, 22 less than in 1989. These forces included 24 SSBNs, 70 tactical boats, and 4 additional submarines. Soviet ballistic-missile forces were significantly upgraded in the 1980s with the addition of 8 Delta-III class SSBNs, each armed with 16 SS-N-8 or SS-N-18 launchers capable of striking US territory from Soviet coastal waters. The Delta-IIIs complement 9 Delta-I submarines carrying a total of 108 missiles, 7 Yankee-I submarines with 128 SSBMs, and 2 Golf-class submarines carrying 18 missiles. Modernization continued in the late 1980s as Delta-IIIs replaced the older Golfs and Yankees. Overall, the number of SSBNs remained constant, while the number of tactical submarines decreased by about 20 percent.

As of 1991, the Soviet Union maintained 63 principal surface combatants in the Pacific (down from 77 in 1989), including two carriers,
together with 65 patrol and coastal combatants, 102 mine warfare
ships, 21 amphibious vessels, and about 230 support and miscellaneous
vessels. Approximately 240 combat aircraft and 99 helicopters, headquartered at Sovetskaia Gavan, comprised the Soviet naval air forces in
the region. Some 65 of these aircraft and 89 helicopters were assigned
ASW missions, reflecting Soviet determination to protect the SSBN
forces in the Sea of Okhotsk in the event of a conflict.

Notwithstanding the overall decline in Soviet Far Eastern forces and
substantial cutbacks in levels of readiness, the Japanese remained
suspicious of Soviet capabilities even after the August 1991 coup. Japan
was disturbed by the large-scale transfer of tanks from Europe east of
the Urals under terms of the Conventional Forces in Europe treaty. In
addition, the Soviet military continued to replace outmoded T-54
tanks with modern T-72s and T-80s through 1991, and strengthened
Soviet air forces in the region with the addition of MiG-29, MiG-31,
Su-24, and Su-27 fighters. Of course, Japan had domestic political
reasons for continuing to emphasize a Soviet military threat.

In sum, Soviet forces in the Far East and Western Pacific underwent
significant quantitative reductions in the late 1980s and early 1990s,
although on a far less impressive scale than in Europe. The bulk of
Soviet reductions in the Far East were along the Sino-Soviet border,
and thus were aimed primarily at influencing reciprocal Chinese
behavior. As perestroika failed to produce results, budget considerations moved to the fore. The forces that remained were restructured
into a more defensive configuration.

Changes in US force structure in the West Pacific

The virtual collapse of Soviet power, together with severe budgetary
problems in the United States, generated pressures in the US Congress
and among the American public for reduced military spending. Questions were raised about the need to maintain US forces in Japan, South
Korea, and the Philippines at previous levels. A series of amendments
to the 1990 defense authorization bill required the Department of
Defense to review the US force posture in the Pacific and draw up
plans for possible reductions. This evaluation led to the cutbacks first
announced by Secretary Cheney in February 1990 and presented to
the Congress in April of that year.[46]

The report noted that although the Soviet Union had undertaken unilateral reductions in forces deployed against China, and had lowered its force posture in Southeast Asia, military capabilities in the Far Eastern district opposite Japan far exceeded what was necessary for defense. In addition, the USSR was continuing to modernize its naval and air forces in the region. Finally, expectations of political volatility and turbulence in key Asian countries during the 1990s recommended against abrupt changes in US deployments. The report concluded that while US forces in Asia should be restructured to address the needs of a changing security environment, the principles of forward deployment, overseas basing, and bilateral security agreements should be preserved.

The Defense Department's plans for the Pacific region envisioned a ten-year plan of reductions and reorganization, carried out in three phases. In the first three years, a total of 14,000–15,000 personnel, mostly ground and support forces but also including some Air Force personnel, would be withdrawn: 7000 from Korea; 5000–6000 from Japan; and 2000 from the Philippines. No significant changes in deployment patterns would be undertaken. In Japan, the squadron of F–16s at Misawa would remain, along with the air base at Yokota and the naval facilities for the carrier *Midway* (to be replaced by the *Independence*) at Yokosuka.[47] In Korea, the 2nd Infantry Division would be streamlined, with Korean forces assuming the mission of departing troops. Reductions would be undertaken in conjunction with continued modernization of both South Korean and Japanese militaries. Both countries were expected to assume a larger share of the costs of basing US forces, and Japan pledged to continue to expand its Overseas Development Assistance to help maintain stable, democratic governments in the region.

In Phase II (3–5 years) and Phase III (5–10 years), possibilities for additional restructuring and reductions in forces were to be considered with reference to the North Korean and Soviet threats to South Korea and Japan, respectively. On the Korean peninsula, much would depend on the internal situation in North Korea following Kim's death. American plans called for South Korea to take the lead in its own defense during Phase III, assuming successful completion of the earlier stages. Continued forward deployment of US forces on Japanese territory was postulated through Phase III, with some additional efficiencies and reductions possible as the Self-Defense forces upgraded their capabilities.

As late as fall 1990, both Washington and Tokyo resisted contemplating significant reductions in US forces in the Western Pacific. The

American perspective, shared by many East Asian politicians, held that a US presence was needed to guard against instability and possible aggression by regional powers.[48] China, Vietnam, and India all field huge armies, have demonstrated great-power ambitions, and are viewed with suspicion by their neighbors. The Korean peninsula is potentially the most explosive area in East Asia. North Korea, ruled by the bizarre Kim dynasty, is close to realizing a nuclear capability, and a change in leadership is virtually assured some time in the next decade. Given these uncertainties, many analysts suggest, a precipitous alteration in the Asian-Pacific strategic balance would be unwise.[49]

By late 1991, US perceptions of the Pacific security regime had changed. The outbreak of the Gulf War and the continued decline of Soviet power, culminating in the abortive August coup and the formal dissolution of the USSR, confirmed that future challenges to American security would be of a substantially different nature. American facilities in Japan, Korea, and the Philippines were still valuable, albeit less so than in the past. When Mount Pinatubo buried Clark Air Base and the Crow Valley training range under tons of volcanic ash, Washington quickly decided to close out the base and transfer American personnel out of the Philippines. President Bush in September announced US plans to eliminate all ground-launched tactical nuclear weapons, which included Lance nuclear-tipped missiles in the Republic of Korea, and by December President Roh Tae Woo could claim that his country was nuclear-free. By the end of the year, no serious observer of Asian-Pacific affairs would identify Soviet aggression as the primary regional threat.

Conclusions

Soviet security policies in Northeast Asia and the Western Pacific during the 1980s reflected changing perceptions of power and of the utility of military force in international relations learned through the experiences of the post-war period. During the Brezhnev era, Soviet military deployments were consonant with the concept of a defense policy that sought superiority, or at a minimum parity, with all possible combinations of opponents, and a foreign policy that demanded equivalence with the United States in Asia. New thinking recognized the counterproductive effects of fielding excessively large forces in the Far East. Rather than intimidating the Asian countries and the United States into accepting the Soviet Union as a legitimate Asian power, aggressive Soviet tactics had encouraged a compensatory build-up and the formation of new alliances directed against the perceived Soviet threat. Extravagant military spending had not bought much security for the Soviet Union in that part of the world.

Under perestroika, the primacy of internal economic development forced a reevaluation and reversal of Soviet policies in the region. The Soviet Far East contained a wealth of natural resources and, considering its location, had immense potential for economic development. However, Moscow's belligerent attitude toward Asia's regional powers, the poor record of Soviet central planning, and effective isolation from the Asian economic miracle had consigned the Soviet east coast to the status of a provincial backwater. Central to the Soviet reform program were attempts at reducing tensions with the major regional powers – China, Japan, and the United States – and initiating measures to achieve comprehensive economic integration with the East Asian regional economy. Substantial reductions in Soviet capabilities and a reorientation of their force posture would demonstrate that new thinking was more than propaganda, clear the path for Soviet participation in regional economic organizations, and free up funds needed for investing in economic development.

Learning in Soviet security policy toward the Asian-Pacific region derived from several factors. First, the imperatives of domestic restructuring led Kremlin reformers to reconceptualize security in terms of economic performance rather than military capabilities. An economics-oriented security program required developing a less threatening military posture, opening up formerly closed areas such as Vladivostok to commercial transactions, and joining regional groupings like the Pacific Economic Cooperation Conference and the Asian-Pacific Economic Conference. More broadly, the Soviet Union would have to abandon an ideologically based approach to international relations, and become a more responsible member of the Asian-Pacific community.

Second, learning in security affairs was facilitated by an enhanced role for civilian advisors who shared Gorbachev's commitment to transforming the Soviet Union's international image. But the security aspect of new thinking encountered resistance from within the Soviet military, and few really substantive proposals for East Asia were advanced during Gorbachev's first two years. From mid-1987 on, however, Moscow demonstrated greater flexibility in a number of areas – the Asian INF missiles, Afghanistan, troops deployed along the Sino-Soviet border, and facilities at Cam Ranh Bay in Vietnam. Intrusive flights along Japan's coastline were curtailed, relations established with South Korea, and discussions initiated on control of the Kurile islands.

Overall, though, developments in Asian-Pacific security issues were less remarkable than in Europe. Does this indicate that for some reason the learning process toward this part of the world was inhibited? Or might political and situational factors have affected Soviet behavior regardless of the security lessons derived?

Evidence suggests the latter explanation is more convincing. The approaches used in East Asia did not differ substantially from those used in Europe, and in some instances (for example, Gorbachev's proposal for an Asian security conference) were adapted from the European experience. In Asia, however, the fragmented security framework did not lend itself to the sort of arms control agreements that were possible in Europe's bipolar context. Moreover, the Soviet Union position of continental dominance was not replicated in the Asian-Pacific region, where the advantage clearly rested with the naval power of the United States. Moscow's force reductions and restructuring, excluding the substantial cutbacks along the Chinese border, did not initially impress US or Japanese strategists. From the perspective of Soviet military analysts, however, these cutbacks had reduced their forces to a minimal, non-threatening defensive stance.

8 Conclusion: Soviet foreign policy learning

In Mikhail Gorbachev's address to the 27th Congress of the Communist Party of the Soviet Union, delivered only eleven months after taking office, he claimed one of the advantages of socialism was its ability

To learn to solve the problems that are posed by life; to learn to avert crisis situations, which our class opponent tries to create and exploit; to learn to oppose attempts to divide the socialist world into layers and set countries against each other; to learn to prevent clashes of interest between different socialist states, to bring about mutual harmony, and to find mutually acceptable solutions to even the most difficult problems.[1]

Contrary to Gorbachev's assertions, Soviet-style socialism collapsed in large part because that system had perfected the means of thwarting, not promoting, genuine learning. The Soviet Union was a closed system, but *imperfectly* closed – not as penetrated nor as receptive to new information as an "open" system, but nonetheless unable to completely preclude the introduction of ideas challenging the status quo. An irreconcilable tension existed between Soviet leaders' efforts to maintain the fiction that Soviet policies were essentially faultless (and hence had no need of learning), and the growing reliance on specialist expertise in an increasingly complex world. Similarly, the Communist Party's development policies had transformed Soviet society and, in the process, laid the foundations for a political culture that was incompatible with the Party's monopolization of political power. A resolution of these strains could not be postponed indefinitely.

Learning in foreign policy had been frustrated by dogmatic adherence to Marxist–Leninist ideology, which stifled creative thought and forced scholars to parrot the official foreign policy line. At best, creative thinkers could under certain circumstances advance tentative policy recommendations through esoteric debates. Ideological blinders were a constant source of tension with other socialist countries – China and

North Korea, for example – and with such capitalist nations as Japan and South Korea. Marxism–Leninism never served as an active guide to decision-making, but it did condition perceptions and foreclose options for Soviet leaders.

Perhaps most important for the present discussion, official Soviet ideology had evolved into a quasi-religion claiming to have a mono-poly on "truth." Soviet leaders manipulated the state ideology in a self-serving and cynical fashion. But this does not mean that they did not believe at some level. Soviet power and position in the world was intricately connected to the fiction of a nearly flawless utopian doc-trine and system that merely required, as they optimistically insisted, "further perfecting." Lacking humility, a crucial quality for genuine learning, Soviet leaders rejected facts and messages that contradicted their view of the world. Nor were they open to outside experiences or criticism – they lacked sensitivity to the fears and concerns of their Asian neighbors, and were unresponsive to their interests.[2]

As Brezhnev and his colleagues began to die off or retire, and evidence of the system's deficiencies mounted, it became increasingly difficult to avoid acknowledging the basic flaws in Soviet-style social-ism. Glasnost was Gorbachev's attempt to subject what he believed was an essentially sound structure to the spotlight of publicity and criticism, but within the boundaries of a Leninist framework. It is ironic that Gorbachev's reforms, which were designed to stimulate learning in a moribund system, and thereby to save it, ultimately conveyed the lesson that the system itself was the problem. A final bit of irony – Mikhail Gorbachev himself was one of the last to master this lesson, as indicated by his behavior following the August 1991 coup.

In most instances, foreign policy learning accompanied or lagged just behind domestic transformations. The explosion of glasnost, the emergence and acceptance of societal pluralism, the call to review and revise "blank spots" in Soviet history, and the first serious efforts at economic reform took place during a two-year period, from 1987 to 1988. As we have seen, 1988 was a watershed year for Soviet relations with Northeast Asia, and Soviet foreign policy more generally. Basic foreign policy principles, including the international application of democratic centralism and the Brezhnev doctrine of limited sover-eignty, became subject to open scrutiny and relatively unconstrained discussion. Reformers charged that the Communist Party's overly centralized, authoritarian approach toward domestic affairs was reflected in its foreign policy. Insularity, elitism, and dogmatism reinforced a hegemonic, great-power mentality that led to the ruptures with Yugoslavia and China. Soviet leaders, prisoners of their own propaganda, could not escape a shortsighted approach to international relations.[3]

The clearest evidence of learning in Soviet policy toward Northeast Asia occurred in Gorbachev's China policy which, not coincidentally, was accorded the highest priority in Soviet Asian affairs. Much of the learning originated from "negative" experiences; that is, through foreign policy mistakes. For example, recognizing that Soviet claims to ideological primacy contributed significantly to Sino-Soviet hostilities, Gorbachev "deideologized" relations among socialist states as he sought to deideologize relations between capitalist systems and the Soviet Union. In addition, the split with China had been immensely expensive, given the large number of troops dedicated to manning the Sino-Soviet border for over two decades. Less tangible costs included foregone trade opportunities, expenses involved in competing with China for influence in the Third World, and tensions which diverted energy from the more immediate requisites of domestic reform.

There was also a more positive type of learning taking place in Soviet relations with the People's Republic of China in the 1980s. The two countries shared common interests in economic reform, and communities along both sides of the border were interested in developing trade. China's experience with liberalized private farms and small businesses, special economic zones, expanded foreign investment, and other market mechanisms within a central planning framework suggested options for reforming the moribund Soviet economy. For many Soviet observers, at least prior to the Tiananmen massacre, the Chinese approach seemed a good example of how to combine effective economic reform with gradual political liberalization.

Soviet learning in relations with Japan occurred at the diplomatic, military, and economic levels. As with China, economic considerations were crucial. From the vantage point of the mid-1980s, when Gorbachev was appointed General Secretary, the future belonged to the world's economic powerhouses. Japan had become a dominant influence in the Asian-Pacific region based on economic rather than military strength. Japan's commanding position in the international economy justified a role in world affairs far beyond what its military stature would seem to justify. By contrast, a large and militarily powerful USSR found itself effectively marginalized as a player in Asian-Pacific regional affairs, excluded from serious consideration except as a potential security threat.

Soviet military power in the region was not only demonstrably ineffective, it also interfered with higher priority objectives under perestroika. Disturbed by the Soviet military presence in the Far East, Washington encouraged Tokyo to build up Japan's military forces and strengthen Japan's alliance with the United States. In addition, Tokyo agreed to cooperate with the United States in developing the Strategic Defense Initiative, and signed a friendship treaty with China directed against the perceived Soviet threat in East Asia. Reliance on force and intimidation, the new Soviet leadership realized, had proved to be ineffectual instruments of statecraft. Economic vitality and skillful diplomacy would be far more useful.

A third aspect of the learning process in Soviet–Japanese relations involves the conflict between learning and political pressures. The Soviet experience indicates that potential for change in foreign policy may be highest in authoritarian systems as they begin to liberalize and become more open to new information, but before they have democratized to the point that political pressures frustrate adoption of new policies. A reformist individual utilizes charismatic personal power to break through the inertia of a corrupt system. The innovator then faces the dilemma of having to wield power arbitrarily in order to create new, institutionalized power structures.[4] This dilemma provides the most plausible explanation for the inability of the two sides to agree on a solution to the Kurile islands quandary. By the time of the Tokyo summit, a number of the more prominent reformers appeared willing to strike a deal on returning the islands. However, public opinion on the islands, in Primorsk krai, and throughout Russia more generally, opposed restitution, and, together with conservative opposition in the leadership, constrained Gorbachev's options.

Soviet relations with the two Koreas exhibited another side of foreign policy learning. Moscow's stubborn support for the rather uncooperative Kim Il-sung regime was dictated less by ideology than by other foreign policy failures; namely, the Sino-Soviet split and the East–West conflict. Soviet Korean policy was also conditioned in large part by simple bureaucratic inertia. This position became increasingly untenable in 1980s as South Korea's economic development far outpaced that of the North. With economic cooperation replacing military confrontation as the centerpiece of Soviet foreign relations, Seoul emerged as both a model and potential partner for the reforming USSR. Pyongyang's value further diminished as the Soviet Union and China moved toward normalization.

South Korea's experience in constructing a strong export-based economy, its surplus investment capital, and its managerial expertise could be tapped for the Far East development program. Given the long history of antagonism between the USSR and Japan, and the lingering dispute over the Kuriles, a Soviet–South Korean *rapprochement* seemed more profitable to Moscow. Furthermore, Soviet leaders realized that Seoul was anxious to enlist Moscow's assistance in its Nordpolitik. In short, a far greater complementarity of interests existed between the Republic of Korea and the USSR than between Japan and the USSR.

One stage in Soviet Korean policy deserves closer examination. What accounts for the Soviet decision to develop stronger defense links with North Korea in the mid-1980s? More specifically, why was Gorbachev willing to approve the delivery of sophisticated jet fighter aircraft to Pyongyang, when his predecessors carefully avoided making such a commitment? And how does expanded Soviet–North Korean military cooperation square with the virtual reversal of Soviet Korean policy toward the end of the 1980s?

During the period from early 1985 to early 1987 – the first two years under Gorbachev – Soviet Korean policy followed the parameters established under Brezhnev and continued under Andropov and Chernenko. Gorbachev apparently encouraged North Korea to take a more accommodative stance toward South Korea and the United States, and convinced Kim to sign the Nuclear Non-Proliferation Treaty. However, Gorbachev was still learning on the job, and the path of least resistance was to continue his predecessors' policies of economic and military cooperation with Pyongyang. For the first two or three years, he largely followed the recommendations of those advisors who had formulated Soviet Korean policies since Khrushchev's time.

In addition, Korea had a lower priority in Soviet Asian policy than either China or Japan, and was therefore accorded less attention. Kim's visits to Moscow in 1984 and 1986, and the exchange of North Korean port facilities for modern Soviet fighters, reflected the usual Soviet attempts at wooing the North Koreans away from the Chinese, and at countering an increasingly aggressive US policy in East Asia. Pyongyang, alarmed by the Reagan administration's bellicose rhetoric, turned to Moscow as the only feasible source for high-tech weaponry, and Moscow seized the opportunity to strengthen ties with Kim's regime.

Clearly it would be misleading to suggest that US pressure in this instance encouraged more accommodative Soviet behavior. If anything, Washington's threatening posture and its decision to send modern F–16 aircraft to Seoul had the opposite effect. Pyongyang pressed for deliveries of comparable Soviet weaponry, for which it was willing to grant concessions – namely, port rights – that consistently had been refused to Moscow in the past. Soviet leaders, including the reformer Gorbachev, reversed a longstanding policy of denying North Korea advanced military equipment. Major changes in Soviet Korean policy occurred long after American pressure had diminished and, the evidence suggests, were due primarily to developments within the Soviet and South Korean systems.

This proposition leads to the broader question of America's role in Soviet foreign policy learning. Supporters of the Reagan administration's confrontational stance toward the Soviet Union contend that American resolve deserves much of the credit for the turnaround in foreign policy, and the ultimate collapse of Soviet communism. Critics assert that hardline policies by the United States contributed little to new thinking, and may even have delayed the reform process. A brief review of US foreign policy in the 1980s may shed some light on this debate.

American foreign policy and Soviet learning

Any nation's foreign policy is, of course, determined by a combination of domestic and external factors. The crux of the problem is to determine the relative impact of each potentially significant variable on a range of foreign policy outputs. This study's learning perspective has emphasized the central importance of internal determinants of policy – ideology, economic constraints, generational change and the succession process, and the role of experts – in reassessing Soviet–Northeast Asian relations. External sources were important in shaping Soviet foreign policy reforms, but domestic factors should be accorded greater weight as the primary motive forces.

The end of the Cold War has prompted a spirited debate among foreign policy specialists. Conservatives argue that it was a series of foreign policy setbacks, occasioned in large part by a hardline US position under President Reagan, that forced major transformations in Soviet foreign policy.[5] The underlying rationale of Reagan's foreign policy held that American isolationism, military weakness, and lack of resolve in the 1970s had encouraged Soviet adventurism and aggression. Reasserting American military power and challenging the Soviet Union around the globe would close off the opportunities for expansionism, contain, and perhaps even reverse Soviet gains in Asia, Africa, and Latin America. America's reinvigorated military posture would place additional pressure on a Soviet economy already in crisis, and in the optimal scenario, "would force the Soviets to choose between external retrenchment and internal collapse."[6]

Those conservatives who were influential in shaping American foreign policy during the Reagan administration viewed world events through a thick bipolar lens. Unlike traditional realists, the Reaganite neo-conservatives seemed intent on changing the internal structure of radical left-wing governments.[7] This perspective assigned much if not all of the blame for leftist radicalism in the Third World to Soviet machinations. Logically, American resistance to Soviet inspired radical movements could reverse the trend. However, the same conservatives were convinced that although the Soviet system lacked popular support, the instruments of repression were so strong that domestic change could not realistically be expected in the near future. American policies could encourage liberalization and democratization in traditional autocracies, but, as Jeane Kirkpatrick observed, "the history of this century provides no grounds for expecting that radical totalitarian regimes will transform themselves."[8]

Reagan's neo-conservative advisers on foreign policy and defense rejected the Nixon–Kissinger premise that East–West detente would draw the Soviet Union into more responsible international behavior through a web of trade and diplomatic linkages, eventually producing a liberalizing effect on the Soviet system. By treating the Soviet Union as a virtual partner in world affairs during the 1970s, they believed, the US had conceded ground to communism. Detente had encouraged the USSR toward expansionism around the globe, and this in turn had supported the emergence of revolutionary movements in the Third World inimical to US interests. Washington, adjusting to the "new reality" of the decline in American power, had refused to resist the growing tide of left-wing radicalism.[9] To correct this damaging policy required a reassertion of American military strength.

Reagan administration hardliners also sought to curtail trade and other forms of economic cooperation between the USSR and the West. Denying the Soviet economy Western technology and investment would exacerbate internal economic problems and increase pressures for change. This strategy was at best ill-conceived and at worst counterproductive. Washington's confrontation with Western Europe over the oil pipeline revealed the difficulties involved in developing a coherent program regulating economic ties with the Soviet Union. Furthermore, it exacerbated tensions within the Alliance. The US government could not effectively control the operation of its domestic businesses, much less corporations in other countries. In any case, increasing the isolation of the Soviet Union – in effect, making the boundaries of a closed system less permeable – would have reduced rather than enhanced the opportunities for learning, had this strategy proved effective.

The Reagan conservatives were on the mark in claiming that Soviet international behavior was aggressive because of its totalitarian character. But their preoccupation with military power led to the conviction that the system was too tightly controlled to allow for internal transformation. They overlooked or discounted many of the signals which indicated the process of change was genuine rather than cosmetic – the emergence after 1987 of hundreds, then thousands of independent interest groups, for example. The Bush administration likewise did not seem convinced by internal Soviet transformations, withholding judgment until the collapse of Eastern Europe's communist governments in late 1989.

If new thinking really was prompted by external reactions to aggressive Soviet foreign policies, changes in Soviet policy toward Northeast Asia should have been evident by the late 1970s or early 1980s. As we have seen, 1978–79 marked a high point of resistance to Soviet expansion in the area, with the normalization of Chinese–American relations, conclusion of a Sino-Japanese treaty, and the resurgence of American military spending. By 1979, the Carter administration had essentially abandoned the proposed withdrawal of American troops from South Korea. Shortly after the Reagan administration came into office, Washington moved to establish closer military ties with Japan and South Korea.

Soviet reactions to these developments, however, consisted of more rather than less assertive behavior in the region. Moscow responded by deploying close to a division of troops in the Kurile islands, assigning naval and air forces to Cam Ranh Bay, upgrading their military equipment in the Far East, and invading Afghanistan to preclude American or Chinese intervention in the region. Soviet leaders did not react to greater military and political pressures by retreating. They responded according to the lessons they had "learned" in the post-war period, under Stalin's tutelage – by seeking to further augment their military power, pursuing confrontational policies, and in general trying to be the political equal of the United States in the Asia-Pacific.

It is also worth recalling that President Reagan softened his highly confrontational posture toward the Soviet Union by early 1984, in time for the upcoming election. Increases in defense spending leveled off,

Secretary of State George Shultz emphasized the United States' willingness to negotiate with the USSR, and Reagan himself spoke favorably of arms control and dialogue. This shift in foreign policy was so striking that prominent conservatives openly decried the President's return to a Nixonian-style detente.[10] And yet major Soviet foreign policy changes did not follow from a more conciliatory American position. The policy stalemate continued through General Secretary Chernenko's brief tenure, and Gorbachev's first two years, as we have seen, were marked by lingering conservatism. Soviet foreign policy does not seem to have been particularly responsive either to US carrots or sticks, reinforcing the hypothesis that the crucial determining variables were internal.

The turning point in Soviet relations with Northeast Asia varied somewhat according to the specific country, but the period from early 1988 through 1989 is clearly pivotal. Moreover, these foreign policy changes closely paralleled the domestic reform process. The most fundamental changes, as I have argued, were linked to a rejection of the dominant ideology and consequently a reconceptualization of Soviet domestic and foreign policy priorities, and to the nascent democratization of Soviet society. A critical turning point was reached in the summer of 1988 when, at the 19th Communist Party Conference, Gorbachev, realizing the difficulties inherent in democratizing the Party, initiated the process of shifting real political power toward elective governmental institutions. A key conference of Foreign Ministry personnel was held immediately afterward, and by the end of the year Gorbachev had formally announced the "deideologization" of Soviet foreign policy.

One consequence of the learning process was a thorough redefinition of power by the Soviet elite. A prominent military presence was recognized as at best irrelevant, and quite frequently counterproductive, for attaining Soviet objectives in Northeast Asia. The Soviet reformist leadership finally understood the importance of non-military elements of power, most notably economics, and sought to add these instruments to its foreign policy repertoire. Military reductions in Northeast Asia and the Pacific, however, did not appear to have been in response to a more confrontational US stance.

The Reagan administration's Northeast Asia policy centered on developing America's strategic advantage in the region, naval power, in a renewed effort to contain Soviet expansionism. America's regional strategy threatened the Soviet Union with the possibility of a full-blown war in the Pacific were Moscow to undertake aggression in

Europe, the Middle East, or elsewhere. Defense Secretary Caspar Weinberger's plan for rebuilding US capabilities and options in the Western Pacific called for substantial increases in Japanese military spending, more Japanese economic assistance to Korea, and (at least after 1983), expanded cooperation with the People's Republic of China.[11]

Were Moscow responding to increased military pressure from the United States in Northeast Asia and the Western Pacific, we would expect reductions or curtailment of military activities to correspond, with an appropriate lag-time, to US actions. Instead, the first major Soviet cutbacks in the region were a reaction not to threats, but to China's troop reductions during the mid-1980s. Soviet forces in the Far East deployed against Japan and the US were virtually unaffected by the cutbacks, a point clearly and repeatedly signaled to both Tokyo and Washington. In contrast, Gorbachev's United Nations speech made clear that Soviet troop withdrawals from Mongolia and along the Sino-Soviet border were made in response to China's earlier gesture. China and the Soviet Union were both reforming systems, and both sides at this point in time were predisposed out of self-interest to pursue a reciprocating strategy.[12]

Washington, however, was more reluctant than Beijing to accept conciliatory Soviet moves as genuine. The Reagan administration's foreign policy had been constructed around the principle of a negative tit-for-tat strategy, to use the language of cooperation theorists.[13] Aggressive moves by the Soviet Union were to be countered resolutely by US actions, as forms of punishment. Despite Gorbachev's accommodating signals, US foreign policy was not sufficiently flexible to immediately reverse the punitive strategy of Reagan's first four years and adopt a positive, conciliatory position toward the Soviet Union. Ideological convictions, political pressures, bureaucratic inertia, and a basic misunderstanding of Soviet internal processes delayed the evolution of new thinking in Washington.

There is another reason to question Reagan's foreign policy as a central variable contributing to Soviet new thinking. American international behavior during the eight years of Reagan's presidency was characterized by many inconsistencies and reversals. A number of US proposals, such as the zero option on intermediate-range ballistic missiles in Europe, were public relations ploys advanced on the assumption that Moscow would reject them as unrealistic. Soviet leaders would have been hard put to know exactly what responses would have satisfied Washington. A wide gap existed between the administration's hostile declaratory policies and its far more cautious operational behavior in East–West relations.[14]

Sino-American relations exemplify the inconsistencies of US foreign policy. During the first year or so after Reagan's election, during Alexander Haig's tenure as Secretary of State, US policy toward China followed the Carter administration's approach, and then cooled considerably under pressure from the right to support Taiwan. After Beijing shifted toward a more independent stance between the two superpowers, Washington moved to strengthen ties with the PRC, sending Commerce Secretary Malcolm Baldridge and then Defense Secretary Caspar Weinberger to China in 1983. Sino-American cooperation in matters of economics and defense then expanded in the latter half of Reagan's administration as China became part of the US plan to "complicate" Soviet strategic planning.[15]

While a more aggressive US policy in the Pacific may have complicated Soviet global strategy, the evidence is lacking for a direct link between a reassertion of American military power in the region and Soviet retrenchment. We have already noted that Soviet Far East troop reductions were in response to Chinese initiatives. Soviet naval operations in the Pacific were curtailed after Gorbachev came to power primarily as a cost saving measure. The withdrawal of Soviet forces from Cam Ranh Bay seems to have been a combination of lowered tensions with China and further attempts to cut expenditures at a facility that no longer had a significant mission.

A far more sophisticated argument can be made that Soviet foreign policy changes originated from broader influences in the external environment. Rather than accept the conservative interpretation that the Reagan administration's assertive policies forced the collapse of communism, Soviet foreign policy change can be portrayed as an adaptive response to a more benign international environment. Following this line of reasoning, the state of crisis in the Soviet system is acknowledged to be primarily domestic in origin, but foreign policy responses are seen as deriving from external sources.[16]

Excluded from this explanation is the centrality of elite perceptions and the rise of a new, younger generation whose perspective on international affairs differed substantially from that of their predecessors. Suggesting that a more benign security environment made it more difficult to justify the need for repression and centralized mobilization of resources is a fundamental misreading of the Soviet system.[17] The older generation did not moderate their policies because they perceived the capitalist liberal democracies as more benign. Detente presented Soviet leaders with a less confrontational international environment, yet the result of Western retrenchment was an adventurous foreign policy based largely on Soviet military potential.

Reformers of the Gorbachev generation rejected these policies as ill-conceived, expensive, and most importantly, counterproductive to the far more important goal of reinvigorating the domestic political-economic system. Although foreign policy learning was clearly evident among institute researchers and other specialists as early as the 1960s, this knowledge was not creatively applied until two decades later, after the new group of decision-makers had supplanted the old. Structuralists seeking more "scientific" explanations for Soviet foreign policy changes may balk at assigning a prominent role to personalities, but the alternative is a superficial and illusory interpretation. A learning perspective, taking into account both internal and external determinants of foreign policy, and incorporating the critical element of perception, contributes significantly to a more thorough understanding of foreign policy change.

Learning and foreign policy

What general observations can be made about the foreign policy learning process from this study of Soviet relations with Northeast Asia? Under what conditions is learning maximized? What circumstances tend to frustrate learning? And what are the conditions under which lessons learned are enacted into policy?

One obvious conclusion is that learning tends to be more difficult under repressive, authoritarian regimes than in a democratic system. Closed systems purposefully attempt to limit the flow of information from outside, and to restrict and compartmentalize access to information within the system. Control over information is integral to preserving the elite's monopoly of political power. Decision-makers may develop highly competent advisory bodies or other mechanisms comparable to those in democratic systems, but the intellectual atmosphere in an authoritarian system invariably constrains the discussion parameters. Real learning is even more difficult if political inquiry and debate is circumscribed by adherence to a quasi-religious philosophy, even if that philosophy does not guide day-to-day decision-making. Genuine learning, then, is more likely in an open system that promotes critical discussion and in which foreign policy specialists are not writing or speaking with an eye to any official canon.

Second, learning is maximized when there exists an element of humility on the part of scholars and decision-makers, institutions, and the larger political system. If past practices and beliefs can be called into question without significant costs, if the major issues of foreign policy are at least open to critical scrutiny, then it is psychologically easier to consider and experiment with alternatives. Individuals in high positions of authority may not be amenable to learning. Such persons are by definition successful, and will resist a critical examination of past policies or decisions with which they may be associated. Leaders who become isolated from society because of their elite position or who may be shielded from negative feedback by aides or other gatekeepers will be poor learners. Should the extant leadership of a country prove incapable of genuine learning, a generational succession may be essential to effect fundamental changes.

To understand learning beyond the individual, it is also important to consider the factors that affect humility within institutions and systems. Institutions are not often humble. Whether public or private, foreign policy organizations generally function in a competitive environment. As specialized bureaucracies seeking to enhance their resources, maximize their influence over policy, and ensure the continued existence of the organization, foreign policy institutions tend to equate their interests with the interests of the country. There is a strong incentive to defend the institutional perspective as the only "correct" one. Such organizations seldom experiment, preferring instead incremental modifications to past positions. In addition, they routinely tailor policy recommendations to decision-makers' supposed preferences, since this improves chances for influencing policy.

At the systemic level, the existence of a messianic ideology clearly interferes with humility. A comprehensive belief system intolerant of competing ideas will dissuade innovation, rewarding those who merely elaborate the status quo. It also stands to reason that superpower status conveys a certain arrogance in foreign policy, which makes learning more difficult. Being a superpower is by definition a mark of success for a country. The leaders of a superpower, confident in the methods by which the state rose to preeminence, will be understandably disinclined to abandon a strategy that has proved successful in favor of experimentation.

Third, the external environment does play a part in foreign policy learning, albeit more contextual than in the form of an immediate and direct influence. Predictable responses from other powers encourage certain behaviors and discourage others, and therefore enhance conditions for learning. If it is clear that one's conduct will entail certain consequences, it is much easier to assess the wisdom of following through on a contemplated course of action. A relatively stable and predictable environment may also encourage innovation, if the perceived costs of experimental strategies are lowered. Conversely, learning is extremely difficult when the subject must contend with conflicting signals emanating from the environment. Uncertainty in the face of contradictory cues will likely heighten suspicions, reinforcing tendencies toward maintaining the status quo rather than toward experimentation or innovation.[18]

Learning may also be impaired in an unremittingly hostile international environment. Consideration and adoption of new ideas will be viewed as excessively risky if leaders decide the country cannot bear the costs of a failed experimental strategy. It is safer to follow familiar terrain, even realizing the long-term inadequacy of business as usual. Thus, countries seeking to encourage foreign policy learning among their adversaries would be well advised not to pursue a highly threatening bargaining strategy, at least not if the adversary is open to cooperation. Conversely, if the opponent is stubborn, and clearly not in a learning mode, the actions of other relevant powers will likely have only marginal effect on changing their policies.[19]

Fourth, while open democratic systems are more conducive to learning than closed authoritarian regimes, conflicting political pressures in democracies may interfere with the application of lessons learned. Timing is critical. Ironically, the ideal conditions for foreign policy learning would seem to be during the transition stage from authoritarianism to democracy. Glasnost liberalized debate and opened up new opportunities for Gorbachev, who in the late 1980s still maintained a relatively authoritarian position within the Soviet Union. The transition period between systems, in other words, provided a "window of opportunity" for a leader intent on radically transforming Soviet foreign policy, decisive enough to carry it through, and not yet constrained by the contradictory demands of a pluralist political system. Assuming the second Russian revolution will emerge from its present tumultuous phase and progress toward greater political equilibrium, we can expect foreign policy innovation to subside.

Fifth, as noted above, learning within one age cohort may be difficult. This study has suggested that a good deal of systemic learning in Soviet foreign policy was linked to the succession process. Although the Gorbachev generation was not uniform in its political attitudes, it was clearly more educated, more politically sophisticated, and more flexible than the Brezhnev generation. The Brezhnev and Stalinist regimes were thoroughly discredited; only fringe elements in the population would seriously have considered turning back the clock in the last year of the Soviet Union's existence. It is difficult to imagine the circumstances that might produce a consensus among the present generation of Russian officials and opinion leaders to revert to the old style of Soviet foreign policy.

Sixth, learning will tend to be enhanced during the process of decentralization. Decentralized political systems, with their multiple access points and overlapping jurisdictions, are more responsive to public pressures, and hence more capable of learning, than highly centralized systems. Unfortunately, extreme decentralization often frustrates effective decision-making. Foreign policy decision-making generally requires strong central leadership and national consensus, both of which were eroded in the Soviet Union's final year. Russia under the leadership of Boris Yeltsin has so far been unable to achieve an effective measure of recentralization. So while decentralization may initially produce a flowering of innovative ideas, the resultant political gridlock tends to interfere with adaptation.

Finally, to the extent that political learning is accompanied by the development of new political institutions, learning itself should over time become institutionalized. This was one of Gorbachev's objectives in creating the Congress of People's Deputies, a Supreme Soviet with real legislative powers, and an elected presidency. A more formalized, constitutional system replacing the narrow oligarchy that dominated Soviet foreign policy in the past would embody procedural restrictions and democratic links to the people that would make extremist or adventurist policies less likely. An open press, less secrecy, and the legitimation of interest group participation add more channels for feedback. Eventually, of course, excessive proceduralism and a growing diversity of inputs into foreign policy can inhibit effective decision-making, and may lead to the sort of policy gridlock evident in many pluralist systems.

Notes

1 Introduction

1 The literature on Soviet learning has expanded dramatically in recent years, most of it linked to the role of specialists in the formulation of policy. One of the best early efforts on Soviet foreign policy learning was Franklyn Griffiths, "Images, Politics and Learning in Soviet Behavior toward the United States," (Ph.D. dissertation, Columbia University, 1972). For assessments of Soviet–Third World relations, the following are especially useful: Elizabeth Valkenier, *The Soviet Union and the Third World: An Economic Bind* (New York: Praeger, 1983); Jerry F. Hough, *The Struggle for the Third World* (Washington, DC: Brookings, 1986); and George W. Breslauer, "Ideology and Learning in Soviet Third World Policy," *World Politics*, vol. 39, no. 3 (1987), pp. 429–48. On learning in the military and strategic realms, see Joseph Nye, "Nuclear Learning and US–Soviet Security Regimes," *International Organization*, vol. 41, no. 3 (Summer 1987), pp. 371–402. On Soviet relations with Western Europe, Neil Malcolm, *Soviet Policy Perspectives on Western Europe* (New York: Council on Foreign Relations Press/Royal Institute of International Affairs, 1989) is a concise, useful work.

The topic of Eastern Europe and its impact both on Soviet domestic transformations and Soviet foreign policy is still relatively unexplored. An excellent early study was Zvi Gitelman, *The Diffusion of Political Innovation: From Eastern Europe to the Soviet Union*, Comparative Politics Series 3, no. 27 (Beverly Hills, CA: Sage, 1972). Also, see Andrzej Korbonski, "Eastern Europe as an Internal Determinant of Soviet Foreign Policy," in Seweryn Bialer, ed., *The Domestic Context of Soviet Foreign Policy* (Boulder: Westview, 1981); and Elizabeth Teague, *Solidarity and the Soviet Worker: The Impact of the Polish Events of 1980 on Soviet Internal Politics* (London: Croom Helm, 1988).

A major recent contribution to the learning literature is George W. Breslauer and Philip E. Tetlock, eds., *Learning in US and Soviet Foreign Policy* (Boulder: Westview Press, 1991). In addition to broad theoretical chapters on learning and case studies on American foreign policy learning, there are excellent papers on Soviet learning in the nuclear age (Coit Blacker), toward Western Europe (Jonathan Haslam), China (Allen Whiting), the Arab–Israeli conflict (George Breslauer), and the United States (Ted Hopf and Franklyn Griffiths). Robert Legvold's chapter on "Soviet Learning in the 1980s" presents a cogent argument for foreign policy analysis on three levels – at the level of the external environment, the level of domestic politics, and the level of belief systems. A learning approach, as Legvold suggests, incorporates all three levels of analysis, each of which is important for a thorough understanding of foreign policy behavior.

Other recent contributions include George W. Breslauer, ed., *Soviet Policy in Africa: From the Old to the New Thinking* (Berkeley: Berkeley–Stanford Program in Soviet Studies, 1992); and James Clay Moltz, "Commonwealth Economics in Perspective: Lessons from the East Asia Model," *Soviet Economy*, vol. 7, no. 4 (1991), pp. 342–63.

2 Learning, adaptation, and foreign policy change

1 Robert Legvold, "Soviet Learning in the 1980s," in George W. Breslauer and Philip E. Tetlock, eds., *Learning in US and Soviet Foreign Policy* (Boulder: Westview Press, 1991), p. 715.

2 James N. Rosenau, "Toward Single-Country Theories of Foreign Policy," in Charles Hermann, Charles Kegley, and James N. Rosenau, eds., *New Directions in the Study of Foreign Policy* (Boston: Allen and Unwin, 1987), p. 61. Rosenau's single-country theory is a variation of the comparative case study method persuasively advocated by Jack Snyder. See his "Richness, Rigor, and Relevance in the Study of Soviet Foreign Policy," *International Security*, vol. 9, no. 3 (Winter 1984–85), pp. 89–108.

3 Ibid., p. 71.

4 The psychological roots of open and closed personalities, and systems, are discussed in Milton Rokeach, *The Open and Closed Mind* (New York, Basic Books, 1960), pp. 54–70.

5 Alexander L. George, "The 'Operational Code': A Neglected Approach to the Study of Political Leaders and Decision-Making," *International Studies Quarterly*, vol. 13, no. 2 (June 1969), pp. 190–222. Elsewhere, George has defined ideologies as comprising *normative commitments* to the realization of a desired end state; *philosophical assumptions* about human nature and the course of historical development; *empirical beliefs* about the character of the contemporary international era; and *strategic prescriptions* for the conduct of foreign policy. Cited in George W. Breslauer, "Ideology and Learning in Soviet Third World Policy," *World Politics*, vol. 39, no. 3 (April 1987), pp. 429–48.

6 James N. Rosenau, *The Scientific Study of Foreign Policy*, revised and enlarged edition (London: Frances Pinter, 1980), pp. 503–4.

7 For a good discussion of the innovation process in organizations, see Everett M. Rogers, *Diffusion of Innovations*, third edition (New York: Free Press, 1983).

8 George Modelski, "Is World Politics Evolutionary Learning?," *International Organization*, vol. 44, no. 1 (Winter 1990), pp. 1–24. Of course, even in open systems most highly structured organizations are extremely resistant to innovation. The point is, authoritarianism exacerbates the problem.

9 For a more extended discussion, see Charles E. Ziegler and Roger E. Kanet, "The Soviet Union," in Gavin Boyd and Gerald W. Hopple, eds., *Political Change and Foreign Policies* (London: Frances Pinter, 1987).

10 William Zimmerman, *Soviet Perspectives on International Relations* (Princeton: Princeton University Press, 1971), pp. 62–64.

11 See Karen Dawisha, *The Kremlin and the Prague Spring* (Berkeley: University of California Press, 1984).

12 On Soviet generational changes, see Jerry F. Hough, *Soviet Leadership in Transition* (Washington, DC: Brookings, 1980).

13 See Yutaka Akino, "Soviet Asian Policy in a New Perspective," in Tsuyoshi Hasegawa and Alex Pravda, eds., *Perestroika: Soviet Domestic and Foreign Policies* (London: Sage, 1990), pp. 226–28.

14 *International Affairs* (Moscow), no. 10 (October 1988), pp. 3–34.

15 See Suzanne Crow, "Reforming the Foreign Ministry," *Report on the USSR*, vol. 3, no. 40 (4 October 1991), and Jan S. Adams, "New Structures at the USSR Foreign Ministry," *Report on the USSR*, vol. 3, no. 40 (4 October 1991).

16 "Mikhail Gorbachev – United Nations Address," Novosti Press Agency, 8 December 1988.

17 See Robert A. Jones, *The Soviet Concept of "Limited Sovereignty" from Lenin to Gorbachev* (New York: St. Martin's Press, 1990).

18 These factors are outlined by Paul Marantz, "Changing Soviet Conceptions of International Security," paper presented at the American Association for the Advancement of Slavic Studies, 19 November 1988, Honolulu, Hawaii.

19 Of course, reformist politicians as a rule become more conservative once ensconced in office. By 1990, Gorbachev's performance on such domestic matters as economic reform and nationalities relations contrasted sharply with the more aggressive positions of Boris Yeltsin, President of the Russian republic.

20 See Ernst Kux, "Contradictions in Soviet Socialism," *Problems of Communism*, vol. 33, no. 6 (November–December 1984), pp. 1–27.

21 This remark, which Gorbachev made in 1987, is cited in Paul H. Nitze, "America: An Honest Broker," *Foreign Affairs*, vol. 69, no. 4 (Fall 1990), p. 6. Nitze erroneously claims that both Gorbachev and Ryzhkov were appointed to the Politburo in 1982.

22 *Pravda*, 16 June 1983, translated in *Current Digest of the Soviet Press* (hereafter *CDSP*), vol. 35, no. 25, 20 July 1983, pp. 1–8.

23 M.S. Gorbachev, *Zhivoe tvorchestvo naroda* (Moscow: Politizdat, 1984).

24 Speech to the Central Committee CPSU, *Pravda*, 7 January 1989, in J.L. Black, ed., *USSR Documents Annual 1989* (Gulf Breeze, Florida: Academic International Press, 1990), p. 9. Gorbachev's speech to the April 1985 plenum is in *Pravda*, 24 April 1985, in *CDSP*, vol. 37, no. 17, 22 May 1985, pp. 1–11.

25 See Mikhail Gorbachev, *Perestroika: New Thinking for Our Country and the World* (New York: Harper and Row, 1987).

26 See especially Elizabeth Kridl Valkenier, *The Soviet Union and the Third World* (New York: Praeger, 1983); Jerry F. Hough, *The Struggle for the Third World* (Washington, DC: Brookings, 1986); Rajan Menon, *Soviet Power and the Third World* (New Haven: Yale University Press, 1986).

27 Ligachev's speech was delivered in Gorkii in August 1988. *BBC Summary of World Broadcasts* (USSR), 8 August 1988.

28 "The Vladivostok Initiatives: Two Years After," *International Affairs* (Moscow), no. 8, 1988, pp. 144–56.
29 Much of the reformist reasoning is closely attuned to Paul Kennedy's argument about imperial overstretch, in *The Rise and Fall of the Great Powers: Economic Change and Military Conflict from 1500 to 2000* (New York: Random House, 1987).
30 Gorbachev's speech on the seventieth anniversary of the Revolution singled out Japan, West Germany, and Italy as examples of countries achieving high rates of economic growth, at least in part as a result of low military expenditures. *Foreign Broadcast Information Service–Soviet Union*, 3 November 1987.

3 Learning and adaptation in the historical context

1 See Richard E. Neustadt and Ernest R. May, *Thinking in Time: The Uses of History for Decision Makers* (New York: The Free Press, 1986).
2 The Soviet Communist Party had at best only weak links with the Vietnamese, Malayan, Australian, and Indonesian communist movements after the war. Ironically, Stalin consistently underestimated the potential of the Chinese communists, who stood the best chance of gaining power.
3 See S. L. Tikhvinskii, "K istorii vosstanovleniia poslevoennykh sovetsko-iaponskikh otnoshenii," *Voprosy istorii*, no. 9 (1990), pp. 3–28.
4 See especially William E. Griffith, *The Sino-Soviet Rift* (Cambridge: MIT Press, 1964); Donald S. Zagoria, *The Sino-Soviet Conflict, 1956–1961* (Princeton: Princeton University Press, 1962); Herbert J. Ellison, ed., *The Sino-Soviet Conflict: A Global Perspective* (Seattle: University of Washington Press, 1982); Klaus Mehnert, *Peking and Moscow* (New York: Putnam, 1963); Zbigniew K. Brzezinski, *The Soviet Bloc: Unity and Conflict* (Cambridge: Harvard University Press, 1967).
5 See Harrison E. Salisbury, *The New Emperors: China in the Era of Mao and Deng* (Boston: Little, Brown, 1992), pp. 83–102.
6 Roy Medvedev, *China and the Superpowers*, translated by Harold Shukman (Oxford: Basil Blackwell, 1986), p. 24. Presumably, at this time Soviet leaders believed little of significance could be learned from their Chinese brethren.
7 See N. Fedorenko, "The Stalin–Mao Summit in Moscow," *Far Eastern Affairs*, no. 2 (1989), pp. 134–48.
8 *Khrushchev Remembers: The Last Testament*, translated and edited by Strobe Talbott (Boston: Little, Brown, 1974), pp. 239–41. The archetype of "old thinking," Gromyko, supports Khrushchev's claim that relations between Mao and Stalin were strained during that first Moscow meeting. Andrei Gromyko, *Memoirs* (New York: Doubleday, 1989), pp. 248–49.
9 O.B. Borisov and B.T. Koloskov, *Soviet–Chinese Relations, 1945–1970* (Bloomington: Indiana University Press, 1975), p. 125.
10 Ibid., especially pp. 108–91.
11 *Khrushchev Remembers*, p. 271.
12 *Pravda*, 28 January 1959, translated in the *Current Digest of the Soviet Press* (hereafter *CDSP*), vol. 11, no. 4, 4 March 1959, pp. 17–25. Khrushchev was

considerably more critical of the Great Leap Forward in his memoirs. See *Khrushchev Remembers*, pp. 272–75.

13 A total of 336 industrial enterprises had been started with Soviet aid, but only 198 were completed. R.K.I. Quested, *Sino-Russian Relations: A Short History* (London: George Allen and Unwin, 1984), pp. 121–24.

14 Roy Medvedev, *China and the Superpowers*, pp. 38–39.

15 *Pravda*, 19 October 1964, p. 2.

16 This is what Georgii Arbatov in his memoirs calls the "China factor" in the ideological struggle of the early 1960s. *Zatianuvsheesia vyzdorovlenie (1953–1985 gg.):svidetel'stvo sovremennika* (Moscow: Mezhdunarodnye otnosheniia, 1991), pp. 86–101. Gilbert Rozman makes a similar argument linking domestic policy discussions with Soviet sinologists' criticisms of the PRC in his book *A Mirror for Socialism: Soviet Criticisms of China* (Princeton: Princeton University Press, 1985).

17 For an extended discussion, see Walter C. Clemens, Jr., *The Arms Race and Sino-Soviet Relations* (Stanford: Hoover Institution, 1968), pp. 85–104.

18 For an excellent history of the Sino-Soviet-American triangular relationship, see Gordon H. Chang, *Friends and Enemies: The United States, China, and the Soviet Union, 1948–1972* (Stanford: Stanford University Press, 1990).

19 Henry Kissinger, *White House Years* (Boston: Little Brown, 1979), pp. 166–67.

20 Ibid., p. 183.

21 *Pravda*, 31 March 1971, in *CDSP*, vol. 23, no. 12, 20 April 1971, p. 7.

22 *Pravda*, 8 June 1969, in *CDSP*, vol. 21, no. 23, 2 July 1969, pp. 3–17. Andrei Gromyko's July 1969 foreign policy report to the USSR Supreme Soviet reiterated Brezhnev's attacks on China, but then denied that an Asian collective security system would be directed against any one country or group of countries. *Pravda*, 11 July 1969, in *CDSP*, vol. 21, no. 28, 6 August 1969, pp. 4–11.

23 See Hemen Ray, "Soviet Diplomacy in Asia," *Problems of Communism*, vol. 19, no. 2 (March–April 1970), pp. 46–49. Ray points out that in addition to seeking to contain the Chinese, the Soviets were also positioning themselves to fill the vacuum that would be left as Britain withdrew its remaining forces from the Indian Ocean by 1971.

24 See George Ginsburg, "The Soviet View of Chinese Influence in Africa and Latin America," in *Soviet and Chinese Influence in the Third World*, ed. Alvin Z. Rubinstein (New York: Praeger, 1975).

25 *Pravda*, 25 February 1976, in *CDSP*, vol. 28, no. 8, 24 March 1976, pp. 6–7.

26 *Power and Principle*, revised edition (New York: Farrar Straus Giroux, 1985), p. 196.

27 See Myles L.C. Robertson, *Soviet Policy Toward Japan: An Analysis of Trends in the 1970s and 1980s* (Cambridge: Cambridge University Press, 1988), pp. 171–74.

28 For a more extended discussion, see Richard H. Solomon and Masataka Kosaka, eds., *The Far East Military Buildup: Nuclear Dilemmas and Asian Security* (Dover, Mass.: Auburn House, 1986). The Soviet military build-up and its implications for Soviet–Asian and Soviet American relations are discussed in greater detail in chapter 7.

29 The definitive study is John J. Stephan, *The Kuril Islands* (Oxford: Clarendon Press, 1974).
30 See Adam Ulam, *Expansion and Coexistence: Soviet Foreign Policy 1917–73*, second edition (New York: Praeger, 1974), pp. 394–98.
31 See Donald C. Hellmann, *Japanese Foreign Policy and Domestic Politics: The Peace Agreement with the Soviet Union* (Berkeley: University of California Press, 1969), pp. 29–40.
32 M.S. Kapitsa, et al., eds., *Istoriia mezhdunarodnykh otnoshenii na dal'nem vostoke* (Khabarovsk: Knizhnoe izdatel'stvo, 1978), pp. 237–42.
33 John J. Stephan, "Japanese–Soviet Relations: Patterns and Prospects," in Herbert J. Ellison, ed., *Japan and the Soviet Quadrille* (Boulder: Westview, 1987), p. 142.
34 However, these container shipments constituted only a minor share of total Japanese trade. Robertson, *Soviet Policy Toward Japan*, pp. 57–61.
35 Michael J. Bradshaw, "Trade and High Technology," in Rodger Swearingen, ed., *Siberia and the Soviet Far East: Dimensions in Multinational Perspective* (Stanford: Hoover Institution Press, 1987), pp. 120–25. Also, see Raymond S. Mathieson, *Japan's Role in Soviet Economic Growth: Transfer of Technology Since 1965* (New York: Praeger, 1979); and Robertson, *Soviet Policy Toward Japan*, pp. 52–87.
36 Arkady Shevchenko, *Breaking with Moscow* (New York: Knopf, 1985), p. 82.
37 See V. Kudryavtsev, "Wandering in Search of New Paths," *Izvestiia*, 2 November 1972, in *CDSP*, vol. 24, no. 44, 29 November 1972, pp. 1–3.
38 See the remarks by Col. A. Leontyev, "A NATO for Asia?," *Krasnaia zvezda*, 17 December 1978, in *CDSP*, vol. 30, no. 51, 17 January 1979, pp. 3–4; and comments in *Pravda*, 13 August 1978, p. 5.
39 Stephan, "Japanese–Soviet Relations," p. 136.
40 Chin O. Chung, *P'yongyang between Peking and Moscow: North Korea's Involvement in the Sino-Soviet Dispute, 1958–1975* (University of Alabama: University of Alabama Press, 1978), pp. 11–13.
41 One authoritative Soviet account states rather defensively that "Many Soviet internationalists were killed defending the Korean and Chinese people." Kapitsa, *Istoriia mezhdunarodnykh otnoshenii*, p. 102.
42 See Joungwon Alexander Kim, "Soviet Policy in North Korea," *World Politics*, vol. 22, no. 2 (January 1970), pp. 237–54.
43 Ibid., pp. 245–47.
44 See Chung, *P'yongyang between Peking and Moscow*, pp. 24–46.
45 Ibid., pp. 98–100.
46 Ibid., pp. 115–33.
47 Ralph N. Clough, "The Soviet Union and the Two Koreas," in Donald S. Zagoria, ed., *Soviet Policy in East Asia* (New Haven: Yale University Press, 1982), pp. 183–85.
48 Ahn Byung-joon, "South Korea and the Communist Countries," *Asian Survey*, vol. 20, no. 11 (November 1980), pp. 1098–107.
49 Mikhail Suslov, "Kommunisticheskoe dvizhenie v avangarde bor'by za mir, sotsial'noe i natsional'noe osvobozhdenie," *Kommunist*, no. 11 (July 1975), pp. 3–10. It is worth noting that the 7th and final Congress of the Comin-

tern, held in 1935, focused on rallying communist parties together in an attempt to isolate and contain fascism through the Popular Front policy.

50 Clough, "The Soviet Union and the Two Koreas," pp. 179–85.

51 See Young Whan Kihl, "North Korea: A Reevaluation," *Current History*, vol. 81, no. 474 (April 1982), 155–59, 180–82.

52 Charles Gati makes a similar argument, in "The Stalinist Legacy in Foreign Policy," Erik P. Hoffmann, ed., *The Soviet Union in the 1980s* (New York: The Academy of Political Science, 1984).

4   The People's Republic of China

1 For an excellent discussion of relations in this period, see Robert C. Horn, "Soviet Leadership Changes and Sino-Soviet Relations," *Orbis*, vol. 30, no. 4 (Winter 1987), pp. 683–99.

2 However, Afghanistan apparently was the least important of China's three preconditions. See Leslie Holmes, "Afghanistan and Sino-Soviet Relations," in Amin Saikal and William Maley, eds., *The Soviet Withdrawal from Afghanistan* (Cambridge: Cambridge University Press, 1989).

3 William E. Griffith, "Sino-Soviet Rapprochement?," *Problems of Communism*, vol. 32, no. 2 (March–April 1983), pp. 20–22.

4 Rakhmanin wrote under his common pseudonym of O.B. Borisov, "Polozhenie v KNR i nekotorye zadachi sovetskogo kitaevedeniia," *Problemy dal'nego vostoka*, no. 2 (1982), pp. 3–14.

5 I.N. Korkunov, "Sotsial'no-ekonomicheskie problemy kitaiskoi derevni," *Problemy dal'nego vostoka*, no. 1 (1982), pp. 58–69.

6 A.N. Zhelokhovtsev, "Apologety 'kitaiskoi modeli' ekonomicheskogo razvitiia," *Problemy dal'nego vostoka*, no. 2 (1982), pp. 117–20.

7 *Pravda*, 31 July 1982, p. 5.

8 Feodor Burlatskii, "Mezhdutsarstvie, ili khronika vremen den siaopina," *Novyi mir*, no. 4 (April 1982), pp. 205–28.

9 The best analysis of this debate is Ernst Kux, "Contradictions in Soviet Socialism," *Problems of Communism*, vol. 33, no. 6 (November–December 1984), pp. 1–27.

10 For a more thorough discussion of the reconciliation process, see Gerald Segal, *Sino-Soviet Relations after Mao* (London: IISS Adelphi Paper No. 202, 1985), pp. 6–15. Hu's speech to the 12th Party Congress was reported in *Pravda*, 9 September 1982, p. 5.

11 R.A. Medvedev, "Kitae v politike SSSR i SShA," *Narody Azii i Afriki*, no. 1 (1990), pp. 79–80.

12 He did claim, however, that China's foreign policy was linked to the interests of imperialism. *Pravda*, 25 March 1982, pp. 1–2.

13 *Izvestiia*, 30 July 1982, p. 4.

14 Brezhnev's Baku speech appeared in *Pravda*, 27 September 1982, pp. 1–2.

15 *Pravda*, 16 November 1982, p. 5.

16 Bovin lived in the Soviet Far East for eleven years as a child, and served as a consultant to Andropov in the Department for Liaison with Ruling Socialist Parties of the Central Committee in the early 1960s.

17 Medvedev, "Kitae v politike SSSR i SShA," p. 80.

18 V.Ia. Portiakov and S.V. Stepanov, "Spetsial'nye ekonomicheskie zony Kitaia," *Problemy dal'nego vostoka*, no. 1 (1986), pp. 37–46.

19 *Pravda*, 11 July 1985, p. 4.

20 *Far Eastern Economic Review*, 19 March 1987, p. 86; Stanislav Kondrashov, "SSSR i ATR," *Izvestiia*, 24 September 1988, p. 5; *The Chinese Economy in 1988 and 1989: Reforms on Hold, Economic Problems Mount*, CIA Report to the Subcommittee on Technology and National Security, Joint Economic Committee, US Congress, Washington, DC, 7 July 1989.

21 *Direction of Trade Statistics Yearbook, 1991* (Washington, DC: International Monetary Fund, 1991), p. 135.

22 *The Chinese Economy in 1988 and 1989*.

23 *BBC Summary of World Broadcasts* (USSR), 18 November 1988; Yufan Hao, "The Development of the Soviet Far East: A Chinese Perspective" *Korea and World Affairs*, vol. 15, no. 2 (Summer 1991) pp. 237–45.

24 Yufan Hao, "The Development of the Soviet Far East," p. 240.

25 See I. Doronin, "Spetsial'nye ekonomicheskie zony v sotsialisticheskom khoziaistve," *Mirovaia ekonomika i mezhdunarodnye otnosheniia*, no. 3 (1989), pp. 69–75; and Kondrashov, "SSSR i ATR."

26 *Pravda*, 24 April 1986, pp. 1, 4.

27 *Gorbachev CPSU Central Committee Political Report*, Moscow Television, translated in *Foreign Broadcast Information Service–Soviet Union* (hereafter *FBIS–SOV*), 26 February 1986.

28 *Soviet Biographical Service*, 1987; *Vjesnik* (Zagreb, 8 March 1988), in *FBIS–SOV*, 14 March 1988. For additional changes in the Ministry of Foreign Affairs, see chapter 5.

29 Ibid.

30 *Pravda*, 29 July 1986, translated in the *Current Digest of the Soviet Press* (hereafter *CDSP*), vol. 38, no. 30, 27 August 1986, pp. 1–8, 32.

31 *Pravda*, 28 November 1986, pp. 1, 3.

32 *Pravda*, 29 November 1986, pp. 1–2.

33 *Pravda*, 23 July 1987, pp. 1–2.

34 Washington had been briefing Beijing regularly on arms control issues since 1984. Samuel S. Kim, "Chinese Foreign Policy after Tiananmen," *Current History*, vol. 89, no. 548 (September 1990), pp. 245–46.

35 Vietnam's Communist Party Congress, at Soviet urging, adopted a program of economic reforms similar to Gorbachev's perestroika. CPSU Secretary and Politburo member Igor Ligachev attended the Congress in December 1986 and announced Soviet intentions to provide an additional $2 billion in economic aid over the next five years, double what Vietnam had been receiving. It is doubtful that, in a period when Soviet policy toward client states was being reexamined in light of cost-effectiveness, such a commitment would have been made without strings attached. Significantly, Vietnamese Party leader Troung urged normalization of ties with the PRC. *Financial Times*, 20 December 1986, p. 2.

36 *Pravda*, 18 March 1988, p. 7. For a more thorough description of this dispute, see Marko Milivojevic, "The Spratley and Paracel Islands Conflict," *Survival*, vol. 31, no. 1 (January–February 1989), pp. 70–77.

37 Mikhail Gorbachev, *Perestroika: New Thinking for Our Country and the World* (New York: Harper and Row, 1987), p. 165.
38 Ibid., p. 166.
39 *The Military Balance, 1985–1986* (London: IISS, 1985) p. 30; *The Military Balance, 1988–89* (London: IISS, 1988), p. 44.
40 Gorbachev's timing may also have been affected by a deterioration in Sino-American relations. Tensions had been exacerbated by American criticism of China over the Tibetan demonstrations and strains over China's sale of Silkworm missiles to Iran, and were further aggravated by technology and trade disputes. See James C. Hsiung, "Sino-Soviet Detente and Chinese Foreign Policy," *Current History*, vol. 87, no. 530 (September 1988), pp. 245–46.
41 Marie Mendras, "Soviet Foreign Policy: In Search of Critical Thinking," in Tsuyoshi Hasegawa and Alex Pravda, eds., *Perestroika: Soviet Domestic and Foreign Policies* (London: Sage, 1990).
42 "The 19th All-Union CPSU Conference: Foreign Policy and Diplomacy," *International Affairs* (Moscow), no. 10 (October 1988), pp. 3–42.
43 Viacheslav Dashichev, "Vostok-Zapad: poisk novykh otnoshenii," *Literaturnaia gazeta*, 18 May 1988, p. 14; and *Komsomolskaia pravda*, 19 June 1988, p. 3.
44 For a more complete discussion, see Saikal and Maley, eds. *The Soviet Withdrawal from Afghanistan*; and Alvin Z. Rubinstein, "The Soviet Withdrawal from Afghanistan," *Current History*, vol. 87, no. 531 (October 1988), pp. 333–36, 339–40.
45 *Pravda*, 2 September 1988, p. 6.
46 *BBC Summary of World Broadcasts* (USSR), 6 December 1988.
47 Nicholas D. Kristof, "Key Talks Open in Beijing," *International Herald Tribune*, 2 February 1989, p. 1.
48 *Pravda*, 6 February 1989, p. 5.
49 *Pravda*, 18 May 1989, pp. 1–2.
50 *Pravda*, 18 May 1989, p. 3.
51 "Sino-Soviet Joint Communiqué," *Beijing Review*, vol. 32, no. 22, 29 May–4 June 1989, pp. 15–17.
52 See Viktor Loshak, "The Echo of Tiananmen Square," *Moscow News*, no. 44 (1989), p. 12; and *Mezhdunarodnaia zhizn'*, no. 7 (1989). For a review of reactions by officials, the media, and the public, see Alexander Lukin, "The Initial Soviet Response to the Events in China in 1989 and the Prospects for Sino-Soviet Relations," *The China Quarterly*, no. 125 (March 1991), pp. 119–36.
53 An editorial in the major Soviet journal on the Far East warned before the summit that while reform successes in one country could energize the other, setbacks could strengthen the hand of those opposed to reform. "Moskva-Pekin: potentsial sotrudnichestva," *Problemy dal'nego vostoka*, no. 2 (1989), p. 9.
54 Moscow TV, in *FBIS–SOV*, 3 July 1989.
55 See Harry Gelman, "Gorbachev and the Sino-Soviet Relationship," paper presented to the Fourth World Congress of Soviet and East European Studies, Harrogate, England, 21–26 July 1990.
56 Kim, "Chinese Foreign Policy After Tiananmen," pp. 246, 248.

57 *Pravda*, 24 April 1990, pp. 1, 5–6; *Izvestiia*, 25 April 1990, p. 4. Military ties had been reestablished early in April with the visit of Song Wen, director of the Chinese Defense Ministry's foreign affairs office. *Beijing Review*, vol. 33, no. 17, 23–29 April 1990, p. 7.
58 Radio Liberty *Report on the USSR*, vol. 2, no. 18, 4 May 1990.
59 *Pravda*, 5 March 1991, pp. 1, 5; *Izvestiia*, 20 March 1991, p. 4.
60 *The Economist*, 23 March, 1991, pp. 37–38. However, other reports suggest any arms deal may have been concluded during an earlier trip by Igor Belousov, chairman of the Soviet State Commission for Military-Industrial Affairs. Sophie Quinn-Judge, "Cannon for Fodder," *Far Eastern Economic Review*, 28 March 1991, p. 11.
61 The optimistic estimates were cited in "Another Milestone in Sino-Soviet Relations," *Beijing Review*, vol. 33, no. 17 (23–29 April 1990), p. 7.
62 Sophie Quinn-Judge, "Cannon for Fodder."
63 *Pravda*, 17 May 1991, p. 1.
64 *Pravda*, 17 May 1991, pp. 1, 4; *Izvestiia*, 16 May 1991, p. 1. Also, see "Sino-Soviet Joint Communiqué," *Beijing Review*, vol. 34, no. 21, 27 May–2 June 1991, pp. 17–19.
65 TASS, 20 June 1991, in *FBIS–SOV*, 20 June 1991.
66 See, for example, the comments by long-time China watcher Vsevolod Ovchinnikov, in *Pravda*, 30 September 1991, p. 4.
67 I. Chernyak, "A Big Success for Soviet Diplomacy," *Komsomolskaia pravda*, 25 June 1991, in *FBIS–SOV*, 27 June 1991; Aleksey Voskresenskiy, "Are Clouds Still Hanging Over the Border?," *Novoe vremia*, no. 19 (May 1991), in *FBIS–SOV*, 11 June 1991.
68 *Beijing Review*, 23–29 September 1991, p. 13.
69 *Far Eastern Economic Review*, 9 January 1992, p. 14.
70 Gorbachev announced plans to develop such zones in the Soviet Union during his Krasnoiarsk speech. See Charles E. Ziegler, "Soviet Strategies for Development: East Asia and the Pacific Basin," *Pacific Affairs*, vol. 63, no. 4 (Winter 1990–91), esp. pp. 453–54.

5 Japan

1 "USSR–Japan: Headed for a New Beginning," *International Affairs* (Moscow), no. 3 (March 1989), pp. 154–55.
2 S.I. Verbitskii, "Formirovanie predstavlenii o Iaponii v Rossii i SSSR," *Iaponiia 1989: ezhegodnik* (Moscow: Nauka, 1991), p. 146.
3 Although I have not found any survey data to support this specific contention, interviews with both specialists and ordinary Soviet citizens conducted in 1989 and 1991 strongly reinforced this impression.
4 *Soviet Foreign Policy, Volume II: 1945–1980* (Moscow: Progress Publishers, 1981), pp. 588–92.
5 See M. Demchenko, "SSSR-Iaponiia: shag k dialogu," *Mirovaia ekonomika i mezhdunarodnye otnosheniia*, no. 4 (1986), p. 78.
6 For a discussion of the various projects, see M.I. Krupianko, *Sovetsko-Iaponskie ekonomicheskie otnosheniia* (Moscow: Nauka, 1982).

7 Leslie Dienes, "Soviet–Japanese Economic Relations: Are They Beginning to Fade?," *Soviet Geography*, vol. 26, no. 7 (September 1985), p. 512.
8 "Gorbachev: Can He Change Soviet Policy on Japan?," *Tokyo Business Today*, vol. 59, no. 4 (April 1991), pp. 28–29.
9 This was the Soviet position as propagandized at an April 1982 conference in Tokyo attended by representatives of various Soviet and Japanese social, cultural, and trade societies. The conference results are summarized in T.B. Guzhenko, "Sovetsko–iaponskie otnosheniia," *Problemy dal'nego vostoka*, no. 3 (1982), pp. 9–20. Guzhenko placed the entire blame for worsening relations on the Japanese side – "The Soviet Union has not taken one solitary step toward destabilizing Soviet–Japanese good-neighborly relations, toward curtailing cooperation. On the contrary, the Soviet side to its credit has taken many actions and initiatives directed toward developing ties and strengthening peace and security in the Asian-Pacific region" (p. 18). For this argument reiterated in the Gorbachev era, see V. Khlynov, "Sovetsko–Iaponskii dialog – vazhnyi faktor mezhdunarodnykh otnoshenii," *Mirovaia ekonomika i mezhdunarodnye otnosheniia*, no. 11 (1986), p. 99.
10 One exception is an article by the reformist Feodor Burlatskii, appearing in *Literaturnaia gazeta* in October 1984, "The Technical Revolution and the Ethics of Robots," translated in *Current Digest of the Soviet Union* (hereafter *CDSP*), vol. 37, no. 9, 27 March 1985, pp. 12–14. In his discussion of the world computer revolution, Burlatskii pointedly excluded the Soviet Union as a contender in the technological struggle among industrial giants. The two most important states in this struggle, he noted, were both in the capitalist world – the United States and Japan. While the discussion was couched in terms of the growing contradictions of capitalism, the message was clear. The USSR could not hope to match the performance of the capitalist systems.
11 Christopher Andrew and Alexander Gordievsky, *KGB: The Inside Story* (New York: HarperCollins, 1990), p. 611.
12 Iu. Kuznetsov, "Kuda tolkaiot Iaponiiu," *Kommunist*, no. 4 (March 1983), pp. 98–109.
13 See, for example, Igor A. Latyshev, "Soviet–US Differences in Their Approaches to Japan," *Asian Survey*, vol. 24, no. 11 (November 1984), pp. 1163–73. At the time, Latyshev was Professor and Department Head at the Institute of Oriental Studies in Moscow.
14 For an elaboration of Japanese concerns over the Soviet threat in the early 1980s, see Hiroshi Kimura, "The Soviet Threat and the Security of Japan," in Roger E. Kanet, ed., *Soviet Foreign Policy in the 1980s* (New York: Praeger, 1982).
15 For an upbeat assessment, see Iu. Bandura, "The USSR and Japan: In Anticipation of Changes," *Izvestiia*, 9 December 1984, in *CDSP*, vol. 36, no. 50, 9 January 1985, pp. 10–11.
16 The citation is in V. Khlynov, "Sovetsko–iaponskii dialog – vazhnyi faktor mezhdunarodnykh otnoshenii," *Mirovaia ekonomika i mezhdunarodnye otnosheniia*, no. 11 (1986), p. 100.
17 Kovalenko's first contact with Japan was apparently in his role as interroga-

tor of Japanese prisoners of war in Siberia. See Tsuyoshi Hasegawa, "Japanese Perceptions and Policies Toward the Soviet Union: Changes and Prospects Under the Gorbachev Era," in Pushpa Thambipillai and Daniel C. Matuszewski, *The Soviet Union and the Asia-Pacific Region* (New York: Praeger, 1989), p. 29.

18 Cited in Kenichi Ito, "Japan and the Soviet Union – Entangled in the Deadlock of the Northern Territories," *The Washington Quarterly*, vol. 11, no. 1 (Winter 1988), p. 39.

19 Rajan Menon, "New Thinking and Northeast Asian Security," *Problems of Communism*, vol. 38, nos. 2–3 (March–June 1989), pp. 7–8; and Hasegawa, "Japanese Perceptions and Policies Toward the Soviet Union," p. 29. Solov'ev served as ambassador until October 1990, when he was replaced by Ludvig Chizov.

20 For various reasons, the summit, which was tentatively scheduled for early 1987, did not materialize for another four years. For the Soviet view of the talks, see *Pravda*, 20 January 1986, p. 5.

21 *Pravda*, 24 April 1986, pp. 1, 4.

22 *Pravda*, 29 July 1986, in *CDSP*, vol. 38, no. 30, 27 August 1986, p. 6.

23 See Leslie Dienes, "A Comment on the New Development Program for the Far East Economic Region," *Soviet Geography*, vol. 29, no. 2 (April 1988), pp. 420–22; and Charles E. Ziegler, "Soviet Strategies for Development: East Asia and the Pacific Basin," *Pacific Affairs*, vol. 63, no. 4 (Winter 1990–91), pp. 451–68.

24 The Toshiba affair seriously affected already strained relations between Japan and the United States, although the impact on a flowering US–Soviet detente was negligible. Several members of the US Congress took the opportunity to engage in some literal Japan-bashing on the steps of the Capitol by hammering a Toshiba radio to pieces, an event that played repeatedly on Japanese television. The Senate voted in June to ban the sale of Toshiba products in the United States for a two-to-five year period, while the House voted to require the State Department to seek compensation for expenses incurred in trying to detect the new, quieter Soviet submarines. Congressional ire was rekindled in March of the following year when a Tokyo district court judge fined Toshiba a paltry 2 million yen ($US 15,750) for violating export restrictions, and gave the two former executives suspended prison terms.

25 On Japan's burden-sharing efforts, see *US–Japan Burden Sharing*, General Accounting Office Report to the Chairman, Committee on Armed Services, House of Representatives (Washington, DC: US GAO, August 1989).

26 *Pravda*, 18 September 1988, in *CDSP*, vol. 40, no. 38, 19 October 1988, pp. 1–7.

27 *Pravda*, 7 May 1988, pp. 1–2.

28 *Izvestiia*, 29 September 1988, p. 5. The story was reported in the *New York Times* (David E. Sanger, "Soviets Make Overtures to Japan to Lease Four Contested Islands"), 22 September 1988, p. 4.

29 *BBC Summary of World Broadcasts* (USSR), 26 July 1988.

30 Daniel Sneider, "Moscow Hopes to Enlist Japanese Business in Solving Economic Woes," *Christian Science Monitor*, 19 December 1988, pp. 7–8.

31 *Izvestiia*, 14 November 1988, p. 1.
32 See Ito, "Japan and the Soviet Union," pp. 38–39
33 Daniel Sneider, "No Big Steps Forward in 'Heated' Soviet–Japanese Talks," *Christian Science Monitor*, 22 December 1988, p. 8.
34 *International Herald Tribune*, 20 January 1989, p. 2.
35 Akio Morita and Shintaro Ishihara, "The Japan that Can Say No: The New US–Japan Relations Card," unpublished English translation, nd.
36 *Pravda*, 1 November 1990, p. 5.
37 The ultimate solutions Yeltsin mentioned included making the islands a joint protectorate of Japan and the USSR; granting the islands self-governing, free status; or possibly even returning the islands to Japan. Vladimir Ovsiannikov, "Boris El'tsin: izbavliat'sia ot gruza proshlogo," *Novoe vremia*, no. 6 (1990), pp. 20–21.
38 Gorbachev's remarks were in response to questions from the president of Asahi Shimbun newspaper, Toshitada Nakae. *Pravda*, 30 December 1990, in *CDSP*, vol. 42, no. 52, 30 January 1991, p. 27.
39 These data, which are collected from various Soviet and Japanese sources, are presented in *SUPAR Report*, no. 10 (January 1991), p. 32.
40 *Japan Times*, 10–16 September 1990, p. 9.
41 Suzanne Crow, "The Soviet–Japanese Summit: Expectations Unfulfilled," Radio Liberty *Report on the USSR*, vol. 3, no. 17 (1991).
42 These obstacles are carefully set out in Rajan Menon, "Gorbachev's Japan Policy," *Survival*, vol. 33, no. 2 (March–April 1991), pp. 158–72.
43 *Izvestiia*, 30 September 1991, p. 1; *Pravda*, 19 October 1991, pp. 1–2. Interestingly, Fedorov cited Alaska and Port Arthur as "lessons" that made the Russian heart ache. Similar sentiments have been expressed to this author during visits to the Soviet Union.
44 Alexei D. Bogaturov, "The Prospects for Soviet–Japanese Rapprochement: A View From Moscow," *Korea and World Affairs*, vol. 15, no. 1 (Spring 1991), p. 104.
45 These points are elaborated in Victor Spandaryan, "How Have the Japanese Done It?" *International Affairs* (Moscow), no. 5 (1990), pp. 80–91. For a detailed discussion of Soviet reformers borrowing from the East Asian model of development, particularly Japan, see James Clay Moltz, "Commonwealth Economics in Perspective: Lessons from the East Asia Model," *Soviet Economy*, vol. 7, no. 4 (1991), pp. 342–363.
46 This view was expressed to the author during a series of interviews conducted in Moscow, April 1989.

6 The Korean peninsula

1 V. Shipaev, "From Silence to Contracts," *Komsomolskaia pravda*, 25 October 1988, trans. in *Foreign Broadcast Information Service–Soviet Union* (hereafter *FBIS–SOV*), 28 October 1988, pp. 17–19.
2 V. Ivanov, "Sovetskii soiuz i aziatsko-tikhookeanskii region: evoltsiia ili radikal'nye peremeny?," *Mirovaia ekonomika i mezhdunarodnye otnosheniia*, no. 9 (1990), p. 102.

3 Yu-Nam Kim, "Changing Relations between Moscow and Pyongyang: Odd Man Out," in Robert A. Scalapino and Hongkoo Lee, eds., *North Korea in a Regional and Global Context* (Berkeley: Institute of East Asian Studies, 1986), p. 174.

4 See *Korea at the Crossroads: Implications for American Policy* (New York: Council on Foreign Relations/The Asia Society, 1987).

5 Rin-Sup Shinn, "North Korea in 1982: First Year for de facto Successor Kim Jong-Il," *Asian Survey*, vol. 22, no. 1 (January 1982), pp. 104, 106.

6 Joseph S. Chung, "Foreign Trade of North Korea: Performance, Policy and Prospects," in Robert A. Scalapino and Hongkoo Lee, eds., *North Korea in a Regional and Global Context* (Berkeley: Institute of East Asian Studies, 1986), p. 86.

7 V.I. Andreev and V.I. Osipov, "SSSR-KNDR: kursom vzaimovygodnogo sotrudnichestva," *Problemy dal'nego vostoka*, no. 3 (1983), pp. 8–22; Young Whan Kihl, "North Korea in 1983," *Asian Survey*, vol. 24, no. 1 (January 1984), pp. 100–11; Harry Gelman and Norman D. Levin, *The Future of Soviet–North Korean Relations* (Santa Monica, CA: RAND, October 1984), pp. 19–21.

8 Young C. Kim, "North Korean Foreign Policy," *Problems of Communism*, vol. 34, no. 1 (January–February 1985), p. 6.

9 Kim Yu-Nam, "Soviet Strategic Objectives on the Korean Peninsula," in Ray S. Cline, James Arnold Miller, and Roger E. Kanet, *Asia in Soviet Global Strategy* (Boulder and London: Westview, 1987), pp. 88–89.

10 Shinn, "North Korea in 1982," p. 105. Other accounts suggest that unofficial Soviet–South Korean trade began as early as 1979. See Dan C. Sanford, *South Korea and the Socialist Countries: The Politics of Trade* (New York: St. Martin's Press, 1990), pp. 19-20.

11 An official history refers to the meeting as a "major landmark" in Soviet–North Korean relations. *SSSR i Koreia* (Moscow: Nauka, 1988), p. 302.

12 *Pravda*, 24 May 1984, p. 2.

13 A. Muratov, "The Friendship Will Grow Stronger," *International Affairs* (Moscow), no. 9 (September 1985), p. 26.

14 Donald S. Zagoria, "The USSR and Asia in 1985," *Asian Survey*, vol. 26, no. 1 (January 1986), pp. 15–29.

15 Michael R. Gordon, "North Korea Joins Pact to Prevent the Spread of Nuclear Weapons," *New York Times*, 27 December 1985, p. 3.

16 *Pravda*, 9 February 1986, p. 4; *Pravda*, 29 November 1986, p. 5.

17 *Pravda*, 4 July 1986, p. 4.

18 *Pravda*, 25 October 1986, p. 1; Peter Polomka, *The Two Koreas: Catalyst for Conflict in East Asia?* (London: IISS Adelphi Papers No. 208, Summer 1986), pp. 23-4.

19 *Pravda*, 23 May 1987, p. 1.

20 See, for example, *Pravda*, 19 November 1987, p. 5; *Izvestiia*, 24 June 1987, pp. 1, 4; and *Pravda*, 4 July 1987, p. 5

21 *The Korea Herald*, 13 March 1988, p.1.

22 *Korean Newsreview*, 10 June 1989, p. 22. The article reported that trade for 1988 was $278 million, an increase of 49.3 percent over the preceeding year.

23 See *Ekonomicheskaia gazeta*, no. 11 (March 1988), p. 23; and statements by Sergei Petrov, deputy councillor of the USSR trade mission in North Korea, on Moscow International Service (in Korean), *FBIS–SOV*, 29 June 1988, p. 27.

24 *The Korea Herald*, 19 July 1988, in *FBIS–SOV*, 19 July 1988, p. 28.

25 KYODO, in *FBIS–SOV*, 12 September 1988, p. 23.

26 Rajan Menon, "New Thinking and Northeast Asian Security," *Problems of Communism*, vol. 38, no. 2–3 (March–June 1989), pp. 25–27; Sophie Quinn-Judge, "Olympic Overtures," *Far Eastern Economic Review*, 14 April 1988, p. 38; TASS, in *FBIS–SOV*, 13 May 1988, p. 14.

27 *Pravda*, 29 June 1988, p. 8.

28 Dmitrii Kosyrev, "Dragons and Computers," *Pravda*, 5 January 1988, translated in *Current Digest of the Soviet Press* (hereafter *CDSP*), vol. 40, no. 1, 3 February 1988, pp. 15–16.

29 *Pravda*, 18 September 1988, in *CDSP*, vol. 40, no. 38, 19 October 1988, p. 7.

30 *Washington Post*, 15 June 1989, p. 35.

31 *Izvestiia*, 4 January 1989, p. 5.

32 YONHAP, in *FBIS–SOV*, 14 September 1988; and Moscow International Service (in Korean), in *FBIS–SOV*, 2 February 1990, pp. 13–14.

33 Roy U. Kim, "Olympics Could Open Soviet–South Korean Relations," *Christian Science Monitor*, 20 September 1988, p. 11. Dan Sanford, who was in Seoul during the Olympics, remarked on "the groundswell of favoritism displayed by the South Korean audiences toward Soviet athletes in opposition to American athletes." *South Korea and the Socialist Countries*, p. 42.

34 *Izvestiia*, 3 April 1989, p. 5.

35 Shipaev, "From Silence to Contracts."

36 *Korea Newsreview*, 16 September 1989, p. 7.

37 See Roy Kim, "Gorbachev and the Korean Peninsula," *Third World Quarterly*, vol. 10, no. 3 (July 1988), pp. 1267–99.

38 *Pravda*, 25 December 1988, p. 4.

39 *Korea Newsreview*, 10 June 1989, p. 22; and 8 July 1989, p. 22.

40 *Economist*, 31 March 1990, p. 32.

41 *Izvestiia*, 6 September 1989, p. 5. South Korea did not become a member of COCOM. It was, however, a Section 5(K) country under the 1979 US Export Administration Act. This Section authorizes the Secretary of State, in consultation with the Secretaries of Defense and Commerce, to negotiate with non-COCOM countries on cooperation in controlling the export of strategic products and technology. In return, Commerce may grant preferential licensing benefits to 5(K) countries. These include, in addition to South Korea, Austria, Finland, India, Ireland, Sweden, Switzerland, and Taiwan. *Export Administration Annual Report, FY 1990* (US Department of Commerce, Bureau of Export Administration, August 1991), p. 13.

42 Roy Kim, "The Soviet Union and the Divided Korea," paper delivered to the University of Hawaii conference on the USSR as a Pacific Neighbor, June 1990.

43 Leonid Mlechin, "Na drugoi storone," *Novoe vremia*, no. 10 (1990), pp. 19–21. One day after Hungary and South Korea established diplomatic ties,

Pyongyang downgraded DPRK–Hungarian relations to the level of chargé d'affaires.

44 *Economist*, 31 March 1990, p. 32.
45 Vsevolod Ovchinnikov, "About the San Francisco Meeting," *Pravda*, 9 June 1990, in *CDSP*, vol. 42, no. 23, 11 July 1990, pp. 5–6.
46 *Washington Post*, 5 June 1990, p. 16.
47 *Izvestiia*, 14 November 1990, p. 4; Mark Clifford and Sophie Quinn-Judge, "Caught in a Vice," *Far Eastern Economic Review*, 29 November 1990, pp. 30, 32; Rhee Sang-Woo, "North Korea in 1991," *Asian Survey*, vol. 32, no. 1 (January 1992), p. 59.
48 Kyodo, in *FBIS–East Asia*, 17 September 1990.
49 See *Izvestiia*, 11 September 1990, p. 5.
50 TASS, in *FBIS–SOV*, 14 December 1990.
51 AFP, cited in Radio Liberty *Report on the USSR*, 15 March 1991, pp. 45–46.
52 Yonhap, in *FBIS–East Asia*, 18 April 1991.
53 TASS, in *FBIS–SOV*, 29 April 1991.
54 *Izvestiia*, 22 April 1991, pp. 1, 4.
55 For example, a two-year cultural protocol was signed in June 1991, and Kim entertained a Russian military delegation in January 1992.
56 See, for example, *Pravda*, 7 October 1991, p. 4.
57 Constantine V. Pleshakov, "Republic of Korea – USSR Relations," *Korea and World Affairs*, vol. 14, no. 4 (Winter 1990), p. 693.

7   Learning and security in the Asian-Pacific region

1 On Soviet attempts to develop new economic ties with the region, see Charles E. Ziegler, "Soviet Strategies for Development: East Asia and the Pacific Basin," *Pacific Affairs*, vol. 63, no. 4 (Winter 1990–91), pp. 451–68.
2 Georges Tan Eng Bok, *The USSR in East Asia* (Paris: Atlantic Institute for International Affairs, 1986), pp. 40–41.
3 Vladimir Ivanov, "Soviet Policy in the Asia-Pacific Region and Economic Reforms," *The Soviets and the Pacific Challenge*, Peter Drysdale, ed., in association with Martin O'Hare (Armonk, NY: M.E. Sharpe, 1991), pp. 130–32.
4 Gerry S. Thomas, "The Pacific Fleet," in Bruce W. Watson and Susan M. Watson, eds., *The Soviet Navy: Strengths and Weaknesses* (Boulder, CO: Westview Press, 1986), pp. 230–31, 235.
5 *The Military Balance, 1985–1986* (London: IISS, 1985); Sheldon Simon, *The Future of Asian-Pacific Security Collaboration* (Lexington, Mass: D.C. Heath, 1988), pp. 30–31, 36–37.
6 *New York Times*, 19 January 1990, p. 6.
7 Associated Press, 21 April 1990.
8 The Japan Defense Agency (JDA) calculated that 435 naval passages per year in the late 1980s (out of a total of 615 through the Soya, Tsushima, and Tsugaru straits) were through the Soya Straits alone. *Defense of Japan 1989*, Japan Defense Agency White Paper, p. 38. However, JDA figures do not differentiate between warships and other craft – supply vessels, barges and landing ships. Other sources suggest that transits through the straits by

major surface combatants comprised a small percentage of total Soviet passages. An article by R. Horiguchi in *Pacific Defense Reporter* (August 1984) claimed that during 1983 only nineteen ships larger than corvettes passed through the Soya and Tsushima straits. Cited in Myles L. C. Robertson, *Soviet Policy Towards Japan: An Analysis of Trends in the 1970s and 1980s* (Cambridge: Cambridge University Press, 1988), p. 133.

9 Raymond L. Garthoff, *Detente and Confrontation* (Washington, DC: Brookings, 1985), pp. 714–15.

10 *The Military Balance 1989–1990*, pp. 29–30.

11 This point is emphasized in Alexei V. Zagorsky, "Confidence-Building Measures: An Alternative for Asian-Pacific Security?," *Pacific Review*, vol. 4, no. 4 (1991), p. 347.

12 Thomas, "The Pacific Fleet," p. 231. Even at their lowest level, US naval forces still outnumbered their Soviet counterparts.

13 Banning N. Garrett and Bonnie S. Glaser, "Arms Control in the Management of US Security Interests in the Asia-Pacific Region," in Frank C. Langdon and Douglas A. Ross, eds., *Superpower Maritime Strategy in the Pacific* (London and New York: Routledge, 1990). Also, see the chapter by Ross Babbage in the same volume.

14 See *The Maritime Strategy*, US Naval Institute Proceedings (January 1986); and Captain M.P. Gretton, "The American Maritime Strategy: European Perspectives and Implications," Seaford House Papers (1987), especially Annex A; Norman Friedman, *The US Maritime Strategy* (London: Jane's Publishing, 1988); Colin S. Gray, "The Maritime Strategy in US–Soviet Strategic Relations," *Naval War College Review*, vol. 42, no. 1 (Winter 1989), pp. 7–18. For a critical view, see William M. Arkin, "Troubled Waters: The Navy's Aggressive War Strategy," *Technology Review*, vol. 92 (January 1989), pp. 54–63.

15 Desmond Wettern, "Ace in the Soviet Hand," *Pacific Defence Reporter* (November 1989), pp. 55–57 notes that the maritime strategy was to compensate for a major decline in the strength of US and Canadian navies in the 1960s and 1970s. US forward deployment in the Pacific would be needed to protect convoys in the event of war or crisis.

16 *Soviet Military Power: Prospects for Change 1989* (Washington, DC: US Department of Defense, 1989), pp. 116–17.

17 Young Whan Kihl and Lawrence E. Grinter, "Changing Security Requirements in Pacific Asia," in Young Whan Kihl and Lawrence E. Grinter, eds., *Security, Strategy, and Policy Responses in the Pacific Rim* (Boulder, CO: Lynne Rienner, 1988), p. 7.

18 *A Strategic Framework for the Asian Pacific Rim: Looking Toward the 21st Century* (US Department of Defense, nd); *New York Times*, 1 December 1991, p. 2.

19 For a good recent treatment of cooperative defense efforts in the region, see Sheldon Simon, *The Future of Asian-Pacific Security Collaboration*.

20 *The Military Balance 1991–1992* (London: IISS, 1991), p. 165.

21 See *US–Japan Burden-Sharing*, Report to the Chairman, Committee on Armed Services, House of Representatives (Washington, DC: General Accounting Office, August 1989).

22 James A. Baker III, "America in Asia: Emerging Architecture for a Pacific Community," *Foreign Affairs*, vol. 70, no. 5 (Winter 1991–92), p. 9.

23 *The Military Balance 1991–1992*, p. 169.

24 Lawrence E. Grinter, "Policy of the United States toward East Asia: Tough Adjustments," in Kihl and Grinter, *Security, Strategy, and Policy Responses in the Pacific Rim*; and Martin L. Lasater, "Chinese Military Modernization," in Stephen P. Gibert, ed., *Security in Northeast Asia: Approaching the Pacific Century* (Boulder, CO: Westview, 1988).

25 See the remarks by Admiral James D. Watkins, in *The Maritime Strategy*, US Naval Institute (January 1986).

26 Frank C. Langdon and Douglas A. Ross, "Superpower Conflict," in Frank C. Langdon and Douglas A. Ross, eds., *Superpower Maritime Strategy in the Pacific* (London and New York, Routledge, 1990), pp. 16–18.

27 Michael MccGwire, "The Changing Role of the Soviet Navy," *Bulletin of the Atomic Scientists*, vol. 43, no. 7 (September 1987), pp. 34–39.

28 Petropavlovsk, a major strategic submarine base on the southeast of Kamchatka peninsula, faces the open Pacific and is not geographically on the Sea of Okhotsk. However, Kamchatka has no rail links to the mainland and Petropavlovsk must be resupplied by air. It is highly vulnerable to being severed from the mainland in the event of a conflict.

29 *Izvestiia*, 5 June 1991, p. 6.

30 Norman D. Levin, *The Strategic Environment in East Asia and US–Korean Security Relations in the 1980s*, A Rand Note, N-1960-FF (March 1983), p. 6. For a more hard-line view of Soviet interests in Korea, see Michael Sadykiewicz, "The Geostrategic Role of Korea in the Soviet Military Doctrine," *Asian Perspective*, vol. 7, no. 1 (Spring–Summer 1983), pp. 101–27.

31 Rajan Menon, "New Thinking and Northeast Asian Security," *Problems of Communism*, vol. 38, no. 2–3 (March–June 1989), p. 26.

32 Edward Warner notes that one significant development in revising Soviet military policy was the growing role of civilian 'institutchiki' in the 1980s. In contrast, the Brezhnev regime had granted the professional military virtually complete autonomy in developing military doctrine. Edward L. Warner III, "New Thinking and Old Realities in Soviet Defence Policy," *Survival*, vol. 31, no. 1 (January–February 1989), pp. 13–33. Also, see G. Kunadze, "Ob oboronnoi dostatochnosti voennogo potentsiala SSSR," *Mirovaia ekonomika i mezhdunarodnye otnosheniia*, no. 10 (October 1989), pp. 68–83; and Gloria Duffy and Jennifer Lee, "The Soviet Debate on 'Reasonable Sufficiency,'" *Arms Control Today*, vol. 18, no. 8, (October 1988), pp. 19–24.

33 During former Prime Minister Nakasone's January 1989 visit to Moscow as a member of a Trilateral Commission delegation, Gorbachev apparently informed his Japanese guest that Soviet reductions in the Far East were in response to Chinese flexibility, implying that Japan would benefit from similar concessions.

34 TASS, 17 September 1988. In October 1989, Foreign Minister Shevardnadze admitted the Krasnoiarsk radar installation was a clear violation of the Anti-Ballistic Missile treaty.

35 Harry Gelman, *The Soviet Military Leadership and the Question of Soviet Deployment Retreats*, Rand Project Air Force Report, R-3664-AF (November 1988), p. 29.

36 See Marko Milivojevic, "The Spratley and Paracel Islands Conflict," *Survival*, vol. 31 (January–February 1989), pp. 70–78.

37 Kyodo, in *Foreign Broadcast Information Service-Soviet Union* (hereafter *FBIS–SOV*), 16 May 1991.

38 Those observers who approached Soviet initiatives in the Asian-Pacific region solely from a military-strategic perspective, without taking into account the domestic context, drew simplistic and highly misleading conclusions about Gorbachev's motives. See, for example, Kenneth G. Weiss, of the Center for Naval Analyses, "Throwing Down the Gauntlet: The Soviet Challenge in the Pacific," *Comparative Strategy*, vol. 8, no. 2 (1989), pp. 149–80.

39 *Gorbachev's Force Reductions and the Restructuring of Soviet Forces*, Committee on Armed Services, House of Representatives (Washington, DC: US GPO, March 1989), p. 44. The head of the Pacific Research Department of IMEMO had stated that the Soviet Pacific Fleet was reduced by fifty-seven ships over the same period, adding that naval activity in the region had been "markedly restricted." Vladimir Ivanov, "Soviet–US Face-off Must End," *Far Eastern Economic Review*, 12 January 1989, pp. 19–20.

40 Harry Gelman, *The Soviet Military Leadership and the Question of Soviet Deployment Retreats*.

41 *Asian Security, 1988–89* (London: Brassey's, 1988), p. 151.

42 Derek da Cunha, "The Growth of the Soviet Pacific Fleet's Submarine Force," *International Defense Review*, no. 2, 1988, pp. 127–31.

43 Tai Ming Cheung, "Holding the Line," *Far Eastern Economic Review*, 27 June 1991, p. 23.

44 Radio Moscow, in *FBIS–SOV*, 23 January 1991. *The Military Balance 1991–92* lists 213 tanks in a motorized rifle division.

45 These and the following data, unless otherwise specified, are derived from the Japan Defense Agency White Papers *Defense of Japan 1987* and *Defense of Japan 1989*; the International Institute for Strategic Studies (London) annual *The Military Balance* for 1985–86, 1989–90; 1990–91, and 1991–92; The US Department of Defense annual *Soviet Military Power, 1989* and *Soviet Military Power, 1990* (Washington, DC: US GPO, 1989, 1990); Richard H. Solomon and Masataka Kosaka, eds., *The Soviet Far East Military Buildup* (Dover, MA: Auburn House, 1986); and Paul F. Langer, "Soviet Military Power in Asia," in Donald S. Zagoria, ed., *Soviet Policy in East Asia* (New Haven and London: Yale University Press, 1982).

46 *A Strategic Framework for the Asian Pacific Rim: Looking Toward the 21st Century* (US Department of Defense, nd).

47 Tokyo television reported in April that the JDA claimed it would not be possible to confine these reductions entirely to management and supply personnel. Cutting 6000 troops would necessitate a reduction in possibly two battalions (about 1000 troops) of the 3rd Marine Corps on Okinawa. Translated in *Foreign Broadcast Information Service – East Asia* (hereafter *FBIS–EAS*), 24 April 1990.

48 The American and Japanese official positions are stated in the 1990 edition of the *Japanese Defense Agency White Paper*, and the Pentagon's *Soviet Military Power* for 1990. Foreign Minister Taro Nakayama, in a statement to the House of Councillors in May 1990, was the first top-level Japanese official to acknowledge that the Soviet menace was receding, although he described the Soviet presence in the region as still constituting a major threat. *FBIS–EAS*, 11 May 1990.

49 For a more optimistic assessment, see "Mission Accomplished in Korea: Bringing US Troops Home," *The Defense Monitor*, vol. 19, no. 2 (1990).

8   Conclusion: Soviet foreign policy learning

1 *Gorbachev CPSU Central Committee Political Report*, Moscow Television, translated in *Foreign Broadcast Information Service*, (hereafter *FBIS–SOV*), 26 February 1986, pp. 32–33.

2 The idea that humility is important to learning is from Karl Deutsch, *The Nerves of Government* (New York: Basic Books, 1966), pp. 229–31.· As in a Greek tragedy, the Politburo protagonists, blinded by hubris, brought about their own downfall.

3 This was the argument of Viacheslav Dashichev's influential article, "Vostok-Zapad: poisk novykh otnoshenii," *Literaturnaia gazeta*, 18 May 1988, p. 14.

4 See Samuel P. Huntington, *Political Order in Changing Societies* (New Haven and London: Yale University Press, 1968), pp. 237–40.

5 See, for example, Richard Weitz, "The Reagan Doctrine Defeated Moscow in Angola," *Orbis*, vol. 36, no. 1 (Winter 1992), pp. 69–86; Paul H. Nitze, "America: An Honest Broker," *Foreign Affairs*, vol. 69, no. 4 (Fall 1990), pp. 1–14; and Burton Yale Pines, "Waiting for Mr. X," *Policy Review*, no 49 (Summer 1989), pp. 2–6.

6 Kenneth A. Oye, "Constrained Confidence and the Evolution of Reagan Foreign Policy," in Kenneth A. Oye, Robert J. Lieber, and Donald Rothchild, eds., *Eagle Resurgent?: The Reagan Era in American Foreign Policy* (Boston: Little, Brown, 1987), p. 5.

7 Coral Bell, *The Reagan Paradox: American Foreign Policy in the 1980s* (New Brunswick, NJ: Rutgers University Press, 1989), pp. 15–16.

8 Jeane Kirkpatrick, "Dictatorships and Double Standards," *Commentary*, vol. 68, no. 5 (November 1979), p. 44.

9 See, for example, Jeane J. Kirkpatrick, *The Reagan Phenomenon and other Speeches on Foreign Policy* (Washington and London: American Enterprise Institute, 1983).

10 Norman Podhoretz, "The Reagan Road to Detente," *Foreign Affairs*, vol. 63, no. 3 (1985), pp. 447–64.

11 Caspar Weinberger, *Fighting For Peace* (New York: Warner Books, 1990).

12 See Alexander L. George, "Strategies for Facilitating Cooperation," in Alexander L. George, Philip J. Farley, and Alexander Dallin, eds., *US–Soviet Security Cooperation: Achievements, Failures, Lessons* (Oxford: Oxford University Press, 1988), pp. 702–7.

13 The concept of "tit-for-tat" is developed in Robert Axelrod, *The Evolution of Cooperation* (New York: Basic Books, 1984). Axelrod's tit-for-tat is based on the Prisoner's Dilemma game, in which players simply react to other players' actions. However, the utility of the model is limited, since communication between players is not possible. Communication and information processing are central to the learning process.

14 Coral Bell, *The Reagan Paradox.*

15 According to Weinberger, "The crux of our Pacific strategy is that by complicating that [sic] Soviet offensive planning we vastly increase our ability to deter any Soviet attack." *Fighting For Peace*, p. 220.

16 Daniel Deudney and G. John Ikenberry, "The International Sources of Soviet Change," *International Security*, vol. 16, no. 3 (Winter 1991–92), pp. 74–118.

17 Ibid., pp. 96–97.

18 George F. Kennan's famous "X" article, which formed the basis for US policy toward the Soviet Union in the post-war period, noted that "the United States has in its power to increase enormously the strains under which Soviet policy must operate, to force upon the Kremlin a far greater degree of moderation and circumspection." However, this policy, Kennan stressed, "must be that of a long-term, patient but firm and vigilant containment of Russian expansionist tendencies ... such a policy has nothing to do with outward histrionics: with threats or blustering or superfluous gestures of outward 'toughness.'" "The Sources of Soviet Conduct," reprinted in *Foreign Affairs*, vol. 65, no. 4 (Spring 1987), pp. 861, 868.

19 This point is made in an excellent study of the INF negotiations: Thomas Risse-Kappen, "Did 'Peace Through Strength' End the Cold War?," *International Security*, vol. 16, no. 1 (Summer 1991), pp. 162–88. Riesse-Kappen's central point is that Soviet domestic politics was critical to explaining the breakthough on the INF treaty in 1987.

Index